Juries

and

Politics

Contemporary Issues in Crime and Justice Series
Roy R. Roberg, San Jose State University: Series Editor

Juries

and

Politics

· · · · · · ·

James P. Levine
Brooklyn College
of The City University of New York

Brooks/Cole Publishing Company
Pacific Grove, California

Consulting Editor: Roy R. Roberg

Brooks/Cole Publishing Company
A Division of Wadsworth, Inc.

Printed in the United States of America
10   9   8   7   6   5   4   3   2   1

Library of Congress Cataloging-in-Publication Data

Levine, James P.
    Juries and politics / James P. Levine.
        p.   cm.
    Includes index.
    ISBN 0-534-14754-2 (pbk.) :
    1. Jury—United States. I. Title.
KF8972.L48   1991
347.73′0752—dc20
[347.307752]   91-11960
                                                CIP

Sponsoring Editor: Cynthia C. Stormer
Editorial Associate: Cathleen S. Collins
Production Coordinator: Fiorella Ljunggren
Production: Victoria A. Vandeventer
Manuscript Editor: Barbara Kimmel
Permissions Editor: Mary Kay Hancharick
Interior and Cover Design: Victoria A. Vandeventer
Typesetting: Bookends Typesetting
Printing and Binding: Malloy Lithographing, Inc.

To Al, Martha,
and the memory of Vivian

About the Author

James P. Levine, who received his Ph.D. from Northwestern University in 1967, is a Professor of Political Science at Brooklyn College. He also teaches at John Jay College of Criminal Justice as a member of the doctoral faculty of the Graduate Center of the City University of New York. Before his present appointments, he taught at Michigan State University and the University of Oregon.

Dr. Levine's specialties are the judicial process and crime policy, fields in which he has published over a score of articles. He has co-authored two textbooks on criminal justice: *Criminal Justice: A Public Policy Approach* (New York: Harcourt, Brace, Jovanovich, 1980) and *Criminal Justice in America: Law in Action* (New York: Wiley, 1986). In recent years he has done considerable empirical research on jury verdicts, resulting in articles in the *American Bar Foundation Research Journal, Crime and Delinquency, Judicature,* and *Trial Lawyers Quarterly.* He also does research on American politics. His most recent work is a book co-authored with David Abbott, entitled *Wrong Winner: The Coming Debacle in the Electoral College* (New York: Praeger, 1991).

Foreword

Through the Contemporary Issues in Crime and Justice Series, students are introduced to important topics relevant to criminal justice, criminology, law, political science, psychology, and sociology that until now have been neglected or inadequately covered. The authors address philosophical and theoretical issues and analyze the most recent research findings and their implications for practice. Consequently, each volume stimulates further thinking and debate on the topics it covers, in addition to providing direction for the development and implementation of policy.

Juries, in their role of "maintaining contemporary community values" through the determination of guilt or innocence, the handing down of sentences, and the awarding of damages, have a significant impact on our society and the criminal justice system. This impact is strongly influenced by the political nature of the American jury system. Contemporary scholars, however, have largely ignored the importance that politicality plays in jury decisions—until now. Levine's work explores the jury process from this unique perspective, from the initial selection of jurors, through deliberation and decision making, to the impact of jury verdicts on society.

This examination of juries from a political perspective is an important contribution to the literature, because it forces us, as Levine suggests, to "search beyond the formal charges and the trial record to better understand what drives jurors to one conclusion rather than another." Such an approach requires that we examine the underlying concerns that are often on the minds of the jurors—that is, the informal nature of what actually transpires in the jury's quest for truth and justice. The author has contributed keen insights regarding the inner sanctum of the modern jury system by reviewing the different types of research utilized to study juries, including mock trials, statistical analysis, and interviews. Some of the more interesting findings include: (1) *who* jurors are has an effect on *what* they decide; (2) the political climate of the time often affects the way jurors view cases, with the current political ethos making jurors more or less eager to convict; (3) *who* sits on the jury can be as important as the evidence in deciding outcomes; and (4) critical jury verdicts often serve as catalysts in producing significant changes in the political and economic system.

The author ends the text with the general conclusion that the jury's decision making processes are far from perfect. In order to improve the current state of affairs, Levine suggests that three goals need to be accomplished by altering the rules under which juries operate. He also offers several proposals that have important policy implications for improving jury verdicts. This work makes a significant contribution to the study of jury behavior and its impact on society; it should be read by all those—both students and policymakers— who have an interest in understanding and improving the American jury system.

Roy R. Roberg

Preface

A century ago Irish-American political satirist Finley Peter Dunne
scathingly mocked the jury through the voice of one of his fictional
characters, the straight-talking "Mr. Dooley." Said Mr. Dooley (in his
Irish brogue): "Whin th' case is all over, the jury'll pitch th' testimony out
iv th' window, an' consider three questions: 'Did Lootgert look as though
he'd kill his wife? Did his wife look as though she ought to be kilt? Isn't it
time we wint to supper?'" (*Mr. Dooley in Peace and War* [Boston: Small
Maynard, 1898], pp. 141–145).

These cutting lines still get a good laugh, but they tell us nothing about
the jury's true nature. They leave unanswered a fundamental question: Are
jurors objective or subjective in rendering verdicts—or something in between?
It is this issue that law professor Harry Kalven and sociologist Hans Zeisel
posed twenty-five years ago in the process of studying *thousands* of verdicts
rendered throughout the United States. In their seminal and now classic book
The American Jury (Boston: Little Brown, 1966), they stated their ultimate concern: "to trace the law in action, to see how juries . . . *really decide cases*" (p.
497, italics added). Their goal then was my goal now—to figure out how juries
exercise the truly awesome discretion entrusted to them and to determine
the extent to which, through their verdicts, they graft onto the law their own
moral perspectives. In short, the key question I am asking boils down to this:
What makes juries tick?

The title of this book, *Juries and Politics*, reveals the gist of my answer:
jurors and juries in large measure act politically. The interdisciplinary research
I assembled and the case studies I compiled for the purpose of drawing an
accurate portrait of the jury in action indicate that jurors rely to a considerable
degree on their own values, ideologies, and biases in the process of coping
with facts that are uncertain and laws that are ambiguous. They work hard
to ascertain the truth in the face of trial inconclusiveness, and they make the

ix

utmost attempt to act rationally in reaching proper verdicts; but in reality they are influenced by all kinds of extralegal considerations. Having been selected from the public-at-large, they mirror many public sentiments and popular feelings. Jurors are partisans who, like everyone else invested with governmental responsibility, are incapable of being totally neutral.

These are strong words. The rest of this book is devoted to backing them up with scores of specific cases, extensive experimental research, reflections of jurors themselves, and analyses of verdict statistics. It is an attempt to review systematically the myriad influences on jurors' behavior: trial evidence and arguments, the demands of justice, assessments of the law, the nature of the political climate, and personal biases. I also explore the impact of jurors on one another—the politicking during jury deliberations that has much in common with other kinds of collective decision making. Finally, I explain the repercussions of jury verdicts: the ways in which what juries do has an impact on the workings of the legal system, on the larger political process, and on society.

This book is germane to many kinds of law-oriented undergraduate and graduate courses. It is suitable for introductory or advanced criminal justice courses focusing on the judiciary, for judicial process courses taught in political science departments, and for courses dealing with the sociology or psychology of law. Because the book draws on ideas and sources from a variety of fields, it is ideal for interdisciplinary courses on law and society.

Beyond the classroom, anyone having either a professional interest in juries, such as attorneys, or a personal curiosity about how juries work should find the book accessible. I have written it for a general audience, including anyone who at one time or another may have been captivated, perplexed, or angered by trials they followed. It is my hope that I have been able to demystify the jury's functioning while at the same time communicating the sense of excitement that jury trials and jury decision making generate.

Just as jurors have biases, so do authors, and here is mine: *I love juries!* My fascination with juries began when I first served on a criminal jury in 1977 and I was struck by the seriousness and the passion of my co-jurors. This budding affection for the jury surfaced two years later during my co-authorship of an introductory criminal justice text, prompting the copyeditor to tell me that I was both more spirited and less cynical in my treatment of jurors than in my descriptions of other participants in the judicial process. Concurring in this assessment, I found myself driven to learn more about the jury, and I spent a good part of the 1980s doing a series of original empirical studies of jury behavior. This research confirmed how much the jury reflects the political culture and gave me an even greater appreciation of its role in making the legal system accountable to the public.

So, although I have tried to be as objective as I could in my discussion of the jury, I must admit that I remain a great admirer. Much of the research that I report reveals shortcomings about the jury, and some of the verdicts described are in my opinion nothing less than horrifying. But for all its weaknesses, the jury in my mind contributes a blessedly democratic element to the legal system.

Acknowledgments

It has been a true joy to work with the people at Brooks/Cole. The entire staff has been helpful, courteous, and competent. Cindy Stormer has been a model editor—demanding but supportive, tough but kind. Editorial Associate Cat Collins handled all kinds of bureaucratic matters with both efficiency and warmth. Vicki Vandeventer smoothly coordinated the production process, and Barbara Kimmel did a masterful job of copyediting. Brooks/Cole's enthusiasm and steadfast commitment to *Juries and Politics* kept me going even during difficult moments over the course of the project.

I was most fortunate in receiving enormously helpful criticisms and suggestions from series editor Roy Roberg and from the following reviewers selected by the publisher to critique earlier drafts of the manuscript: Theodore Becker of Auburn University, Valerie P. Hans of the University of Delaware, Martha A. Myers of the University of Georgia, David Neubauer of the University of New Orleans, and Neil Vidmar of Duke University School of Law. I would also like to thank John Beatty, Dan Claster, Philippa Strum, and Vera Tarr, who are colleagues of mine at Brooklyn College, and Jo Dixon of New York University for reading parts of the manuscript and offering sound advice. Also deserving of thanks is Lynn Mather of Dartmouth College for her support of my jury research at an early stage. Finally, I express my appreciation to Michael Musheno and Dennis Palumbo of Arizona State University, to David Abbott and Robert Abrams of Brooklyn College, and to Victor Rosenblum of Northwestern University for their moral support over the years.

My family has been behind me all the way during the writing of this book, putting up with the long and sometimes odd hours that I devoted to it. I thank them for their backing, which has meant so much to me.

James P. Levine

Contents

The jury is, above all, a political institution,
and it must be regarded in this light
in order to be duly appreciated.

Alexis de Tocqueville, *Democracy in America* (1835)

Jury Politics in Microcosm: The Bernhard Goetz Case

(Question) What Happened?
(Answer) Who Knows?

They called him the subway vigilante. From the moment the fragmented story first emerged, sides were formed. Four young men were seriously wounded by gunshots fired at them while they were riding a crowded New York City subway train. The assailant at first fled but later turned himself in to a New Hampshire police station where he confessed to the shooting. His reason? He was surrounded by a bunch of hoodlums who were demanding his money. His name? Bernhard Goetz.

Goetz soon became a household word, not just in New York but nationwide, as his face adorned the covers of the major news magazines. The reaction of the legal system was confused and contradictory: the district attorney first charged him with (among other things) attempted murder; the grand jury threw the charges out, refusing to indict Goetz; a new grand jury was formed, hearing the case anew (presumably on the basis of new evidence); the second grand jury reversed the actions of the first one and charged Bernhard Goetz with a series of very serious felonies. Goetz pleaded not guilty on the basis of self-defense, saying that when the youths demanded five dollars from him, "I was acting out of goddamn fear." The prosecution, noting that two of the victims were unarmed and a third was cowering when shot, argued that Goetz had

1
· · · · · · ·
Juries
and Politics

conducted a one-man vendetta against the criminal world and had taken the law into his own hands. It became the responsibility of a jury of twelve ordinary citizens to sort out the murky events of December 22 and to decide what had happened and who was to blame. Was Goetz a hero, a villain, or a tragic figure somewhere in between? Determining guilt or innocence is a legal decision on one level but an agonizing political and moral decision on another.

As trials go, this one was thorough and probing. But despite a seven weeks' duration and more than 10,000 pages of testimony, the trial raised as many questions as it answered. What was the tone of the victims' requests for money? Were they begging or were they menacing when they said to Goetz, "Do you have five dollars?" Of what significance was the "shine" in the eyes of one of Goetz's victims, which Goetz took as a sign that he was about to be attacked? Did Goetz's previous experience as a mugging victim make him excessively afraid or angry? How many bullets did Goetz fire and what were their trajectories? Was the youth who was permanently paralyzed by one of Goetz's bullets backing away when Goetz said, "You seem to be all right. Here's another"? Why did Goetz flee through a subway tunnel and hide for over a week? What was the significance of the emotional confession he made on videotape to New Hampshire police officers after he surrendered?

In the end, the evidence remained clouded. The jury acquitted Goetz of all charges except the illegal weapons count. Some of the jurors stated that the prosecution simply had failed to prove beyond a reasonable doubt that Goetz had *not* been threatened with serious bodily harm and that he had *not* responded unreasonably. As one juror put it, "There was a lot of conflicting testimony. A lot of people said a lot of different things, including Goetz himself. . . . It was so hard to establish what the facts were. Some of the witnesses saw people that other witnesses didn't see, people saw people who weren't there—and this was over two years after it happened."[1]

What really happened? Unfortunately, that is an unanswerable question. Because the truth never emerges with 100 percent certainty, doubt is an inevitable part of the trial process. And it is this doubt that opened the door for juror politics, in the Goetz case as in so many cases. It is such politicization that is the focus of this book.

What the following pages will show is that the Goetz jurors, faced with contradictory and confusing evidence produced at the trial, looked outward to the social milieu and inward to their own personal feelings to get answers. They acted politically, bringing subjective sentiments and social interests to bear in exercising the power that the legal system entrusted to them. And their decision had political consequences, touching the emotions of many people far removed from the trial and helping redefine the "law in action"— the nature and limits of the right to self-defense. The Goetz verdict was in large measure a political judgment.

Justice for Goetz

This book will show that juries do more than assess the evidence and apply the law; they consider blameworthiness in the process. Issues of right and wrong are intertwined with questions of guilt and innocence. Jurors seek justice while looking for truth.

Faced with conflicting evidence, the Goetz jury arrived at a rendition of the facts favorable to the defendant. They refused to accept the eye-witness account of the prosecution's strongest witness, a passenger who said that one youth was sitting down when shot. "Too many inconsistencies" in his testimony, said one juror. Regarding the infamous final shot that paralyzed the fourth victim, the jury concluded that it might never have been fired at all: the bullet might have struck him during the initial flurry.

And how did the jury deal with Goetz's incriminating New Hampshire confession on videotape where he said (among other things): "[I am] a cold-blooded murderer, . . . a vicious rat, . . . a monster. A person has to be reduced to this kind of animal to survive in the city"? They dismissed it as the irrelevant ramblings of a distraught man who had temporarily lost control of his senses. Said one of the jurors: "He was so agitated . . . he just wasn't being rational."[2] In the words of another juror: "I felt he was not far from the edge of hysteria. . . . He had been driving for nine days before that. . . . We took all that into consideration."[3] At every turn, the jury construed the facts in ways that were partial to Goetz's cause.

Underlying the jury's pro-Goetz disposition was undoubtedly a feeling that Goetz was no wanton criminal. Granted, it was irresponsible of Goetz to travel on a crowded subway with a loaded gun, and perhaps he *was* a little too jumpy for everyone's good. But the jury believed that Goetz was the victim and his accusers were the culprits, not the other way around. Goetz was not out to harm innocent people, he was not a vicious person, and he was not a danger to society—unlike his adversaries who appeared to be all of those things combined.

This was a common outlook. No sooner had Goetz been brought back to New York as a defendant than the local press routinely featured headlines using his nickname: "Bernie this"; "Bernie that"; "Bernie something else." This is quite an endearing way of referring to someone accused of attempted murder and aggravated assault and reflects the popular perception that he was no villain. In contrast, both the media and the jurors described Goetz's victims as "dangerous punks" who looked liked "caged animals." So when confronted with someone who may have broken the law but basically was not at fault, the jury "let him off" because it seemed the just thing to do. In fact, a few days after the trial, juror Mark Lesly was photographed wearing a tee-shirt with a picture of Goetz, next to an enlarged *New York Post* headline: "Goetz Off the Hook."[4]

3

But justice is often more complicated. The "good guys" often have flaws and the "bad guys" sometimes have redeeming qualities. Consequently, verdicts are sometimes mixed, with neither across-the-board acquittal nor conviction on all charges. So it was in the Goetz case: the jury found Goetz *mostly* innocent but *a little* guilty. Although Goetz was cleared of twelve out of the thirteen charges against him, he was found guilty of the felony of illegal gun possession. As criminologist Franklin Zimring put it, "The verdict had all the hallmarks of a compromise,"[5] but it was hardly a down-the-middle compromise. Goetz came out ahead—chastised, subject to punishment, but spared the potential of life imprisonment that conviction on the more serious charges could have brought. The accompanying cartoon conveys the jury's sense of justice better than words: a slap on the wrist and a pat on the back!

The presiding judge who sentenced Goetz on the gun conviction apparently had a similar perspective. Goetz could have received seven years imprisonment, or he could have received probation, as recommended in the probation department's presentence report. But the judge, eschewing both extreme harshness and extreme leniency, took a middle course, sentencing Goetz to six months in jail, five years probation, and mandatory psychiatric counseling. The judge and the jury apparently concurred: Goetz was no saint but he surely was no sinner.

Ironically, both judgments reflected and vindicated Goetz's initial assessment of himself made in the videotaped confession that was largely disregarded by the jurors: "What happened here is I snapped. People are looking for a hero or they're looking for a villain and neither is . . . [the] truth."[6] The jury, which deliberated more than thirty hours, was groping for the truth: not just factual truth (destined to remain obscure) but moral truth as well. In post-trial accounts, the jurors all denied such soul-searching, claiming that they were only following the law and sifting through the evidence. But in reality the Goetz case was also about right and wrong, and the jury played a significant role in evaluating a terrified citizen's impulsive but understandable response to perceived threats.

By concluding that Goetz was largely but not totally blameless, the jury was acting as a moral arbiter. And by rejecting both extremes in its quest for justice, the Goetz jury was acting in classic political fashion—searching for middle ground. Juries do this time and time again.

Crime, Conservatism, and the Goetz Jury

The jury's partiality toward Goetz is no mystery. The case was played out against a backdrop of seemingly rampant crime that had been engulfing cities like New York for decades and that showed no signs of abating. Frightful experiences with crime, fear of being attacked, and seething anger at criminals were common for most New Yorkers. And the nationwide conservatism

Source: Courtesy of Steve Kelly, *San Diego Tribune.*

spurred by high crime rates was surely a key political element in the jury's handling of the Goetz case.

Six of Goetz's jurors had been victimized by crime; three by subway crime. Most of them knew people who had been mugged or assaulted, and all had been bombarded day after day and year after year by grisly stories in the media of violence and bloodshed. This was a crime-saturated jury, and to a greater or lesser degree, each juror was quite upset about the dangers lurking in the city.

In New York, the subway symbolizes the perilous state of the city. It is on the subways that people often find themselves shoulder to shoulder and eye to eye with unsavory characters whom they can often avoid in the normal course of their lives. And it is in the subway that they feel at the mercy of the criminal element, with nowhere to flee and usually with no help around. The subway situation is so unnerving that many would rather endure the enormous cost and aggravation of commuting by bus or car than expose themselves to that terrifying situation.

This is the context in which jurors heard the evidence in the Goetz case. To decide whether Goetz's self-defense claim was legitimate and whether his use of deadly force was excessive, the jurors had to put themselves into Goetz's situation. Said one juror after the verdict: "The jurors live in New York. I ride the train every day. We know what the confines of the subway are. We felt that Mr. Goetz had no chance to retreat in that situation."[7] Ordinary experiences of ordinary people become very real elements in the crucible of judgment. The trials and tribulations of everyone who has to cope with crime on a daily basis were the unspoken testimony that had to weigh on the minds of the jurors trying Bernhard Goetz.

JURIES AND POLITICS

As is often the case, the law gave jurors ample latitude in bringing their own convictions to bear. To determine that deadly force could be used in self-defense, jurors had to answer two questions in the affirmative: (1) Did the defendant subjectively believe he was about to be attacked? and (2) Objectively, were these beliefs reasonable? The problem is that the notion of reasonableness is inherently unclear, revealing nothing about the circumstances under which it is normal to be afraid. The rules governing self-defense beg the key question, When is fear of crime reasonable?

The law itself thus gave little guidance to help jurors decide certain issues germane to Goetz's defense. Are body language and facial expressions accurate cues to distinguish the harmless panhandler who asks for money from the felon ready to use violence if the request for money is denied? Does it matter that Mr. Canty, who "requested" the five dollars, had three companions nearby? Was that different from a situation in which a person is accosted by someone acting alone? What about the fact that the youths' only potential weapons, filed-down screwdrivers, were never revealed or even mentioned to Goetz and were only discovered later buried in their pockets? Might a reasonable person have *assumed* that they were armed?

Because the law's standard of reasonableness is hopelessly vague, the jurors had to look within themselves to decide Goetz's guilt or innocence, unavoidably taking into account their personal feelings, that crime in the city was out of hand. Said New York University law professor Bert Neuborne: "The jurors had so little faith in the criminal justice system, both to protect us and to bring the guilty to justice, that they were willing to tolerate a degree of vigilante behavior that I think rationally cannot be justified."[8] Whether justifiable or not, the jury's conclusion that Goetz was confronted by a band of thugs and was within his rights to shoot them in self-defense had to have been influenced by personal and public attitudes toward crime and urban life. The facts were unclear and the law was vague, so the jurors drew on their own ideology in rendering judgment. "Enough is enough," was the response of a crime-weary jury.

Black and White: The Impact of Race

Two critical facts have been left out of our discussion until now: Goetz is white and his victims were black. Racial conflict is one of the major political issues in many cities and in the country at large. Whether we look at electoral battles where voters have voted overwhelmingly for candidates of their own race or whether we just eavesdrop on social conversations, a stark conclusion emerges: racial conflict permeates the United States in almost every walk of life—in the schools, in neighborhoods, at the workplace, and on the jury.

The crime issue is often enmeshed with the race issue. To be black is often to be branded a criminal; and to be a white juror dealing with blacks alleged to have committed crimes is perhaps to have an opportunity to strike out at what is widely thought of as a "black peril" in our society. It was not just Goetz who was on trial; it was the entire black race, law-abiding citizens and lawbreakers alike. Racial prejudice was surely one element in Goetz's defense.

To be sure, jurors rarely acknowledge race as an issue. The ten white and two black jurors on the Goetz jury specifically disavowed any concern about race. Said one juror after the verdict: "It didn't matter if he was a white man or a black man. Crime doesn't know color."[9] The professed view of the jurors was that Goetz's victims were young toughs who just happened to be black, a sentiment echoed by black columnist William Raspberry: "We should stop pretending that the four black youths were coming home after choir practice. . . . Goetz was right to be afraid."[10]

But we might ask, How would the jury have decided had Goetz been black and his four victims white? In the words of *Washington Post* columnist Dorothy Gillian: "If you doubt that racism was a factor, just try to imagine whether a pistol-toting black man would have had such a sweeping vindication [from the jury] had he shot 4 white teen-agers because 2 of them approached him and one of them had a 'shine' in his eyes and a 'funny' smile. . . . If you believe that, I have a cheap bridge I want to sell you."[11]

The point here is not to decide the matter one way or the other; it is to recognize that personal characteristics of defendants and victims that have little if anything to do with the evidence sometimes impinge upon jurors' perceptions of guilt and innocence. Dressing Goetz's victims in suits and ties when they testified before the jury could not change their color or the stereotypical image of lawlessness associated with young black males. The prosecution's portrayal of Goetz as paranoic, antisocial, and trigger-happy could not eradicate his white skin and frail appearance, so stereotypical of the beleaguered victim. The judge instructed the jurors to base their verdict on the law and the evidence, but jurors can hardly disregard impressions and attitudes built up over the course of a lifetime. American society is deeply affected by racial consciousness, and jurors drawn from such a society will inevitably bring this awareness to bear when deciding criminal culpability.

The Legacy of the Verdict

The Goetz case, like so many, didn't end with the verdict; it had political reverberations. Jurors were quick to deny that they had "sent a message," but others were just as quick to read all kinds of things into the jury's decision.

Many feared an unleashing of vigilantism as a result of Goetz's almost complete exoneration. One such critic was Manhattan Borough President David Dinkins (later elected mayor of New York) who called the verdict "a clear and open invitation to vigilantism."[12] Responding to such concerns, then Mayor Ed Koch immediately warned the public *not* to read such a message into the verdict: "There may be some who misperceive the case and will think that somehow or other vigilantism is acceptable. We're saying now to those who are concerned, we will never permit that."[13] Since the Goetz case, however, there have been very few incidents in which crime victims struck back violently at their assailants. Anxiety about citizens taking the law into their own hands seems to have been unfounded.

But although this potential threat did not materialize, a less tangible effect of the case still echoes throughout New York: race relations suffered a serious blow. Even though a good number of blacks empathized with Goetz's plight, especially since blacks are far more likely to be victimized by violent crime than whites are, many worried that the verdict would encourage the further stereotyping of blacks as criminals. The president of the largely black Bronx Community College minced no words: "The climate in which this decision was made, whether it be by white jurors or black jurors, is one of racism and fear of black young men."[14]

The verdict, correctly or incorrectly, was perceived by many as antiblack. When juries speak, society often listens and places its own interpretation on the jury's actions. No matter how scrupulously jurors try to decide cases objectively, their verdicts are political acts that transcend the specific facts of the case. Jury leniency toward Goetz contributed to racial polarization in an already racially tense city.

8

The Moral of the Goetz Case

We will never know what happened on that rush-hour subway train underneath New York City in late 1985: who said what, who was sitting where, what the exact trajectories of the bullets were, and what everyone was thinking. We cannot accurately reconstruct events, let alone figure out what was going on in people's minds, and neither could the jurors. They had no recourse but to rely to a considerable extent on their own predispositions and preferences. The conservative tenor of the times, attitudes toward blacks, feelings about self-defense, and deep pangs about justice—these were the hidden elements that tilted the jurors in Goetz's direction. The Goetz case thus illustrates the fundamental theme of this book: jury decision making—judgment by peers—is an intensely political process.

Political Dimensions of Jury Verdicts

Looking at the jury politically focuses our attention on certain kinds of questions that will be examined in the rest of this book. It prompts us to search beyond the formal charges and the trial record to better understand what drives jurors to one conclusion rather than another. And it forces us to look at the undercurrents of cases, the often hidden concerns that are on the minds of jurors.

In this first chapter, we lay the groundwork for studying the jury as a political entity. After an introductory look at the trial process and the role of the jury (Chapter 2), we will examine the following factors as we try to make sense out of jury behavior:

1. the skewing of juries through the juror selection process, which results in the disproportionate representation of certain political views in the jury (Chapter 3)
2. the power struggles that go on during the trial—the way that courtroom participants sway, influence, and sometimes manipulate jurors (Chapter 4)
3. jurors' concerns about justice—the moral elements that go into a determination of whether and to what degree people on trial ought to be held responsible for the acts they are accused of committing (Chapter 5)
4. jury "legislating"—the manner in which jurors bend the law and sometimes disregard it altogether because they disagree with it (Chapter 6)
5. the political climate—how the ascendancy of liberal or conservative ideologies in an area affects jury verdicts (Chapter 7)
6. the role of bias—the impact of jurors' likes and dislikes of certain kinds of people such as racial minorities on their judgments (Chapter 8)
7. jury room politics—the use of various collective choice processes that enable jurors with different viewpoints to reconcile their discords to obtain verdicts (Chapter 9)
8. the political consequences of jury verdicts—how verdicts *in toto* contribute to the constant reshaping of public policy and how certain publicized verdicts act as catalysts in the broader political arena by highlighting social issues (Chapter 10)

As we examine juror decision making in Chapters 4 through 8, we move progressively from the external factors that directly affect jury decision making, such as the trial process and the culpability of defendants, to the forces that are more inward, like political ideologies and personal prejudices. Similarly, when discussing jury deliberations in Chapter 9; we first look at the give-and-take of juror dialogues with one another and then explore the more subliminal processes of peer pressure, leadership, and negotiation. Whether looking at the cogitations of individual jurors or the workings of the jury as a whole, this book moves progressively from the outward stimuli influencing jurors to what is going on within the jurors themselves.

Studying the Jury

The jury has been studied in a variety of ways. Jurors themselves have furnished accounts of how verdicts have been reached, either in response to interviews by reporters and scholars or on their own initiative. Insights have also been offered by other participants at trials—judges, prosecutors, lawyers, witnesses, and defendants. Although the views of all those involved in the trial, including the jurors, must be treated with some skepticism because of their peculiar vantage point and self-interests, all have something to contribute in determining how juries function. The jurors have a special advantage for shedding light on what went on in the jury box and in the jury room: they were there.

Statistical analysis of verdicts—searching for trends and patterns in outcomes—is another method of studying actual trials. Unfortunately, when individual verdicts are grouped together and studied as a whole, unique elements of each case that might be the true bases of judgments (such as the evidence!) are lost. But identifying variation in conviction rates from crime to crime, place to place, and time to time does permit us to draw inferences about political and social influences on juries. I myself have engaged in a fair amount of such empirical research, some of it done expressly for this book.

Finally, virtually every potential influence on jurors has been studied in mock jury research—simulations of juries in which experimental subjects are exposed to representations of trials and respond as if they were jurors. Characteristics of crimes, trials, defendants, witnesses, and the mock jurors themselves are varied, but all other factors are held constant as the mock trial is run repeatedly. By using such experimental controls, these studies enable us to pinpoint a good number of the factors that affect the rendering of verdicts.

The word *mock* exposes some weaknesses in this line of inquiry.[15] Some of the re-creations of trials have been contrived, such as the use of brief written summaries that bear little resemblance to what happened in court. Many of the studies use college students as role players; they are not representative of actual juror pools. And all of the experiments are by definition artificial, lacking a crucial ingredient of real jurors' decisions: control over people's destinies. But the methodology of this line of research has undergone vast improvement over the years, and a voluminous body of findings has accumulated that emerged from some rather sophisticated research designs. So as we probe the juror's mind and the jury's interactions, we shall cautiously incorporate the discoveries of mock jury research into the analysis.

The jury is a difficult body to investigate. Direct observation or taping of deliberations is, with rare exceptions, prohibited. The jurors' self-reports are always somewhat suspect, and in any event jurors are usually gone from the courthouse within minutes of the verdict, making them poor targets for systematic interviewing. Statistics on verdicts never speak for themselves; interpreting them is risky business. And simulations, good as they may be, do not study the real thing.

So we utilize every kind of research possible to analyze the jury. As we try to ferret out the politics behind jury verdicts, we adopt an eclectic strategy-relying on multiple methodologies to get a sense of how the jury works. They all have shortcomings, but put together they provide a quite adequate portrayal of the jury in action.

The Discretion of Juries

When trials are over, jurors are on their own; they have virtually unfettered authority to decide outcomes. It is their right to resolve any legal ambiguities that may remain after the judge has instructed them about the law, and it is their province to determine the facts. They issue no reports, they need provide no explanations, they are monitored by no one in the legal system, and with rare exceptions, their decisions cannot be overturned. They are to a very great extent the masters of their own ship.

This is what is meant by *discretion*: flexibility in the handling of assigned tasks. Just as police, prosecutors, and judges have some leeway in applying the law, jurors also exercise their own prerogatives in making choices. Indeed, the nature of the juror's job impels such discretion: there are no unequivocally correct solutions to the disputes put before them. Trials are supposed to clarify reality, but in fact they often leave jurors awash in a sea of confusion. As the noted trial attorney F. Lee Bailey has remarked, "A trial by jury . . . is in fact a terrifying experience, riddled with uncertainty and often happenstance."[16]

Factual Uncertainty

One source of juror discretion is the uncertainty about facts that remains after trials are over. This idea, sometimes called *fact-skepticism*, was propounded years ago by Judge Jerome Frank, who called into question the effectiveness of the adjudication process. He claimed that no matter how thorough trials are, "facts are guesses."[17] Every trial has two sides: two competing lines of argument, two opposing lawyers trying to convince the jury. Indeed, the adversary process works best when it confuses the most. The prosecution and the defense both make valiant efforts to make their evidence seem sound and the opposition's evidence seem shaky, if not ridiculous. As Chapter 4 will show, the persuasive tactics of lawyers in quest of courtroom victories can hide the truth as much as illuminate it.

Police rarely come across criminals *in flagrante delicto*—"caught in the act," or literally, "while the crime is blazing." Even when that happens, jurors must wrestle with the accused's state of mind: for instance, did the defendant *know* the gun was loaded? Moreover, the cases in which criminals are caught with a "smoking gun" are the very cases likely to be resolved through guilty pleas without ever going to trial. What juries hear are mixed-up states of affairs, and unfortunately even relatively thorough trials often leave jurors in the dark.

There are many fact-finding difficulties in the trial process. Eyewitness accounts of crimes, especially by victims who are under great stress, are always open to question. Witnesses can lie, and it is not always easy to distinguish liars from those telling the truth. Relevant information is sometimes inadmissible because of the rules of evidence. Defendants often invoke their constitutional right and refuse to testify, thus depriving the jury of one side of the story. Experts testifying about such things as ballistics, insanity, or the cause of injuries often contradict one another. And inferences drawn from evidence, such as about a defendant's state of mind, are always questionable. Problems like this, to some extent, leave jurors with tough questions of judgment that cannot be decided in a mechanical fashion.

A couple of recent cases illustrate this point. Bewilderment reigned after the Los Angeles trial of a preschool director and her adult son, charged with molesting eleven children in their school over a period of five years. The trial ran from April 1987 to January 1990, and featured testimony from 124 witnesses, produced 800 exhibits, and included reels of videotaped interviews with the children who described their experiences. It resulted in 60,000 pages of transcripts and cost the taxpayers $13 million. And where did this copious outpouring of information leave jurors? One juror said, "When I went into the jury room I was as confused and uncertain as I was on the first day of the trial."[18] The jury could not reach agreement, and after another trial a second jury deadlocked. One frustrated juror stated "I felt like I went in there [the jury room] with more questions than evidence."[19] A newspaper headline captured the jurors' dilemma: "For Jurors, Facts Could Not Be Sifted from Fantasies."[20]

Another case shows that facts can be elusive even when many people have observed the crime in progress. On November 3, 1979, the Communist party held a "Death to the Klan" rally in Greensboro, North Carolina. Armed members of the Ku Klux Klan (KKK) and the American Nazi Party showed up for a counterdemonstration. A confrontation took place, during which thirty-nine shots were fired and five of the Communists were killed. The five Klansmen tried for murder claimed that they shot the victims in self-defense after being fired upon.

The key question was simple: Who shot first? Unlike many cases that lack eyewitnesses, this violence was actually videotaped in its entirety by television newscasters covering the rally. But despite the longest and costliest trial in North Carolina history, doubt about the facts remained. The jury accepted the KKK–Nazi version and acquitted the defendants. But federal prosecutors thought the jury had erred and later tried the same people for civil rights violations on the grounds that they had in fact shot first. When that trial resulted in another acquittal, many people were left skeptical, and to this day no one can say *for sure* what really happened: "facts are guesses."

The Los Angeles child molestation case and the Greensboro shoot-out trial are unusual examples: they were both thorough and probing searches for the truth. If after such extensive efforts to determine the facts, confusion still abounded, imagine how much less satisfactory are the results of the typical trial that lasts a few days or less. Individual jurors are often left "up in the air," perplexed about events, motives, alibis, and the veracity of witnesses.

Legal Ambiguity

Another source of juror discretion is legal ambiguity. The laws that jurors must apply often include concepts that cannot be understood easily or that are inherently susceptible to varying interpretations. Although judges spend considerable time giving jurors instructions about the meaning of legal provisions, the jury is still often left with rather vague standards to be applied to the case at hand. The key element in first-degree murder, premeditation, is not clear-cut: just how much forethought or planning must a defendant exhibit? A woman's consent to sexual intercourse is a valid defense in rape cases, but the term *consent* is also subject to many definitions. The imprecision of the law opens the door to juror subjectivity.

Certain legal norms are so loosely defined that they virtually defy objective application. Such is the case regarding obscenity laws. The United States Supreme Court has ruled that people can be convicted of obscenity charges only when the materials in question are so patently offensive that they violate "contemporary community standards" about sexual expression. But the Court, in *Miller* v. *California*, straightforwardly refused to provide any guidelines to clarify the criteria to be used to determine these standards:

> It is neither realistic nor constitutionally sound to read the First Amendment as requiring that the people of Maine or Mississippi accept public depiction of conduct found tolerable in Las Vegas, or New York City. People in different States vary in their tastes and attitudes, and this diversity is not to be strangled by the absolutism of imposed uniformity.[21]

13

The result of leaving the law so open-ended has been enormous inconsistency on the part of juries in resolving obscenity cases. This is well illustrated by three verdicts in separate cases rendered in a single month, October 1990. In one of them, a Cincinnati jury acquitted an art museum director of obscenity charges for displaying Robert Mapplethorpe's photographs of homosexual sadomasochism, which included pictures of a finger inserted into a penis and a man urinating into another man's anus. Said one juror, "It's not my cup of tea, I don't understand it, but if people say it's art then I have to go along with it."[22]

This verdict contrasts with a Fort Lauderdale jury's conviction of the owner of a local record store on obscenity charges for selling an album by the black rap group "2 Live Crew," which specializes in lewd rhymes about oral sex, anal sex, and other forms of sexual intercourse. In many of the songs, the singer uses vulgar language to brag about the power of his penis and his exploits with women. Despite contentions that both the content and the wording of the group's songs were perfectly acceptable in the ghetto subculture, the jury applied a more restrictive standard.

Further incongruity is illustrated in a third case decided the same month by another Fort Lauderdale jury, dealing with charges against "2 Live Crew" itself for performing in public. It took about two hours for the jury to acquit the group. In the words of the jury foreman: "As the cross section of the communty that we are, it was just not obscene. People in everyday society use these words."[23] Perhaps, but a jury from the same town reached exactly the opposite conclusion about the very same lyrics only two weeks earlier!

The seemingly contradictory results in these three cases are not surprising. The legal definition of obscenity as devised by the courts is fraught with ambiguity. It was not the facts in the three cases that were in doubt: the jurors could see the disputed photographs and hear the controversial songs. It was the law that caused uncertainty, because the meaning of "contemporary community standards" is not readily apparent. When juries are presented with such elusive legal standards, they have considerable freedom in reaching verdicts.

Jurors do seek the truth about facts and the correct meaning of the law, but they are not always there for the finding. It is therefore not surprising that a major study of jury behavior revealed that in 69 percent of all cases,[24] jurors are initially split when they first begin deliberations. The speculative nature of adjudication makes the exercise of juror discretion an inevitable fact of life.

The Jury as a Political Institution

This book interprets jury behavior politically. We accept as a premise the 150-year-old dictum of Alexis de Tocqueville, the French commentator on American government, whose sage observations in the classic *Democracy in America* have in many respects stood the test of time: "The jury is, above all, a political institution, and it must be regarded in this light in order to be duly appreciated."[25]

To understand how the jury acts politically, we must first define the word *political*. Scholars have endlessly argued about its true meaning, but the 1938 definition of Professor Harold Lasswell remains sound: politics has to do with "who gets what, when, and how."[26] Politics involves the *process* of taking sides, choosing among conflicting interests and values, and it involves certain *outcomes*: government decisions that affect the way a society is run. In summary, actions are political when people use personal discretion to produce authoritative decisions about public issues.

The jury is a political institution because it "plays politics": in exercising discretion, jurors at times rely on extralegal personal preferences to decide who wins and who loses. The jury is political in another sense: by contributing to the making of public policy. Although juries rarely think about the ramifications of their decisions while making them, the aggregate impact of multitudes of verdicts parlays the jury into a significant role in the resolution of important public issues.

This perspective is hardly earth-shaking. A hundred years ago a school of jurisprudence called *legal realism* articulated the notion that courts respond to social realities and political pressures in making decisions. In the oft-quoted words of Oliver Wendell Holmes (who later became a Supreme Court justice), written in 1881:

> The life of the law has not been logic; it has been experience. The felt necessities of the time, the prevalent moral and political theories, intuitions of public policy, avowed or unconscious, even the prejudices which judges share with their fellow-men, have had a good deal more to do than the syllogism in determining the rules by which men should be governed.[27]

These ideas, iconoclastic when written, are now orthodoxy in the understanding of legal development. The political role of the judiciary is now taken for granted, and it has been unequivocally shown how courts make policy decisions. It is widely recognized that the United States Supreme Court makes policy in construing the Constitution, and in the last two decades the political role of trial courts has come to light through a myriad of empirical studies (emphatically destroying the "upper court myth," according to which only appellate courts shape the direction of law).[28]

Strangely enough, however, de Tocqueville's profound insight about the jury's political nature has *not* been explored by many contemporary scholars. Behavioral scientists have studied the intrusion of extralegal factors on juror judgments, but this phenomenon has been seen generally as a perversion of a normally objective fact-finding process. As Gary Jacobsohn pointed out in 1977 in his own trenchant analysis of the jury's policy-making role, even political scientists "have done very little to advance an understanding of [the jury's] political character."[29] And in 1991, political scientist Lynn Mather still lamented that "although the . . . jury has a long and rich political history, discussion of juries frequently ignores their political features."[30]

Political Conflict and the Jury

Fortunately, however, there is an intellectual tradition in the broader study of American politics that points the way to the type of jury analysis undertaken in this book. James Madison, in *Federalist Number Ten* written in 1788, emphasized the ubiquity of conflict and how the various factions dividing the country used government to advance their causes. Since then, many others have explored the way conflicts over interests and values can creep into the most unexpected places, wherever decisions of public consequence are being made. Political scientist E. E. Schattschneider made the point well in 1960:

> Political conflict is not like a football game, played on a measured field by a fixed number of players in the presence of an audience scrupulously excluded from

the playing field. Politics is much more like the original primitive game of football in which everybody was free to join, a game in which the whole population of one town might play the entire population of another town, moving freely back and forth across the countryside.[31]

The jury room is in fact a perfect arena for social conflict to be fought and resolved. Jury service for most people is one of the few opportunities to participate firsthand in the making of important government decisions. One reason why most ex-jurors report having positive feelings about their experience,[32] despite long, boring waiting periods and disruption of their normal routines, is that they are given a rare chance to exercise power in a political system where their individual impact is indirect at best. Consequently, whether they are aware of it or not, jurors may use their ballots as personal statements about issues that transcend the specific facts of the case.

Occasionally jurors frankly acknowledge the politicized nature of the task in which they were engaged. Here, for example, are the words of a member of a jury that acquitted a group of black militants accused of planning violence during the early 1970s:

> Jury duty seemed to have a special value in this phase of United States history. The killings of Kent State students that went unprosecuted, along with countless killings of blacks by white authorities. The fighting in Vietnam could not be stopped. Even—yes—crime in the streets: Its profound causes seemed hopelessly out of control. Our chance to get the jury view put us exactly in the center of at least one problem, with the responsibility of making a decision about it. Jury duty was a citizen's rare opportunity not to be helpless in the functions of the system.[33]

Such candor is unusual, but the intrusion of political input into jury decision making is a standard phenomenon. There are all kinds of issues and political conflicts that present themselves to juries and become hidden agendas: disputes between liberals and conservatives about crime policies; clashes over gender, race, and ethnicity; discord about moral standards; and disagreements about every imaginable public policy issue—the right to self-defense, euthanasia, consumer protection, the environment, and the homeless. Burning controversies of the day are not neatly confined to the polling booth or legislative chamber: they find their way into all kinds of places, including the jury box.

The trial of the head of the Seminole Indian tribe illustrates how seemingly mundane cases can put important social conflicts in the jury's lap. James Billie went on trial in Florida for violating the Endangered Species Act by killing a rare Florida panther as part of a religious ritual. The jury had to cope with more than the factual question about how hard it was to distinguish the endangered panther from other nonendangered members of the cougar family. Billie claimed not only that the First Amendment's freedom of religion protected this tribal rite but that treaties between the United States Government and the Seminoles protected Indian hunting rights. Although the judge ruled against him on both counts, stating that the only issue was whether Billie knowingly killed the protected animal, the jury was faced with a pointed conflict pitting Indian rights against wildlife conservation. The federal jury deadlocked, but a subsequent state prosecution resulted in an acquittal. Did the juries' verdicts simply reflect doubts about the evidence, or were they responding to the deeper issues underlying the case? That will never be known, but the Seminoles certainly felt vindicated by the outcome. Said one member of the tribe: "We feel good about it. At least somebody's on our side."[34]

Civil cases, too, raise issues that transcend the legal dispute in the courtroom. Marian Guinn's invasion of privacy suit against local officials of the Church of Christ for denouncing her before the entire congregation as an adulteress gave the jury deep political issues to ponder. Although technically the jury's function was simply to apply the standards of the civil law of torts to the case at hand, the jurors who awarded her $390,000 later admitted seeing their mission more broadly. Several minced no words in stating that they had weighed a woman's right to live according to her own sexual standards against the right of churches to discipline their members and had come out strongly in favor of the former.[35] The broad issue of sexual morality is unmistakably a political issue, whether it is debated in a legislature or decided upon in a jury room.

Any political feud that engulfs communities or the society as a whole has the potential for spilling over into the jury room. Verdicts are much more than simply the application of legal standards and the ascertainment of facts. They are in some measure political outcomes. Juries and politics are inextricably linked.

Juries and Populism

The jury is not only a political institution but also a very special kind of political institution. Unlike so many governmental bodies, which are more or less elitist in nature, the jury to a considerable extent mirrors popular values and sentiments. Although there are selection biases (to be discussed in Chapter 3) that keep the jury from being anywhere near a perfect reflection of the entire body politic, it is a means for the expression of majoritarian sentiment. Dominant social values often become the underlying basis for resolving the perplexing factual quandaries left unanswered by the trial process. Elected officials may at times reflect the will of the people, but their views are an indirect representation of current feelings. Jury decision making, on the other hand, is literally the *vox populi*—the voice of the people. It is populism in action.

17

The Jury Decision-Making Process

Jurors and juries very rarely consider political factors explicitly: the decision-making process is far more subtle. In fact, when asked how she or he decided a case, a juror almost invariably answers "I stuck to the facts." And jurors who so respond are not lying, for it has been shown that they generally make sincere efforts and often use dogged determination to get at the truth.[36] But as the truth is often hard to discover, jurors must use their own political sentiments to shed light on shadowy facts and legal concepts. The intrusion of political beliefs is normally a subconscious phenomenon: jurors tend to construe the facts in a way that produces decisions that they find personally satisfying.

This idea was developed by Professors Harry Kalven and Hans Zeisel of the University of Chicago in their classic work on the jury published in the 1960s. Recognizing that "fact-finding and value judgments are subtly intertwined," they developed what they called the "liberation hypothesis": the ambiguities in the evidence and vagueness of legal concepts *liberate* jurors to decide relatively close cases in accordance with their own values. The jury yields to their own sentiments in the process of resolving doubts.[37]

The very nature of the adversary process, with the presentation of opposing arguments and evidence, provides some legitimate basis for whatever verdict is rendered. There is always some piece of evidence, line of argument, or legal definition for jurors to seize upon in order to justify the outcome they prefer. There are different ways of seeing things and different conclusions that can be drawn from the same information. In the words of British scholar Patrick Devlin, jurors who want to acquit take a "merciful view of the facts";[38] those desiring convictions look at the facts vindictively.

The psychological theory of cognitive dissonance is useful for explaining how politics can undermine the jurors' best intentions to be objective. Leon Festinger, who propounded the theory in the 1950s,[39] cogently argued that people confronted with inconsistent ideas (cognitive dissonance) feel very uncomfortable with the ensuing contradictions, especially when external evidence conflicts with deeply held sentiments. To avert or relieve this anxiety, they may employ various cerebral techniques for reducing the inconsistency, including distortion of reality to conform to preconceived opinion and to comport with instinctive feelings. A classic example of this psychological phenomenon is the heavy smoker who, by disparaging the use of statistics, rejects the incontrovertible scientific evidence that smoking causes cancer, bringing up examples of 90-year-olds who smoked three packs of cigarettes a day or claiming that smoking prevents other health problems such as overeating.

This adeptness at rationalization to avoid the unpleasantness of cognitive dissonance is the key to understanding jury behavior. As the jurors cope with the gamut of issues confronting them, they must also deal with their personal feelings and opinions. To the extent that they are strongly committed to their points of view, they will use their mental prowess to bring the law and the evidence in line with these views.

For example, jurors who are avid hunters and resentful of strict game laws may choose to believe that a defendant charged with hunting out of season was simply engaged in target practice in the woods when a herd of deer bounded into his or her line of fire. Those eager for acquittal may well accept as exonerating evidence tin cans supposedly used as targets found near the scene of the shooting, even if the cans were rusty and lacked any bullet holes. "Their aim was terrible," a sympathetic juror might reflect; "the unshot cans show just how desperately they needed practice!" Politics, in this case disdain for restrictions on the right to hunt, becomes the largely hidden but nonetheless quite powerful driving force behind the jurors' thought processes.

Several current approaches to jury decision making emphasize the cognitive processes involved as jurors simultaneously juggle facts and feelings. It is doubtless true, as advocates of "information processing" theory contend,[40] that logic is a major component of juror fact finding; but it is the juror's politics that so often provide the premises and fill in the gaps that pure reasoning leaves open. Similarly, the "story model" devised by Hastie, Penrod, and Pennington;[41] stresses that jurors try to reconstruct reality by creating a credible story that ties together all the evidence. Of course, not every juror would compose the same story. Professor Phoebe Ellsworth, commenting on the story model, makes the point well: "It is well known among psychologists that much of what is perceived is a function of the perceiver; it is a particular *construct* of the events perceived, rather than a true reflection."[42] Which scenario of events among many plausible ones is most believable to a juror may well depend on the verdict that a particular juror prefers.

There are cases in which the evidence is so overwhelmingly one-sided that only one verdict seems plausible, and under such circumstances jurors rarely decide the other way unless they are fanatically committed to the values that would lead to the preposterous outcome. After all, one of the values to which almost all jurors are dedicated is coming up with truthful verdicts. Total denials of reality, although not unknown, are rare: jurors do not often convict those who are undoubtedly innocent or acquit those who are unquestionably guilty.

The chapters that follow stress the political dimensions of jury decision making. It is contended that politics is as central to the exercise of jury discretion as it is to all other acts of government. When the trial doesn't present clear answers, jurors to a greater or lesser extent rely on their political instincts as they grope for the proper verdict.

Conclusion

Benjamin Franklin would have understood jurors. Writing two centuries ago in his *Autobiography*, he made this pithy observation about human nature: "So convenient a thing it is to be a *reasonable* creature, since it enables one to find or make a reason for every thing one has a mind to do."[43] A juror who "has a mind" to convict can normally find plenty of reasons to do so, just as an acquittal-oriented juror usually can find grounds for exoneration.

In this chapter and in this book, we put forth the theory that jurors act politically in going about the business of reaching verdicts. Normally faced with contradictory evidence and arguments, they lean toward one side or the other on the basis of their personal views on the many social issues that underlie cases. Trials are more than fact-finding exercises; they entail conflicts of values, interests, and ideologies. The jury, from this perspective, is an inherently political institution.

Notes

1. Quoted in David Pitt, "Goetz Jurors Found Both Sides Evidence Difficult to Accept," *The New York Times* (June 20, 1987), p. A1.
2. Quoted in "Not Guilty," *Time* (June 29, 1987): 10.
3. Quoted in Pitt, "Goetz Jurors Found Both Sides Evidence Difficult to Accept."
4. Mark Lesly, "Diary of a Juror," *The New York Post* (June 19, 1987), p. 5.
5. Franklin Zimring, "Why the Goetz Verdict Was Not a Landmark Precedent," *The New York Times* (June 21, 1987), p. E25.
6. Quoted in Margaret Hornblower, "Jury Exonerates Goetz in 4 Subway Shootings," *The Washington Post* (June 17, 1987), p. A15. © 1987, *The Washington Post*. Reprinted with permission.
7. Ibid., A14.
8. Quoted in Joseph Berger, "Goetz Case: Commentary on Nature of Urban Life," *The New York Times* (June 18, 1987), p. B6.
9. Quoted in Hornblower, "Jury Exonerates Goetz in 4 Subway Shootings."
10. William Raspberry, "Let's Stop Pretending," *The Washington Post* (June 19, 1987), p. A25.
11. Dorothy Gillian, "Law of the Monster," *The Washington Post* (June 18, 1987), p. D3. © 1987, *The Washington Post*. Reprinted with permission.
12. Quoted in David Pitt, "Blacks See Goetz Verdict as Blow to Race Relations," *The New York Times* (June, 1987), p. A1.
13. Quoted in Kirk Johnson, "Goetz Is Cleared in Subway Attack: Gun Count Upheld," *The New York Times* (June 17, 1987).
14. Quoted in Pitt, "Blacks See Goetz Verdict as Blow to Race Relations."
15. For more elaboration of methodological problems of mock jury research, see Wayne Weiten and Shari Seidman Diamond, "A Critical Review of the Jury Simulation Paradigm: The Case of Defendant Characteristics," *Law and Human Behavior*, 3 (1979): 71–93. Also see Kathleen Carrese Gerbasi, Miron Zuckerman, and Harry Reis, "Justice Needs a New Blindfold: A Review of Mock Jury Research," *Psychological Bulletin*, 84 (1977): 323–345.
16. Quoted in L. Wrightsman, "The American Trial Jury on Trial: Empirical Evidence and Procedural Modifications," *Journal of Social Issues*, 34 (1978): 138.
17. Jerome Frank, *Courts on Trial: Myth and Reality in American Justice* (New York: Athenium, 1967), pp. 14–36.
18. Seth Mydans, "For Jurors, Facts Could Not Be Sifted from Fantasies," *The New York Times* (January 1, 1990), p. A18.
19. Seth Mydans, "7 Years Later, McMartin Case Ends in a Mistrial," *The New York Times* (June 28, 1990), p. 1.
20. Seth Mydans, "For Jurors, Facts Could Not Be Sifted from Fantasies, *The New York Times* (January 1, 1990), p. A18.
21. 413 U.S. 14 (1973).

22. Quoted in Anna Quindlen, "Grand Juries," *The New York Times* (October 25, 1990), p. A27.

23. Sara Rimer, "Rap Band Members Found Not Quilty in Obscenity Trial," *The New York Times* (October 22, 1990), p. 1.

24. Harry Kalven and Hans Zeisel, *The American Jury* (Chicago: University of Chicago Press, 1971), p. 488.

25. Alexis de Tocqueville, *Democracy in America*. Translated by Henry Reeve, revised by Francis Bowers, edited by Phillips Bradley. (New York: A. A. Knopf, 1946), Vol. I, p. 282.

26. Harold Lasswell, *Politics: Who Gets What, When, and How* (New York: McGraw-Hill, 1938).

27. Oliver Wendall Holmes, *The Common Law,* edited by Mark deWolfe Howe (Cambridge, Mass.: Harvard University Press, 1963), p. 5.

28. See John Gates and Charles Johnson (eds.), *The American Courts: A Critical Assessment* (Washington, D.C.: CQ Press, 1991).

29. Gary Jacobsohn, "Citizen Participation in Policy-Making: The Role of the Jury," *The Journal of Politics*, 39 (1977), p. 74.

30. Lynn Mather, "Policy Making in State Trial Courts," in John Gates and Charles Johnson (eds.), *The American Courts: A Critical Assessment* (Washington, D.C.: CQ Press, 1991), p. 139.

31. E. E. Schattschneider, *The Semisovereign People: A Realist's View of Democracy in America* (Hinsdale, Illinois: Dryden Press, 1975), p. 18.

32. W. Pabst, G. Munsterman, and C. Mount, "Myth of the Unwilling Juror," *Judicature*, 60 (1976): 164–171.

33. E. Kinnebeck, *Juror Number Four: The Trial of Thirteen Black Panthers as Seen from the Jury Box* (New York: Norton, 1973).

34. "Mistrial Declared in Panther Killing," *The New York Times* (August 28, 1987), p. A32.

35. "Award in Church-Privacy Suit," *The New York Times* (March 16, 1984), p. A13.

36. D. Bridgeman and D. Marlowe, "Jury Decision-Making: An Empirical Study Based on Actual Felony Trials," *Journal of Applied Psychology*, 64 (1979): 91–98.

37. Kalven and Zeisel, *The American Jury,* 163–167.

38. P. Devlin, *The Enforcement of Morals* (London: Stevens, 1959), p. 21.

39. Leon Festinger, *A Theory of Cognitive Dissonance* (Stanford, Calif.: Stanford University Press, 1957).

40. M. Kaplan and L. Miller, "Reducing the Effects of Juror Bias," *Journal of Personality and Social Psychology*, 36 (1978): 1443–1455.

41. Reid Hastie, Steven Penrod, and Nancy Pennington, *Inside the Jury* (Cambridge, Mass.: Harvard University Press, 1983).

42. Phoebe Ellsworth, "Are Twelve Heads Better than One?" *Law and Contemporary Problems*, 52 (Autumn 1989): 206.

43. Benjamin Franklin, *Autobiography,* edited by L. Labaree, P. Kelchan, H. Boatfield, and H. Fineman. (New Haven: Yale University Press, 1964), p. 87.

21

2
. . . .
Trial by
Jury in the
United States

A Brief History of the Jury

The origins of the jury are obscure, but as in so many democratic institutions, we can trace some of its roots to the Greeks. In his play *The Eumenides*, Aeschylus refers to the concept of peer justice—the idea of having ordinary people sit in judgment of those accused of crimes. The goddess Athena, confronted with a man accused of murder, calls forth the first jury, the Areiopagica:

> This is too grave a cause for any man to judge; nor, in a case of murder, is it right that I should by my judgement let the wrath of Justice loose. . . . [S]ince decision falls to me, I will choose out jurors of homicide, for a perpetual court, in whom I vest my judgement. . . . I'll pick my wisest citizens, and bring them here sworn to give sentence with integrity and truth.[1]

Although this calling forth of citizens takes place in a drama, it reflects a practice that emerged around 500 B.C. The Greek dicastery was made up of between 501 and 6,000 *dicasts*, volunteers from the public who deliberated the fate of individuals accused of crime. It was they who convicted Socrates of, among other things, corrupting the youth in 399 B.C. The dicasts were belittled by many of Athens' elites, including Plato and Apollodorus, but nonetheless they were entrusted with the responsibility of deciding the facts, the law, and often the sentence.

The Romans, the Franks (under Charlemagne), and the Anglo-Saxons in England also experimented with the concept of the jury, but its modern development began with William the Conqueror, the Norman leader who subdued England in 1066 A.D. William used panels of citizens to help the Crown record financial information, and a century later Henry II began the process of using British townspeople to consider criminal matters.

These precursors of the modern jury served mainly the needs of the ruling monarchs by obtaining better information about local affairs. Rather than protectors of the accused, they were replacements for less enlightened forms of trial, trial by battle and trial by ordeal. Under trial by battle, people in conflict fought each other in jousts or duels: the victor was absolved, and the loser condemned on the grounds that God had sided with the winner. Under trial by ordeal, accused persons were subjected to endurance tests, such as being burned with hot irons: those who survived were said to have received God's blessings and were therefore proclaimed innocent.

These trials, based on divine guidance, were gradually supplemented by a process akin to the modern procedure of grand jury indictment. Before a person was subjected to ordeal or battle, a group of people knowledgeable about community affairs decided whether there was sufficient evidence to accuse the suspect. The turning point of the jury's development occurred in 1215, when a group of barons forced King John to accept trial by jury as a right of the accused. In the *Magna Carta*, King John promised that "no free man shall be taken or imprisoned . . . or outlawed or exiled or in any way destroyed except by the lawful judgment of his peers." This concession was an acceptance of the idea that ordinary citizens would be not only witnesses and accusers but ultimate decision makers on the issue of guilt or innocence. Significantly, it was in the same year that the Lateran Council forbade clerical participation in ordeals; this left a gap in legal procedures that the jury filled. Thus, popular participation in the judicial process was established centuries before the "bloodless revolution" of 1688 established the notion of parliamentary supremacy and democratic control over the legislative process in England.

At first, people on British juries decided guilt or innocence on the basis of personal observation. Jurors were eyewitnesses or members of the community who had some special knowledge. Basically, they were neighbors of the accused who investigated the incident in question and rendered judgment accordingly. Their role in law enforcement was equal to or greater than their judicial role.

Later, juries were composed of people unconnected to the criminal incidents in question. Their job was to listen to the evidence presented by both sides and use their common sense to figure out what really happened and whether the law had been violated. These juries also determined what the meaning of the law was and whether it applied to the specific circumstances at hand. They became central institutions in the process of adjudication.

The jury's new role went well beyond fact finding. During this period, from roughly 1200 to 1600 A.D., the jury developed a spirit of independence. In fact, the jury played an important role in the social history of homicide,

23

substituting its own judgment about culpability for that of the law. The jurors at the time balked at the law of England that required the imposition of death against all those convicted of homicide, and so returned a verdict of guilty in only a small percentage of cases.[2] Instead, juries either acquitted or produced findings of self-defense, often in contradiction to the facts. In this way, the harshness of British law was mitigated by the jury's willingness to stretch the facts to spare the accused. From the early stages of jury development, politics became an accepted part of jury decision making, with jurors occasionally using popular judgments to curtail unacceptable dictates of the British government.

The American colonies adopted the jury system at the outset, and juries played a prominent role in the American process of adjudication. Thus, in 1735, when publisher Peter Zenger was accused of seditious libel, lawyer Andrew Hamilton successfully urged the jury to use its position to support the precious value of freedom of the press. Said Hamilton to the jurors: "Jurymen are to see with their own eyes, to hear with their own ears, and to make use of their own conscience and understandings, in judging of the lives, liberties or estates of people."[3]

So central were juries to the colonial value system that King George's curtailment of juries was one of the major grievances listed in the Declaration of Independence. The jury had come to be seen not merely as a sensible fact-finding device but as a means of protecting individual rights from despotic governments. The jury was hailed by colonists as "a valuable safeguard of liberty" and the "palladium of free government."[4] Even leaders of the incipient republic who were skeptical about democratic governance, such as Alexander Hamilton, not only approved of the jury but advocated a robust role for it.

It is little wonder that the framers of the United States Constitution and the Bill of Rights made trial by jury a right of defendants not only in criminal cases but in most civil cases as well. It was virtually the only procedural right embedded in the original constitution: Article III, Section 2, states that "the trial of all Crimes, except in cases of impeachment, shall be by jury." This right was reaffirmed in the Sixth Amendment. Judgment by peers—people lacking rank, title, or position—was to be a means of holding the new government accountable to the people. To be sure, many were excluded from the jury—the same people who were also denied the franchise in many states: blacks, women, non-Christians, and those without property. But these juries *were* bodies of ordinary citizens with the power not only to decide the facts but to interpret the law and to apply their own moral standards. The politicized jury was considered *de rigueur* and a legitimate infusion of social values into the administration of justice.

In the first half of the nineteenth century, the jury dominated the judicial process—a period that has been called the "golden age" of trials. Not only were most criminal cases resolved before juries, but jurors had enormous leeway to draw on their own feelings about the cases in addition to the evidence laid out in the courtroom. Trials were relatively informal processes, technical rules were at a minimum, and the jury reigned supreme. Criminal justice historian Samuel Walker characterized the jury of the nineteenth century as "the direct voice of the community, expressing its irrationalities and prejudices."[5]

This all changed in the latter part of the nineteenth century and during the twentieth century. Prosecutors and judges gained more control over cases, dismissing many and working out guilty pleas in many others. An administrative process replaced an adversarial process in dealing with the growing number of burglary, theft, robbery, and assault cases coming before the courts. Jury trials became somewhat rare luxuries affordable by rich defendants or the last resorts of those accused of the most serious crimes.

The jury's freedom of action was also restricted, perhaps in part as a result of the growing professionalism of the legal system and the disdain that many prominent lawyers of the late-nineteenth century had for the nation's growing masses.[6] Instead of being given general mandates to follow in deciding for one side or the other, judges gave juries detailed instructions about the law that they were supposed to follow. The law of evidence was developed, depriving jurors of all kinds of information considered irrelevant, biased, or illicitly obtained. Warnings to jurors to disregard their own sentiment about the law and their own feelings about proper punishment became commonplace. The "directed verdict" of English law was embraced by American judges, enabling them to find defendants not guilty on the grounds that there had been insufficient incriminating evidence to justify sending the case to the jury. Disposition of cases without juries became commonplace, as lawyers and judges assumed much control of the judicial process. Gradually the jury was stripped of much of its authority by legislatures and judges.

However, the political role of the jury did not disappear. In the rest of this book we shall see that the jury's political function, which used to be aboveboard, continues to affect the decision-making process but in a sub rosa fashion. We will also show that the jury's importance today lies not in the number of cases it hears but in the types of cases it decides and the impact their decisions have. Not only does jury power remain substantial, but jury politics remains alive and well.

The Jury and the Constitution

The vitality of the jury has been enhanced by the constitutional blessings it has received from the Supreme Court. Although both Article III and the Sixth Amendment provide for trial by jury in criminal cases and the Seventh Amendment gives litigants the right to trial by jury in any cases involving at least twenty dollars, early constitutional decisions limited these rights to cases arising in federal court. The only way that constitutional protections found in the Bill of Rights could be extended to state law and state cases was through the Fourteenth Amendment's due process clause, which forbids states to deny life, liberty, or property without due process of law. And in 1937, the Supreme Court ruled that only "fundamental" rights essential to

25

the "principle of justice" were to be incorporated into the coverage of the due process clause.[7] Jury trial was *not* deemed to be one of these rights, leaving state legislatures and state courts free to deprive defendants of juries if they were so inclined. Although the constitutions of most states provided the right to jury trial in certain kinds of cases, the United States Constitution had no bearing on how this right was to be explicated.

This all changed in the 1960s, when liberalism surfaced in many parts of American government, including the courts. Many of the rights deemed nonfundamental in earlier years were reevaluated, one of them being the right to trial by jury. In *Duncan* v. *Louisiana*[8] in 1968, the Supreme Court ruled that jury trial in criminal cases *was* fundamental to the American scheme of justice. Thus, the due process clause of the Fourteenth Amendment guaranteed a jury trial in state courts in any kind of case that, if tried in federal court, would entitle defendants to a jury trial under the Sixth Amendment. Applying this guideline, the Court has subsequently ruled that if defendants are subjected to the potential of at least six months imprisonment—whether they are being tried for felonies, misdemeanors, or criminal contempt of court because of improper courtroom behavior—they have the right to be tried by a jury.[9] Moreover, in *Blanton* v. *North Las Vegas,* the Supreme Court declared that there may be a right to a jury trial when less than a six-month sentence is permissible if there are other penalties that are so severe that they indicate the legislature treated the crime as serious rather than petty.[10] On the other hand, the Seventh Amendment's provision for jury trials in civil cases has *not* been incorporated into the Fourteenth Amendment, because less is at stake than in criminal trials. So states are permitted to use their own discretion in determining the extent to which the civil jury is used.

The rationale of the Supreme Court is noteworthy. The Court does not allege that it is the jurors' adeptness at fact finding that makes their role in sorting out the guilty from the innocent imperative. Rather, it emphasizes the political dimensions of the jury's decision making: protecting defendants from government oppression, giving defendants the opportunity to benefit from jurors' sympathetic reactions, and preventing miscarriages of justice. It is the jurors' values, not their brains or knowledge, that make their participation critical to due process.

Consistent with this reasoning, the Court has held that a jury is not required in juvenile court delinquency proceedings. In *McKeiver* v. *Pennsylvania*,[11] emphasis was placed on the fact that the juvenile court system is based on the premise of *in loco parentis*: the court plays the role of the parent. The community is specifically excluded from hearings: visitors are not allowed, there is no press coverage, and court transcripts are permanently sealed. Only those constitutional rights that have a bearing on fact finding are extended to juveniles to make certain that mistakes about guilt are avoided. "But," in the words of the Supreme Court, "one cannot say that in our legal system the jury is a necessary component of accurate fact-finding." What the court implicitly is saying is that the major virtue of the jury is as a source of political input from the public; but where such politicization is undesirable (as in juvenile hearings), the justification for the jury disappears.

The issue of jury politics also arises with regard to the question of a defendant's waiver of a jury trial in favor of a bench trial heard by a judge alone. Federal rules and most state procedures require consent of the prosecutor and/or the judge, and the Supreme Court has upheld this limitation on the right to waive the jury. Despite the fact that trial before a jury might well, under some circumstances, subject defendants to public passions and prejudices detrimental to them, the Court in *Singer v. United States* dismissed such objections on the grounds that the jury is the "normal and preferable" way of deciding criminal cases.[12] Again, the implication is that the idea of populism is to be given substantial weight in working out constitutional law.

The constitutional right to a civil jury in federal courts also is rooted in the desire to give ordinary people a chance to determine the allocation of responsibility and obligations in civil disputes—decidedly political questions. According to Judge Patrick Higgenbotham of the United States Court of Appeals, an expert on the Seventh Amendment, the framers of the Constitution saw the civil jury as a means of granting political power to the citizenry.[13] Giving this right to litigants was a way of bringing popular justice and the "distinct values" of jurors into the judicial system.

Consequently, there has been reluctance to exclude juries even from the so-called complex case involving technical and detailed evidence, which presumably are beyond the grasp of laypersons. The third circuit of the United States Court of Appeals has ruled that there is a "complexity exception" to the Seventh Amendment,[14] but this ruling has not been adopted by other federal courts. Although giving jurors the job of dealing with complicated economic or engineering data is arguably a deprivation of due process because of the potential for miscomprehension, appellate courts have deemed jurors capable of resolving the fundamental issues of fairness and equity that confront them. Keeping the jury—even in mass disaster cases involving multiple plaintiffs, multiple defendants, and millions of dollars in possible damages—is a way of allowing democratic processes to determine "who gets what, when, and how," which is what politics is all about.

The Structure of the American Jury

The Constitution says almost nothing about the composition of the jury other than mandating that it be "impartial." This simple word has engendered an enormous body of constitutional law dealing with the qualifications of jurors—criteria for inclusion and exclusion. These rules will be dealt with in Chapter 3 in the discussion of jury selection procedures.

Finding nothing in the text of the Constitution about the makeup of the jury, the courts decided quite early that the model for the federal jury should be the jury that existed in colonial America at the time of the country's founding. Thus, the use of twelve jurors and the requirement of unanimous verdicts are features of the jury that were grafted onto the Sixth Amendment. Practices of the colonies regarding the civil jury were less clear-cut, so the Seventh Amendment's assurance of a jury in federal cases was never interpreted as mandating any particular jury characteristics. The only requirement is that the structure used assures a "fair and equitable resolution of factual issues."[15]

The Supreme Court, however, has asserted that both the size of the criminal jury and the unanimous decision rule established at the outset of the nation were merely "historical accidents," transplanting British customs in the development of American institutions. These features of the jury have been characterized as not necessarily related to the quality of jury decision making—the ability to reach the proper verdict. Consequently, the Supreme Court has ruled that states need not adhere to age-old definitions of the kind of jury that states are required to afford those accused of serious crimes.

Specifically, it has been ruled that it is constitutional for states to save money by using juries with as few as six members. In *Williams* v. *Florida*, it was held that participation of the community could be adequately achieved with a jury smaller than the traditional jury of twelve, a number the Supreme Court said had no importance "except to mystics."[16] Because the smaller size did not make the jury significantly less reliable in reaching correct verdicts, did not threaten the representative nature of the jury, and did not in itself make group deliberation less vigorous, the jury of six passed constitutional muster. However, the Court alluded to the possibility that the jury *could* be made too small to serve justice well, and recognized that they were on a "slippery slope" that might become too sharp if the number were reduced below six.

This decision, which cited empirical evidence on jury functioning to support its contention, was sharply criticized by scholars as misinterpreting and overrelying on studies that were methodologically flawed. As one professor put it, "ignorance of science is no excuse" for misusing it.[17] The Supreme Court may have been responding to this academic rebuke when it drew the line at six, striking down Georgia's jury of five in *Ballew* v. *Georgia*.[18] The Court's opinion brought in more sophisticated studies than were dealt with in the *Williams* case, studies that tended to cast doubt on the reliability of the smaller jury. However, its main concern was not fact-finding effectiveness but adequate political representation. Echoes of the political theory of jury decision making described in the first chapter of this book reverberate in Justice Blackman's characterization of jury functioning in the *Ballew* case:

> Because juries frequently face complex problems laden with value choices, the benefits [of the larger group] are important and should be retained. In particular the counterbalancing of various biases is critical to the accurate application of the common sense of the community to the facts of any given case.

The other area in which states have been permitted to deviate from the constitutional standard for federal courts is the imposition of the decision rule.

The Supreme Court approved the use of nonunanimous jury verdicts in non-capital cases in a pair of decisions directed at avoiding the wastefulness of "hung juries" that fail to reach complete agreement: Louisiana's statute permitting 9–3 verdicts of guilt and Oregon's law allowing 10–2 convictions.[19] Justice Douglas, in dissent, argued that nonunanimity denied due process because it permitted convictions even if some jurors had reasonable doubt, and it eliminated the "earnest and robust argument necessary to reach unanimity."[20] The majority of the Court, in confronting this argument, ruled that group conformity effects (to be discussed later in chapter 9) normally result in capitulation of jury holdouts, so the impact of unanimity requirements was inconsequential. Moreover, using analysis quite similar to that used in cases on jury size, the Court stressed that the jury's main function was *not* accurate fact finding: it was to act as "a group of laymen representative of a cross section of the community" who go about the business of reaching "common-sense judgment."[21]

Taking this tinkering with the structure of the jury one step further, the state of Louisiana tried to combine a jury of fewer than twelve with a non-unanimity rule, and the Supreme Court unanimously struck it down.[22] Louisiana's arrangement, whereby those accused of misdemeanors could be convicted by five out of six jurors, was invalidated on the grounds that, in criminal cases, conviction by at least six people is necessary to maintain the safeguards that the jury is intended to provide—mainly, sufficient community sentiment in favor of a guilty verdict.

To some degree, this host of decisions and the scholarly debate surrounding it are a tempest in a teapot. Ironically, England has dispensed with the unanimity rule in criminal cases and now permits convictions by a margin of ten to two, provided the jury first deliberates for at least two hours. But few states in this country have followed suit. As of 1988, only five states permitted nonunanimous convictions by juries: Louisiana, Montana, Oklahoma, Oregon and Texas. However, thirty-four states now require something less than 100 percent juror agreement in civil cases. Thus, most states follow the practice of the federal courts, even though they are not required by the Constitution to do so.

Reduced jury size is also a phenomenon that affects a limited set of states and cases. Only six states have reduced the number of jurors deciding criminal cases involving felonies to below twelve: Connecticut, Florida, Louisiana, and Oregon use six; Arizona and Utah use eight. Twenty states, however, use fewer than twelve jurors in cases entailing misdemeanors only. And a substantial majority of states, as well as most federal district courts, use smaller-size juries in civil cases.

Trial Procedures

Trial by jury is a complex affair. Over the years, legislatures and courts have created an extensive series of procedural steps to be taken before, during, and after trials. The rules governing these procedures, such as hearings on

29

the legitimacy of police line-ups, are highly technical. The total process is an elaborate one, so complicated that law schools devote entire courses to criminal procedure and civil procedure. Here we can only give a rudimentary sketch of the various stages, so that the jury's role can be seen in its appropriate legal context.[23]

Criminal Procedure

In criminal cases, courts take over after police make arrests. The accused soon has an *initial appearance* before a judge, a hearing in which formal charges are made, the defendant is advised of his or her rights, counsel is appointed if the accused cannot afford a lawyer, and bail is set. Shortly thereafter there is a *preliminary hearing,* in which the judge decides whether there is sufficient evidence to justify proceeding further. If not, the case is dismissed. If so, the case moves on, in some states to the grand jury, where the twenty-three members receive the prosecutor's evidence. If the jurors decide by a majority vote that the evidence is adequate to justify a trial, they issue an *indictment.* In states like California that have abolished the grand jury, the prosecutor alone decides whether to move forward, issuing an *information* if a trial is warranted.

Soon thereafter, an *arraignment* is held, during which the defendant enters his or her plea. In the plea bargaining process, the defendant pleads guilty to some charges and waives the right to a jury trial in exchange for some form of leniency. If the defendant pleads innocent, the case moves to the trial stage. A whole set of pretrial activities then ensues, including a process known as *discovery,* in which the prosecution and the defense are allowed access to the evidence availing to the other side. Under some circumstances, adverse witnesses can be interviewed under oath and recorded by a court reporter in what is known as a *deposition.*

Then comes the trial, the first step of which is jury selection (to be discussed in detail in the next chapter). Each side makes an *opening statement,* in which each provides an overview of what it intends to prove and the evidence it will be presenting. The prosecution then interrogates witnesses, and after each one testifies, the defense is allowed to *cross-examine* in an attempt to expose weaknesses in the witnesses' testimony (sometimes known as *impeaching the witness*). The prosecutor can then engage in another round of questioning, known as the *redirect,* to be followed by a last opportunity for the defense, known as the *recross.*

After the prosecution rests its case, the defense can present its own witnesses, but it need not if the defense believes that the prosecution failed to prove guilt beyond a reasonable doubt. If the defense does present witnesses, the prosecution gets the same chance to break their testimony down through cross-examination. Defendants may testify on their own behalf, but the Fifth Amendment's *privilege against self-incrimination* means they cannot be forced to do so.

At the end of the trial, lawyers for each side present *closing statements*, which include both summaries of the evidence and allusions to broader questions raised by the case. This is the point at which lawyers can overtly bring in political issues. The prosecutor may emphasize how ghastly a crime is to appeal to jurors' conservatism; the defense may discuss the legitimacy of the defendant's motives, as in cases in which women retaliate against wife-beaters. The last word comes from the judge, who gives *instructions* explaining general legal principles and the various verdict options open to the jury. The instructions include specific definitions of the laws applicable to the case at hand and what *elements* of a crime must have been proved for the jury to convict.

The case then goes to the jury for deliberation. If the jury returns a guilty verdict on any or all charges, a *sentencing hearing* takes place some time later, normally without a jury at which time the judge decides the punishment. Defendants who are found guilty can file *post-verdict motions*, alleging either that the jury had no basis for a conviction or that prejudicial errors were made that justify a retrial. If the jury is unable to reach a verdict, a *mistrial* is declared and the prosecution has the option of deciding whether to try the defendant again.

Civil Procedure

Civil law is private law, involving the rights and duties that people and institutions have with regard to others. A person who claims to have been wronged by someone can sue for *damages*, the monetary equivalent of the losses suffered. The person suing is called the *plaintiff*; the person sued is the *defendant*. A pedestrian injured in an automobile accident, for example, can sue the negligent driver and claim the cost of medical treatment, lost earnings, the economic loss of permanent injuries, and even the dollars-and-cents estimate of intangible harm, such as emotional distress. In certain situations, a wronged party can get court protection by means of *injunctions*, which are court orders restraining an individual's actions.

The first step in civil cases is the filing of a *complaint* by the plaintiff. The defendant is sent a copy of the complaint (a step known as *serving process*) and must file an *answer* with the court; the complaint and the answer together are called the *pleadings*. Thereafter, a long period of negotiations ensues, including *pretrial conferences* before a judge, during which issues are clarified and bargaining between the adversaries takes place. Most cases result in *settlements*, in which the defendant agrees to pay the plaintiff some amount less than what was originally demanded in the suit.

Cases that are not settled go to trial. What transpires is similar, although not identical, to criminal court procedures. In civil cases, judges have a bit more control. If the judge thinks the plaintiff has no real case, a *summary judgment*, in favor of the defendant can be issued before the trial or a *directed verdict* can be issued after the trial. After the case is presented, the jury deliberates to determine if the plaintiff proved the defendant's *liability*, on the basis of the *preponderance of the evidence*—a less stringent burden of proof than the criterion of *beyond a reasonable doubt* used in criminal cases. If the jury decides for the plaintiff, the jury must also resolve the question of damages. In some states, trials are "bifurcated": one jury decides the liability questions and a different jury decides damages. In either case, following the verdict and damages award, a posttrial motion may be made, such as a request that the jury's damage award be set aside as excessive and unwarranted.

Appeals

In civil cases, both parties may file an *appeal* with a higher court to review the legality of lower court procedures. In criminal cases, however, only the defense may file appeals; acquittals are final under the *double jeopardy* provision of the Fifth Amendment, which prevents a person from being tried twice for the same crime. At the appellate stage, legal rulings made during the trial can be challenged, such as the introduction of inadmissible evidence or the definition of law provided in the judge's instructions; but the jury's findings of facts are by and large untouchable. When an appellate court overturns a conviction or a civil court judgment, it either terminates the case or, more commonly, *remands* the case back to the lower court. There the trial judge has the option of permitting a new trial free of the damaging legal errors that caused a reversal.

The Jury's Contemporary Role

Functions of the Jury

The jury's role in criminal cases is primarily to determine the guilt or innocence of defendants. In the trial, jurors are confronted with arguments made by lawyers, testimony of witnesses, physical evidence presented to the court, and instructions about the law given by the judge. The jury need make no decision about specific issues—who was lying, what the defendant's motive was, whether an alibi stands up, or whether an expert witness is credible. The jury looks at the body of evidence as a whole and decides whether the charges against the defendant have been proved beyond a reasonable doubt. Jurors issue no report and give no reasons for their judgment; they simply file into the courtroom when their deliberations are over and give single word decisions. The judge asks, "Have you reached a verdict?" and the jury spokesperson answers, "Yes, Your Honor, guilty" or "Yes, not guilty."

The process isn't always so simple. In many cases there are multiple charges against a defendant. A person accused of shooting someone during a mugging may be accused of attempted murder, robbery, and assault; so the jury must decide not only whether the defendant committed the crime but also which laws were violated. In addition, jurors often must choose what degree of crime was committed—for example, first-degree assault requiring intent to do serious physical harm versus second-degree assault involving serious injuries but without malicious intent. Moreover, there are sometimes multiple counts: a person engaged in a brawl can be charged with a separate count for every person who was attacked. And on top of multiple charges and counts, there are sometimes multiple defendants charged with involvement in the same criminal events. So jurors, despite not having to give explanations or justifications, often have their work cut out for them.

Aside from adjudicating guilt and innocence, juries sometimes have a role in sentencing. However, only seven states continue the once common practice of letting juries determine punishment in noncapital cases. In some of these states the judge has the right to overrule the jury, and in others the defendants can choose whether they want the jury to decide the sentence. In practice, therefore, the right of juries to determine prison length or to grant probation is fading out.[24]

On the other hand, juries have a truly awesome sentencing role in the thirty-seven states that have capital punishment. The Supreme Court, in declaring that the death penalty was not unconstitutional per se, ruled that after a person is convicted of a capital crime there must be a separate hearing on mitigating and aggravating circumstances to determine if the murderer deserves death. It is the jury that usually makes this fateful decision, a role approved of and applauded by the Supreme Court as a sound means of "maintaining a link between contemporary community values and the penal system."[25] The repetition of the phrase "contemporary community values" emphasizes that the Court uses the jury's *political* function to justify the jury's responsibility for making life-and-death decisions.

In civil cases, the jury regularly has a twofold and sometimes a threefold role to play. First is the issue of liability: are the plaintiff's allegations true and was the defendant legally at fault? In a negligence case, for example, the jury must decide not only whether the defendant's icy sidewalk caused the plaintiff to fall and break a hip but whether failure to shovel and salt the sidewalk immediately after a storm constituted unreasonable behavior. The jury's discretion is wide-ranging: questions of law and fact are mixed; the standard of proof is less stringent than in criminal cases; and legal concepts, such as what constitutes a "reasonably prudent person" in negligence cases, are quite open-ended.

If the jury finds for the plaintiff, compensatory damages must be ascertained—how much the plaintiff was injured and how that translates into dollars-and-cents. Some aspects of this decision are relatively straightforward, such as medical expenses, salary lost from being out of work, and the cost of repairing a wrecked automobile. But how do you assess how much a lost eye is worth? How do you convert the pain and suffering caused by severe injuries into money? And what about the emotional hardships caused by debilitating illnesses, such as black-lung disease contracted by so many

33

miners? These are questions hardly susceptible to any exactitude, and juries have enormous latitude in making such determinations.

In recent years, juries have awarded enormous amounts of damages in selected cases. More than 400 awards of over $1 million were made annually in the 1980s. The median amount given to winning plaintiffs was much, much less, however. A study of civil jury verdicts in forty-three sites in ten different states showed typical awards of $78,218 in Los Angeles, $20,702 in Phoenix, $10,382 in Cook County (Chicago), and $19,172 in Dallas.[26] When jurors do grant huge amounts, they may well be making judgments about the gravity of the underlying social harms and the proper assigning of blame, as when a jury in 1988 required a tobacco company to pay a New Jersey man $400,000 in compensation for his wife's death from lung cancer following forty years of smoking.

Jurors are doing more than compensating people for losses; they are also making statements about the rights and responsibilities of people and businesses. The old saying "Put your money where your mouth is" describes the power afforded to jurors by a legal system that entrusts them with the job of allocating damages. Jurors are thus able to back up what are essentially political judgments with sanctions and rewards that have a direct bearing on human life. That gives jurors a lot of power.

A final function of the civil jury that arises in certain kinds of cases is the assessment of punitive damages, which goes beyond compensation for loss. The word *punitive* has the same root as the word *punishment;* the law allows juries to punish defendants who intentionally have caused injuries by forcing them to pay damages over and above the losses sustained by plaintiffs. The criteria for making these kinds of judgments are virtually nonexistent. The jury simply decides how "bad" the defendant was—a quintessentially political judgment. And despite the complete absence of standards to guide juries, the Supreme Court in March 1991 upheld the jury's broad discretion in setting punitive damages.[27]

Jury Utilization

In criminal law, a jury trial is the rare exception. Only about 5 percent of all felony cases are resolved through jury trials, although there are local variations, as indicated in Table 2-1. Recognizing the unpredictability of jury behavior and the potential for harsh punishment if convicted, most defendants who are unable to get their cases dismissed at the pretrial stage plead guilty, often by plea bargaining for a reduction in charges and/or a lighter sentence. This arrangement saves time, money, and manpower and serves the interests of the overloaded criminal justice system well.

In the civil courts, jury trials are avoided to an even greater extent than in criminal courts. It is estimated that no more than 1 percent of all suits filed in state court result in jury trials, although the percentage of cases in

Jurisdiction	Percentage of cases resulting in jury trials	Number of cases filed	
			TABLE 2-1
			Felony cases
			resulting in
Seattle, Wash.	15%	3,126	jury trials
New Orleans, La.	10	3,659	
Washington, D.C.	9	8,442	
Des Moines, Iowa	8	1,401	
Lansing, Mich.	7	1,358	
Portland, Ore.	7	3,892	
Denver, Colo.	6	3,772	
Minneapolis, Minn.	6	2,364	
St. Louis, Mo.	6	3,649	
Dallas, Tex.	5	14,784	
Salt Lake City, Utah	5	2,754	
Brighton, Colo.	4	1,142	
Colorado Springs, Colo.	4	1,484	
Philadelphia, Pa.	4	13,796	
Tallahassee, Fla.	4	2,879	
Davenport, Iowa	3	1,312	
Fort Collins, Colo.	3	776	
Geneva, Ill.	3	1,263	
Manhattan, N.Y.	3	30,810	
Rhode Island	3	5,485	
San Diego, Calif.	3	11,534	
Chicago, Ill.	2	35,528	
Cobb County, Ga.	2	4,427	
Golden, Colo.	2	1,838	
Greeley, Colo.	2	630	
Miami, Fla.	2	21,313	
Pueblo, Colo.	1	339	

Source: U.S. Department of Justice, Bureau of Justice Statistics, *Report to the Nation on Crime and Justice,* 2nd ed. (Washington, D.C.: U.S. Department of Justice, 1988), p. 84.

federal courts that go to the jury is somewhat higher—between 2 and 3 percent.[28] Most cases are resolved through settlements, in which the plaintiff and defendant work out a mutually acceptable agreement on damages. As is true in criminal cases, risk avoidance is a primary factor. It is normally far better to settle for less than to run into the possibility that a jury might absolve the defendant completely. This is precisely what happened to a Pennsylvania couple who in 1984 turned down a $2.2 million settlement offer from a hospital where their daughter was born with severe permanent handicaps. A jury subsequently ruled that the hospital was not negligent during the delivery of the baby and therefore owed the couple nothing. Not only can such ghastly fates befall litigants, but the cost and aggravation engendered by trials are major deterrents to entering into them.

In the face of the facts and figures about the low proportion of jury trials, one might wonder whether this book or any book on juries is worth reading. It may seem as silly as reading a volume on the intricacies of the triple play or stealing home plate in baseball—interesting occurrences but of virtually no relevance to the typical game. But the small fraction of all cases that actually go before juries is a statistic that misleadingly downplays the significance of the jury whose legal and political role is far from trivial.

First, the absolute number of jury trials is not so small: there are about 300,000 every year.[29] The small proportion of cases going to juries may be more a reflection of the huge caseloads of the courts than an indication of the insignificance of the jury. More than 10 million nontraffic criminal cases were filed in state criminal courts annually in the 1980s, in addition to about 30,000 federal criminal cases.[30] The figures for the civil courts are even more staggering: in 1985 about 14,000,000 suits were started in state courts, not to mention the quarter of a million civil suits commenced in federal courts annually.[31] The point is that the jury role pales somewhat in the broader context of the enormous amount of judicial business being conducted.

Second, although only a small percentage of those accused of crimes opt for jury trials, the number of persons accused of serious crimes who receive jury trials is much higher. In Salt Lake City, for example, 64 percent of those accused of murder go before the jury, in contrast to 19 percent of accused robbers and 7 percent of accused burglars.[32] In states with the death penalty, twice as many defendants charged with capital crimes as those charged with noncapital crimes resort to jury trials.

Third, celebrated cases involving public figures, sensational crimes, or highly visible social conflicts are much more likely to be disposed of through jury trial. These are the cases that one author described as being the top layer of the "criminal justice wedding cake."[33] Cases involving assassinations, mass murders, big-stakes corruption, or public scandals such as Watergate and "Contragate" may be relatively few in number, but the public cares about them a great deal, and the jury is often the decision maker that has the final word.

So the jury is *not* a minor institution in terms of either the amount of business they get or the importance of that business. In monetary terms, jury service is also big business, with well over $200 million spent annually on juror fees paid by the courts. And the salaries that many employers continue to pay their employees while they are on jury duty totals more than one billion dollars.

These large expenditures are not the result of lavish pay scales for jurors. On the contrary, the average daily compensation for jurors is paltry, as Table 2-2 demonstrates. States typically pay between $10 and $15 a day—less than half the minimum wage—and some pay even less.

The reason for the high budget for jurors is the numbers of people involved. Jury service is in fact a mass enterprise. Approximately 5 million

TABLE 2-2

Jury fees

in state and

federal courts,

1990*

Jurisdiction	Juror fees per day		Jurisdiction	Juror fees per day
Federal	$30.00	:	Mississippi	$15.00
		:	Missouri	6.00
Alabama	10.00	:	Montana	12.00
Alaska	25.00	:	Nebraska	20.00
Arizona	12.00	:	Nevada	15.00
Arkansas	5.00	:	New Hampshire	30.00
California	5.00	:	New Jersey	5.00
Colorado	0.00*	:	New Mexico	26.80
Connecticut	0.00*	:	New York	15.00
Delaware	15.00	:	North Carolina	12.00
District of		:	North Dakota	25.00
Columbia	30.00	:	Ohio	10.00
Florida	10.00	:	Oklahoma	12.50
Georgia	5.00	:	Oregon	10.00
Hawaii	30.00	:	Pennsylvania	9.00
Idaho	5.00	:	Rhode Island	15.00
Illinois	4.00	:	South Carolina	10.00
Indiana	7.50	:	South Dakota	10.00
Iowa	10.00	:	Tennessee	10.00
Kansas	10.00	:	Texas	6.00
Kentucky	12.50	:	Utah	14.00
Louisiana	12.00	:	Vermont	30.00
Maine	20.00	:	Virginia	20.00
Maryland	10.00	:	Washington	10.00
Massachusetts	0.00*	:	West Virginia	15.00
Michigan	15.00	:	Wisconsin	16.00
Minnesota	15.00	:	Wyoming	30.00

*These are the basic rates for a full day of service. Some states pay more to those who actually serve as jurors; others pay more after a juror has served a certain number of days. There are some variations within some of the states.
**No fees are paid for the first three days of jury service; thereafter jurors are paid $50.00 per day.
Source: U.S. Department of Justice, Office of Justice Programs, Bureau of Justice Statistics, Sourcebook of Criminal Justice Statistics—1989 (Washington, D.C.: U.S. Department of Justice, 1989), p. 76.

people are called for jury service annually, about 2 million of them come to court, and roughly one million actually serve on juries.

This is quite a phenomenon: hordes of private citizens from various walks of life are entrusted with profound public responsibilities. In this country, one person serves as president, 50 as governors, 535 as members of Congress, and about 5,000 as state legislators. But *one million* annually serve as jurors, making it quite an exercise in participatory democracy. The French commentator de Tocqueville justifiably called the jury one of the foremost instruments of republican government. In 1830 he wrote, "The institution of the jury consequently invests the people . . . with the direction of society."[34] The jury is a political body not only because it brings its interests and values to bear in making decisions, not only because it engages in political processes to arrive at verdicts, and not only because its decisions affect the workings of society. The jury is a political institution because it truly allows a substantial segment of the population to run powerful government machinery if only for a fleeting period of time.

The entire citizenry does not serve, however. The jury may be one of the nation's most democratic institutions, but some people are better represented than others. Giving juries a significant role in the administration of justice by all means entails the infusion of populism into the administration of justice, but some parts of the community provide greater input than others. Who gets on the jury has a good bit to do with the kind of politics practiced by the jury, and as the next chapter reveals, there are marked biases in the juror selection system.

Notes

1. Aeschylus, *The Eumenides*, in *The Oresteian Trilogy*, translated by Phillip Vellacott (Harmondsworth, Middlesex, England: Penguin Books, 1972) pp. 163–164.
2. Thomas Green, "The Jury and the English Law of Homicide, 1200–1600," *Michigan Law Review*, 74 (January 1976):498.
3. Quoted in Valerie Hans and Neil Vidmar, *Judging the Jury* (New York: Plenum Press, 1986), p. 35.
4. Quoted in Charles Whitebread and Christopher Slobogin, *Criminal Procedure: An Analysis of Cases and Concepts*, 2nd. ed. (Mineola, New York: Foundation Press, 1986), p. 596.
5. Samuel Walker, *Popular Justice: A History of American Criminal Justice* (New York: Oxford University Press, 1980), p. 111.
6. Jerold Auerbach, *Unequal Justice: Lawyers and Social Change in Modern America* (New York: Oxford University Press, 1976), pp. 14–73.
7. *Palko* v. *Connecticut*, 302 U.S. 319 (1937).
8. *Duncan* v. *Louisiana*, 391 U.S. 145 (1968).
9. *Baldwin* v. *New York*, 399 U.S. 66 (1970); *Codispoti* v. *Pennsylvania*, 418 U.S. 506 (1974).
10. *Blanton* v. *North Las Vegas*, 489 U.S. 539 (1989).
11. *McKeiver* v. *Pennsylvania*, 403 U.S. 528 (1971).
12. *Singer* v. *United States*, 380 U.S. 24 (1965).
13. Patrick Higgenbotham, "Juries and the Complex Case: Observations about the Present Debate," in *The American Civil Jury* (Washington, D.C.: Roscoe Pound-American Trial Lawyers Foundation, 1987), 72–73.
14. *In re* Japanese Electronic Prod. Antitrust Litig., 631 F.2d 1069 (3rd Cir. 1980).
15. *Colgrove* v. *Battin*, 413 U.S. 149 (1973).
16. *Williams* v. *Florida*, 399 U.S. 78 (1970).
17. Michael Saks, "Ignorance of Science Is No Excuse," *Trial*, 10 (1974):18.
18. *Ballew* v. *Georgia*, 435 U.S. 23 (1978).
19. *Johnson* v. *Louisiana*, 406 U.S. 356 (1972); *Apodaca* v. *Oregon*, 406 U.S. 404 (1972).
20. *Johnson* v. *Louisiana*, 406 U.S. 356, 389 (1972).
21. *Apodaca* v. *Oregon*, 406 U.S. 404, 410 (1972).
22. *Burch* v. *Louisiana*, 441 U.S. 130 (1979).
23. For more details on criminal procedure, see David Neubauer, *America's Courts and the Criminal Justice System*, 3rd ed. (Pacific Grove, Calif.:Brooks/Cole, 1988), chap. 14. For an outline of

civil procedure, see Lawrence Baum, *American Courts: Process and Policy* (Boston: Houghton Mifflin, 1990), pp. 227–230.

24. For a succinct discussion of the practice of jury sentencing, see Michael Tonry, "Jury Sentencing," in Sanford Kadish (ed.), *Encyclopedia of Crime and Justice*, IV (New York: Free Press, 1985), pp. 1465–1466.
25. *Witherspoon* v. *Illinois*, 391 U.S. 510 (1968).
26. Stephan Daniels and Joanne Martin, "Jury Verdicts and the 'Crisis' in Civil Justice," *The Justice System Journal*, 11 (Winter 1986): 336–337.
27. *Pacific Mutual Life Insurance Co.* v. Haslip, No. 89–1279 (1991).
28. See Lawrence Baum, *American Courts: Process and Policy*, 2nd. ed. (Boston: Houghton Mifflin, 1990), pp. 245; Marc Galanter, "Jury Shadows: Reflections on the Civil Jury and the Litigation Explosion," in *The American Civil Jury*, pp. 18–21.
29. Interview with Tom Munsterman of the Center for Jury Studies, April 3, 1986.
30. Administrative Office of the United States Courts, Statistical Analysis and Report Division, *Federal Judicial Workload Statistics* (Washington, D.C.: U.S. Government Printing Office, 1983).
31. National Center for State Courts, *State Court Caseload Statistics: Annual Report 1985* (Williamsburg, Va.: National Center for State Courts, 1987), pp. 46–47.
32. United States Department of Justice, Bureau of Justice Statistics, *Report to the Nation on Crime and Justice*, 2nd. ed. (Washington: U.S. Department of Justice, 1988), p. 84.
33. Samuel Walker, *Sense and Nonsense about Crime: A Policy Guide* (Pacific Grove, Calif.: Brooks/Cole, 1985), pp. 16–18. (The wedding cake model was first proposed by Lawrence M. Friedman and Robert V. Percival in *The Roots of Justice: Crime and Punishment in Alameda County, California, 1870–1910.* Chapel Hill: University of North Carolina Press, 1981.)
34. Alexis de Tocqueville, *Democracy in America.* Translated by Henry Reeve, revised by Francis Bowen, edited by Phillips Bradley (New York: Alfred A. Knopf, 1946), Vol. I, 282–283.

39

3

. . . .

Jury
Selection
Processes

I n the late 1960s, black militant Warren Wells was accused of attempted murder and assault of a police officer in Oakland, California. The first time he was tried, there were two blacks on the jury; the jury could not agree on a verdict, voting 10–2 for acquittal on two counts and 6–6 on two counts. After a retrial, a second jury with two blacks on it again could not agree; this time the jury voted 11–1 for acquittal. There was a third trial, with *no* blacks on the jury; this jury convicted Wells of two counts of assault with a deadly weapon.

What this suggests is that *who* sits on the jury can be as important as the evidence in deciding outcomes. It certainly seems that the presence of blacks on the first two Wells' juries had a decisive impact on the other members. Perhaps the black jurors presented a different point of view on the threats posed to blacks by some white police officers and the necessity for blacks to exercise self-defense. Is the Wells case a rarity, or does the jury selection process normally function to give one side or the other an advantage? This chapter is devoted to answering that question.

The Right to a
Representative Jury Panel

The idea that a person's background and attitudes affect his or her public decision making is hardly controversial. Voters routinely consider a candidate's characteristics in deciding how he or she is likely to act in office if elected. The United States Senate probes deeply into the personal characteristics of judicial nominees to determine whether they deserve confirmation. Political scientists have discovered all kinds of connections between the nature of political recruitment and the subsequent political behavior of the individuals who have been recruited. It should not surprise us that who serves on juries also has a signficant impact on the nature of jury verdicts.

Certainly the United States Supreme Court has accepted this as a premise of its decision making regarding the composition of the jury. The justices have been quite concerned about the meaning of the concept "impartial jury"—the institution that the Constitution requires the federal government and the states to use in criminal cases. And they have stated in no uncertain terms that "selection of a petit jury from a representative cross section of the community is an essential component of the Sixth Amendment right to a jury trial."[1] But the application of this guiding principle has not been simple, and as this chapter will show, the present methods of selecting juries still leave much opportunity for bias. Some kinds of people are chosen more often than others.

The Supreme Court has not required that all juries reflect perfectly the makeup of the community. Rather, it has handled the issue of nonrepresentativeness by ruling that certain kinds of people cannot be systematically kept off of juries. As early as 1880, it struck down Virginia's law that explicitly prohibited blacks from serving on juries,[2] and it has in recent years ruled that the Fourteenth Amendment's equal protection clause prevents severe underrepresentation of blacks on juries. Moreover, the Supreme Court has ruled that the Sixth Amendment makes it illegitimate to exclude intentionally *any* "cognizable" group from jury pools; to deny large, identifiable groups (such as women) a chance to participate on the jury unless there is sound reason for doing so is unconstitutional.

Thus, the requirement that juries represent a cross section of the community refers to who is kept *off* juries rather than who is put *on*. In January 1990, in *Holland* v. *Illinois* the Supreme Court reiterated the idea that no single jury need be an accurate representation of the community; there is no constitutional right to have poor people or rich people, blacks or whites, youngsters or the elderly, mail carriers or teachers on any particular jury.[3] The Constitution requires that groups who have a right to be represented have a fair chance to be called for jury service; if they do not end up on the jury, that is just an unfortunate fact of life.

In order for a jury pool to be constitutionally deficient, two things must be demonstrated. First, it must be established that it is an identifiable group that has been excluded. To date, only racial groups and women have been placed in this category. Thus, even though the preponderance of defendants are young adults, the courts have not held age groups to be entities that deserve a fair share of seats on jury panels.

The second issue is, What is a "fair" share? The Supreme Court has been inconsistent in answering this question. In the 1960s, the Court said that fair representation existed as long as no group was banned absolutely or

41

the jury empaneling procedures were not purposefully manipulated to keep blacks off of juries. Thus, in 1965, a conviction in *Swain* v. *Alabama* was upheld despite the fact that 26 percent of the eligible voters in the jurisdiction were black but only 10–15 percent of jury panels were black. Said the Court: "We cannot say that purposeful discrimination based on race alone is satisfactorily proved by showing that an identifiable group is underrepresented by as much as 10%."[4] But a Harvard statistician later showed that having 5 or fewer blacks on 30 consecutive panels of 100 prospective jurors (as occurred in the setting where Swain was tried) was a degree of underrepresentation of blacks that could have resulted from chance in only 1 out of 100 *million trillion* groups of such panels.[5]

Despite this demonstration of the Supreme Court's statistical naiveté, the courts have by and large remained insistent that only striking disparities in percentages between an identifiable group's proportion of the underlying population and its proportion of the jury panel are unconstitutional. A situation in which only 10 percent of the persons on jury panels were women in a Louisiana community that was 53 percent female was unacceptable according to the Supreme Court.[6] But closer cases in which differences are of only a few percentage points have generally not been constitutionally offensive to the courts, even in cases in which the disparities were quite unlikely to have occurred by chance.

In a nutshell, jury selection methods are subject to scrutiny if they function in a way that seriously dilutes the representation of racial minorities and women on jury panels. In Alameda County, a "clear thinking" test used to screen prospective jurors was struck down because the poor performance by blacks on the culturally biased test resulted in the exclusion of large numbers of blacks from jury panels.[7] However, in the absence of a demonstration that some particular facet of the jury selection scheme works to a protected group's disadvantage, only extreme cases of exclusion are said to violate the Constitution. The "numbers test" imposed on anyone challenging the composition of juries is a difficult one to pass; that is, it is hard to prove discrimination.

This leaves federal, state, and local authorities with substantial latitude in devising and implementing the mechanics of jury selection. As we shall now see, no matter what plan is utilized, there is a multistep screening process that winnows out many people and leaves those actually sitting in judgment in the jury box a rather select lot. Jurors are not elites, but just as surely they are not random samples of the community. Defendants are judged by *some* of their peers, but not by all of them.

The Skewing of the Jury Panel

The Master Wheel

The first stage in the selection of juries is the gathering of names of prospective jurors. This is sometimes called the *master wheel* (akin to a roulette wheel) from which jurors are to be selected by some random method. Until the 1960s, the prevalent method of securing names for the wheel was the *key man* system, according to which jury commissioners or court clerks chose people of presumably high character from the community. Thus a Philadelphia "jury master," when asked in 1963 what he looked for in his search for jurors, said, "The Masters look for a reasonably intelligent person, in good health, and of good moral background. . . ."[8] This method obviously vested enormous discretion in such officials and resulted in highly unrepresentative lists of people. In fact, it may be legitimate to continue to refer to it as the "key man" system, rather than the gender-free term "key person," because so few women were chosen. Although the Supreme Court has ruled that, in principle, such a method can be constitutional,[9] it has recognized the inherent subjectivity of this approach and has more readily found discrimination if the approach results in underrepresentation of an identifiable group.[10] Because of such challenges, as well as the trend toward making juries more democratic, the key man system has largely fallen into disuse.

The general approach currently used to create the master wheel is to use standard lists of citizens, primarily voter registration rolls. Use of such lists was mandated for the federal system in 1968 through the Jury Selection and Service Act, and most states followed suit. Such lists are longer and broader than those secured through the key man system, but they too do not perfectly mirror the community. Voting is far from universal in the United States, despite get-out-the-vote campaigning by government groups and moralizing in high-school civics classes. Only about 50 percent of all those eligible to vote *do* vote in presidential elections, and turnout is lower for other contests. Moreover, failure to register to vote is not random: some groups vote less than others and so get underrepresented on the master wheel. Those who are ineligible to vote, such as resident aliens, do not get on the master wheel at all.

Consequently, research on the use of voter lists has discovered substantial biases. One study of the Eastern District of the United States District Court in Massachusetts found a "middle America" coloration to the jury pools: whites, males, the middle aged, the middle class, and the moderately educated were overrepresented; nonwhites, females, the very old, and the very young were underrepresented.[11] Some of these biases have cumulative impacts, assuring the virtual exclusion of certain subgroups. Thus, in the entire federal jury pool of 1,095 persons serving the Boston area in 1970, not one young, black woman appeared; on the basis of their numbers in the general population, there should have been six.

The increased voting of blacks in recent years, partially as a result of energetic voter registration campaigns, has somewhat diminished the bias against blacks getting on the master wheel. In fact, studies of Dade County, Florida, and Los Angeles actually show an *over*representation of blacks on jury panels.[12] However, other slighted groups whose voting participation lags have not fared as well: Hispanics, the poor, and the young continue to show up with insufficient frequency on master wheels driven by voter lists.

43

To remedy some of these biases, some jurisdictions have supplemented voting lists with other sources of names. Such rosters include driver's licenses lists, tax rolls, telephone directories, utility records, and welfare lists. In attempting to ferret out names of people normally hidden from public view, some states have used unusual sources. Alaska, for example, has resorted to registering people who secure fishing and hunting licenses, which has the effect of locating Eskimos whose names would otherwise be unavailable. Just how successful these kinds of efforts are at expanding the net of potential jurors is illustrated by the example of San Diego County, California: utilizing drivers' lists added to the master wheel 410,359 people who have driver's licenses but who are not registered to vote.[13] The use of sophisticated computer technology has enabled jurisdictions to merge various sources to make sure that names appear on the master wheel only once.

There is no doubt about it: we have come a long way from the often highly skewed lists of the key man system. Before 1960, most people could go through an entire lifetime without being contacted for jury service, and the relatively small group of potential jurors were biased in terms of race, gender, class, and age. Thus, it was perfectly fitting that the twelve jurors portrayed in the aptly titled 1950s movie *Twelve Angry Men* were white males over the age of forty. The juror selection apparatus now reaches much deeper into the community, and a wide assortment of individuals are sought out. Being called for jury service is no longer a special calling.

44

The Venire

The problem of unrepresentative juries does not end with the master wheel. Not everyone who is contacted shows up at court, and not everyone who does arrive is required to serve: in fact, far from it. And there are significant differences between those who manage to escape service and those who make it to the *venire*—the group of people who assemble at the courthouse prepared to become jurors.

There are any number of ways that people evade the jury recruitment system, thereby creating biases in the composition of juries. First, a substantial number of people do not respond to their jury notices. Although theoretically people can be held in contempt of court and punished by fine or jail for refusing to respond, realistically many assume that the judicial system has better things to do with its time and money than to chase after derelict jury recruits. Add to these legions of willful defiers the many who never receive their notices in the first place and you come up with an incredible shrinkage of the master wheel. It is estimated that only about two out of five people targeted for jury service actually come to court.

The least of the problems created by this low appearance rate is an occasional shortage of jurors to hear cases. This can result in *judicial gridlock*, as occurred in New York City on September 17, 1981, when the beginning of all new civil and criminal cases was halted because only 300 out of the

3,000 people notified actually came to court. Such shortfalls, while rare, can lead frustrated jury officials to resort to strange remedies: in 1987 a Houston judge invoked an nineteenth-century "roundup" law and sent deputy sheriffs to a nearby mall where they rounded up shoppers for immediate jury duty!

This anecdote does make us laugh, and in fact enough people usually do show up through normal channels for the courts to function. But large-scale nonresponsiveness has a deadly serious side: it biases the venire. Those who show up tend to be richer and older than those who do not, and they are disproportionately white men. To deal with such skewing, some jurisdictions have, with some success, stepped up efforts to find those whose notices went astray and to coax those who shirked to come forth. Another more dramatic reform that has been even more successful in improving response rates is the so-called one-day-one-trial system: courts that call people for one day only unless they are actually seated as jurors for a trial, find that people are much more willing to fulfill their obligations. Still other jurisdictions, which consider it too expensive to dispatch court marshals and send certified letters, make no attempt to prod people into court but instead stratify the source lists used to construct the master wheel to compensate for biases stemming from the no-show problem.

There are other threats to the representativeness of the venire aside from no-shows. For a variety of reasons, most states automatically exempt certain people from jury service on the basis of their occupations. Police officers are generally excused because of the likelihood that they will side with the prosecution; lawyers are kept off because they might unduly influence their co-jurors; and doctors, nurses, and firefighters are often excused because their services are so vital to the community. Why people in other occupations are frequently excluded in some states—morticians, schoolteachers, soybean farmers, airline pilots, and telephone operators, for example—is less readily understandable. Perhaps it simply represents legislative bowing to organized pressure. Since there are inherent demographic biases in the kinds of people who hold different jobs (for instance, most nurses are women and most firefighters are men), such biases carry over into the venire when automatic exemptions are made.

For many years, certain situations entitled individuals to exclusion from jury service. The most serious source of biasing were the old "housewives" and "mothers" clauses that excluded people in these positions on the grounds that they were needed at home. Because by definition it is only women who fall into these categories, this exclusion was a major cause of the underrepresentation of women on juries. And because the Supreme Court has ruled that women are an "identifiable" group whose presence gives "a flavor" and "a distinct quality" to a jury, arrangements such as that of Louisiana, which automatically exempted women unless they volunteered for jury service, have been struck down.[14]

The tendency in recent years has been to do away with automatic exemptions and handle juror problems on a case-by-case basis. Even parents of young children are no longer excused without question, with courts preferring to encourage alternative child-care arrangements. This reduces built-in biases that lead to the underinclusion of certain types of people, but it increases the discretionary power of jury officials who routinely hear a wide gamut of pleas for exemption from jury service: students who will miss examinations, farmers whose fields will go unploughed, cardiac patients with hypertension who are worried about too much stress, store owners who are faced with having to close their businesses, and employees who would be unable to pay their rent or feed their families if forced to survive for a couple of weeks on jurors' pay. Deciding which of these appeals are meritorious is quite subjective, and it creates the potential for discriminatory treatment based on race, ethnicity, status, or some other characteristic unrelated to the justification for being excused. The overt biasing of the venire caused by automatic exclusions may inadvertently be replaced by more subtle but equally pernicious partiality on the part of jury officials. The inescapability of bias when granting excuses has led some states to make virtually everybody serve except those with the most compelling hardships; but such toughness has the drawback of securing a good number of very resentful jurors who might well take their anger out on the accused.

A final potential source of venire bias are disqualifications based on presumed incompetency. Almost all states exclude convicted felons as morally unfit, which nationally keeps several million people off the jury. Many states exclude individuals who have ever been committed to psychiatric hospitals on the grounds that they are emotionally unequipped to serve. These policies may or may not be legitimate, but they are not neutral in the way they affect the selection of jurors. Those who have been convicted of major crimes and who are therefore ineligible for jury service are more likely to be black, poor, and young than the society at large; so excluding them on the basis of their previous misdeeds removes from the venire some of the very people most similar to those going on trial in the criminal courts. Staring at the venire, which often is totally devoid of young black males, the accused might well ask, Whose peers are they?

Again, however, it must be observed that the net of the venire catches many more people now than it used to. Gone are the days of the "professional" juror who serves repeatedly for lack of anything better to do and who is in the jury box because, one way or another, so many others managed to elude service. No longer can we stereotype the juror with any degree of accuracy, as a more diverse batch of people now get on the master wheel than in years past. Happily, the venire is not nearly as skewed as it once was.

The Haphazardness of the Voir Dire

The venire that assembles at the courthouse is more or less randomly divided and assigned to the different trials as they come up. Groups of possible jurors, called the *panel*, go to a courtroom where the second stage of the jury selection process takes place—the *empaneling* of the jury. About three or four times as many people as will ultimately serve on the jury go through this next stage of the jury selection process—the *voir dire.*

The voir dire is a procedure for investigating whether the jurors have prejudices and preconceptions that would prevent them from considering the evidence objectively. The term is derived from the French words *voir,* meaning "true," and *dire,* meaning "say." The combination of these words has been translated in various ways, including "to speak the truth" and "to see what is said." The idea behind the phrase is that prospective jurors should truthfully answer questions about themselves to see if there is anything about their attitudes that would prevent them from deciding the case before them objectively. In the federal judiciary and in a few state courts, this questioning is done primarily by the judge; but in most state courts it is the attorneys on both sides who play the dominant role in trying to ferret out prejudices.

Responses indicative of bias can result in a challenge *for cause.* The judge has the prerogative, indeed the duty, of removing panelists whose answers demonstrate that they are incapable of being objective. Potential jurors can be removed for *specific bias*—some connection to the case at hand, such as being related to the victim, that would color the juror's judgment of the facts. In the United States (but not in England) they can also be eliminated from the jury for *nonspecific bias*—negative feelings toward specific types of people or strong moral convictions that would impair them from being open-minded. In the case establishing the right to challenge for nonspecific bias, Chief Justice John Marshall, in the trial of Aaron Burr for treason, ruled that potential jurors could be questioned about their political biases because Burr was such a politically controversial figure.[15] Today, a person confessing that he or she despises homosexuals could be challenged if the defendant were on trial for burning down a bar catering to gay people; a person passionately against alcohol abuse would be susceptible to a challenge in a reckless homicide case involving allegations of drunk driving. It is up to the judge to decide if a panelist's remarks suggest bias and whether the bias is sufficiently intense to prevent an individual from being fair.

What is open to question are the kinds of biases that are legitimate targets of the voir dire. The Supreme Court has been loathe to give defendants the constitutional *right* to expansive questioning and removal of potential jurors who show bias. This right has been established in cases involving racial prejudice, but even this right is circumscribed: the trial must be one in which racial issues permeate the case, rather than just a case where the defendant is black and the victim is white.[16] Also, cases entailing considerable pretrial publicity entitle the defense to determine whether venire members have already made up their minds as a result of media accounts. Even in this situation, however, the issue is not merely whether panelists were exposed to publicity but whether as a result of this exposure, panelists had formed indelible opinions about guilt that would mandate excusing them for cause.[17] The Supreme Court has summarily refused to extend the constitutional right to voir dire questioning to other potential prejudices, such as negative attitudes toward people with beards.[18] The net result is that judges currently have enormous leeway in regulating the scope of the voir dire and assessing whether responses given are manifestations of bias.

Ironically, the one area in which the Supreme Court has made exclusion based on voir dire admissions almost automatic works to the advantage of the prosecution. In *Lockhart* v. *McCree,* the Court upheld the elimination of jury candidates who voice scruples about the death penalty.[19] The American Psychological Association, in an *amicus curiae* ("friend of the court") brief, concluded on the basis of experimental data that "the research studies show that death-qualified juries are prosecution-prone."[20] But the Court disregarded these findings, preferring to grant legitimacy to the state's interest in securing a jury free of people biased against capital punishment who would be unable to consider the death penalty at the sentencing stage of the trial. The voir dire, intended to eliminate partiality, was turned on its head: in trying to make the jury more open-minded to life-or-death decisions, the Court opened the door to a jury biased toward the prosecution.

Practically speaking, the voir dire is often incapable of eliciting expressions of bias except in the rare case where jurors are asked something as precise as their views on capital punishment. Suppose, for example, that a member of the venire being interrogated about, say, feelings toward people on welfare was asked, "Would you think negatively of a person just because he or she was receiving government welfare payments?" Most people would probably say "No." The follow-up question "Do you think people on welfare are more likely to rob or steal than those who are working?" would probably elicit another negative response. "In your opinion, does being on welfare for a long period of time generally mean that a person has a character deficiency?" Most people would hesitate to say yes in open court. Then, to the ultimate question, "In evaluating the evidence, would the fact that the defendant is a welfare recipient prevent you from deciding her guilt or innocence on the basis of the evidence only?" The answer would probably be "Absolutely not."

Would such a dialogue prove freedom of bias against those on welfare? Probably not. Many Americans have deep-seated animosities to those on welfare; for many, the mere mention of the word unfortunately and unfairly conjures up images of lazy freeloaders. But very few would admit such hostilities publicly, and many others may be unaware of the intensity of such feelings. Because society now frowns on outright displays of prejudice and most people have an intuitive understanding of the socially "correct" attitudes, many of us hold such prejudices within us and reveal them only in the company of friends and family. Consequently, the voir dire is not generally a very suitable mechanism for uncovering contemptuous feelings and discredited views.[21]

However, it is important to note the word *generally* in the previous sentence. Some voir dires are better than others. The typical one is very superficial, lasting a few hours. In federal court, where judges do the questioning, a half-hour voir dire is not unusual.[22] These quick searches for bias are likely to come up with little.

48

On the other hand, lengthy and persistent probing can uncover more guarded prejudices. Lawyer Charles Gerry, patiently questioning a suburban woman during jury selection for the murder trial of a black militant, received nothing but innocuous replies on the subject of racism—until he asked her whether she had ever moved out of a neighborhood because too many blacks had moved in. Her single-word response, "Yes," was enough to get her removed for cause.[23] Identifying true biases can take a long time: in the 1982 case of Angelo Buono, Jr., accused of being the California "Hillside Strangler" who had sexually molested and killed at least ten women, it took over three months and the interrogation of 350 people to select a jury.

Giving lawyers a relatively free hand to explore the attitudes and ideas of venire members is one way, albeit a time-consuming way, of uncovering biases. Another method is to question individual prospective jurors privately, rather than in the presence of others in the venire. Jurors are more likely to be honest when they are not on public display and subject to ridicule or condemnation. To mention one's hatred of blacks while being watched and heard by a roomful of black panelists would require a boldness that most people lack. But because the en masse voir dire is quicker and less cumbersome, it is the standard way of proceeding despite its potential for eliciting studied responses that lack forthrightness.

In reality, the voir dire better serves purposes other than that of screening out those unsuited for jury service. First, it plays a role in sensitizing jurors to the importance of certain values that they ordinarily may not sufficiently appreciate, such as the presumption of innocence. Members of the venire spend considerable time listening to the judge and the lawyers ask people whether they can be fair, and this pounding away at prospective jurors may cause some of them to set aside the very prejudices they are reluctant to reveal. This has been called the "socialization function"[24] of the voir dire, teaching jurors about their important responsibilities and the attendant special ground rules.

Second, the lawyers on both sides sometimes use the voir dire to start their attempts at persuading jurors to favor their side in the case at hand (a phenomenon discussed in the next chapter). During the course of asking panelists about prejudices they may harbor, lawyers can start the argumentation process. For example, a lawyer may ask, "Do you believe that just because a person is a police officer he or she is telling the truth?" The purpose of such a question may be more to sow doubts about key prosecution witnesses than to elicit a pro-police bias as grounds for challenge for cause. This practice can be taken even one step further; it can be used to implant positive biases under the guise of trying to eliminate negative ones. For example, prospective jurors who might be anti-Semitic may be asked if they are aware of successful Jews, like musician Leonard Bernstein and baseball star Sandy Koufax, in an attempt to get them to exert favoritism *toward* a Jewish defendant. Judges play a role in constraining such perversions of the voir dire, but using the questioning process to influence venire members goes on nonetheless.

49

This brings us to what may be the most effective use of the voir dire—to gather information about prospective jurors. Voir dire does not eliminate partisans, partly because of the relative superficiality of the process itself and partly because everyone has sentiments that affect his or her judgments; value-free, apolitical jurors do not exist. But, ironically, voir dire may help accomplish the exact opposite of its ostensible purpose by enabling each side to do a better job of packing the jury with sympathizers. The whole questioning process may be a device best suited to making the next stage of the jury empaneling process, the exercise of peremptory challenges, a more rational process. The voir dire is a political sounding board, and as we shall now see, it is a device often used to get people with the "right" politics on the jury.

The Use of Peremptory Challenges

Because the voir dire system is a rather sloppy means of identifying bias, both sides of a case are given a certain number of *peremptory challenges*. These are carte blanche opportunities to exclude members of the venire without having to give a reason. Generally, more peremptory challenges are permitted in criminal cases than in civil cases, and more in serious criminal cases than in minor ones. In murder cases, some states allow up to twenty-six peremptory challenges for each side.

50

The theory behind this procedure is that members of the venire may give some sign or have some characteristic that makes them seem biased to one side or the other, even though such bias cannot be proved. The assumption is that both sides will rely on intuition and savvy to exclude people with hidden biases. The prosecutor might excuse a professor simply on the assumption that academics tend to be too liberal; the defense might remove someone who kept giving the defendant "dirty looks." Both sides engage in the process of "sizing up" people, challenging those suspected of underlying prejudices that would hinder impartiality. In principle, this activity eliminates extremists and leaves as jurors those who are best suited to deciding cases on the basis of the evidence alone.

Until 1986, both sides could use any criteria whatsoever to conclude that members of the venire were objectionable: race, gender, name, looks, smell, clothing, tone of voice during the voir dire—anything. Thus, when two southern Arizona ranchers went on trial in 1980 for robbing and torturing three Mexican farm workers, the ranchers' lawyers used their peremptory challenges to strike all Mexican-Americans from the jury, and the presiding judge lamented that he was powerless to do anything about it.[25] But total freedom in the use of peremptory challenges has been slightly limited: the Supreme Court ruled in *Batson* v. *Kentucky* that the equal protection clause of the Fourteenth Amendment precludes prosecutors from striking blacks from the jury simply because the prosecutors think that blacks will be partial toward black defendants.[26] When prosecutors challenge blacks, they may now be required to give an explanation of their grounds for objection apart from the matter of race. In 1990, New York State's highest court relied on the state constitution in imposing a similar constraint: defense attorneys in that state are no longer allowed to use race as the sole criterion in making a peremptory challenge.[27] But except for these qualifications, both sides are still free to do whatever they please in making use of peremptory challenges, including striking all poor people, old people, short people, or bald people! Even after the *Batson* decision, race continued to be used as a basis for peremptory challenge because trial judges have yet to engage in searching probes of the reasons for such challenges. In the 1990 drug case against Washington, D.C., Mayor Marion Barry, the prosecution used *all* of its peremptory challenges to eliminate blacks, and the defense used ten out of its twelve challenges to eliminate whites. In deciding to exclude people, lawyers can be capricious and discriminatory; they have almost full rein.

How do they use this almost unbridled discretion to remove jurors? They try to "stack the deck." Card players use this phrase to refer to a form of cheating that entails rearranging the cards in such a way as to ensure being dealt favorable cards. This meaning has been expanded to include any practice that involves setting things up in advance in a rather illicit way so that preferred outcomes are more likely to materialize. And this is exactly what lawyers try to do when they use their peremptory challenges to pick a jury predisposed to their side. They seek juries that are *politically* stacked.

Reality thus clashes with theory. The use of peremptory challenges is supposed to eliminate people who are biased and leave a batch of open-minded jurors. But lawyers use their prerogatives to try to accomplish just the opposite—a jury packed with sympathizers or at least devoid of antagonists. A manual prepared for incoming assistant district attorneys in Dallas minces no words: "WHAT TO LOOK FOR IN A JUROR: 1. You are not looking for a fair juror, but rather a strong, biased and sometimes hypocritical individual who believes that defendants are different from them in kind, rather than degree."[28]

Defense attorneys are just as cynical in their search for jurors. Attorney Herald Price Fahringer, an expert on jury selection, candidly describes the harsh realities of the courtroom: "It's really foolishness for lawyers to tell jurors that they want them to be impartial. We all do it, and it's a lie. I don't want an impartial jury. I want a jury that is compatible to my client's cause."[29]

As blasphemous as that statement sounds, it is undebatable: lawyers want to win, and getting a favorable jury is part of a winning strategy. The only real questions are: How do lawyers go about trying to handpick the jury? and How successful are they?

Jury Selection Strategies

There is endless folklore among lawyers about the best kinds of jurors for different kinds of cases—"best," of course, meaning biased in the right direction. Some of the most successful trial attorneys have proffered advice on jury selection, and these suggestions tend to circulate in the legal profession. In 1936, Clarence Darrow thought that Catholics and Episcopalians made more defense-oriented jurors than Baptists and Methodists.[30] Melvin Belli claimed that farmers side with the prosecution, whereas bartenders, who are forgiving in nature, are good for the defense.[31] James Bouska, a distinguished district attorney in Kansas, urged prosecutors to choose Scandinavians and Germans over Jews and Southern Europeans.[32]

It is not just religion, occupation, and ethnicity that are linked to jury biases; any human trait is fair game for lawyers' predictions. Reading habits, style of clothing, and hobbies have been used to gauge jurors' tendencies. Even baseball team preferences have been utilized: lawyers who practiced in New York City in the 1950s recall that the prosecution often excused Dodger fans, the defense eliminated Yankee fans, but both sides found Giant fans acceptable because they were less passionate in their views.[33]

These kinds of suggestions and admonitions are generally bandied about informally by lawyers, but some attempts to codify the "state of the art" of jury selection have been made. Table 3-1 is a summary of some of the accumulated wisdom about certain characteristics that are used to type jurors as either leaning toward the prosecution or leaning toward the defense. The presentation in this table is completely unsystematic; it is simply a hodgepodge of factors supposedly correlated with biases.

Lawyers rely on these kinds of generalizations as well as on the remarks and demeanor of prospective jurors during the voir dire in their attempts to get juries that tilt in their direction. They pride themselves in their ability to use given clues cleverly and flexibly, sometimes even by rejecting common sense. Such craftiness is illustrated in a story told about noted lawyer Percy Foreman's unusual reaction to an answer given to him by a member of the venire:

> In questioning a prospective juror in a murder case, he asked, "Do you know me by reputation?"
>
> "Oh, yes, I certainly do," the man replied.
>
> "And would you be prejudiced against my client by what you know about me?" asked Foreman.
>
> "I certainly would," the venireman promptly answered, "because I know what a shyster you are. Nobody would hire you unless he was guilty."
>
> By all the rules, an answer like that should have immediately disqualified him. But Foreman, to everyone's amazement, declared, "I'll accept this juror. He's an honest man."[34]

Foreman's sagacity notwithstanding, there are problems that hinder rational use of the peremptory challenge. First, many of the "rules of thumb" about the propensities of prospective jurors are overgeneralizations at best and falsehoods at worst. Referring again to Table 3-1, is it really true that blue-collar workers are partial to the defense and school teachers are pro-

Pro-defense characteristics	Pro-prosecution characteristics	TABLE 3-1
Antiauthoritarian	Authoritarian personality	A lawyer's list of desirable juror characteristics
Single or divorced	Woman	
Unemployed	Affiliation with law enforcement	
Minority member	Victim	
Uneducated	Acquainted with victim of crime	
Unaffiliated	Club member (especially officer)	
Nonconforming appearance	Manager or supervisor	
Intellectual	Secretary	
Had prior brushes with law	School teacher	
Union man	Likes prosecutor	
Factory worker	Prior experience as juror	
People person (by occupation)	Career military	
Very rich	Retired	
Laughs, jovial	Paper person	
Raised in large family	Never married	
More than three children	Dour, sour countenance	
Similar to defendant	Raised in small family	
Book reader	Has few children	
Heavy drinker	Accountant	
Artist	Banker	
Blue collar	Bookkeeper	
Clerk	Engineer	
Housewife	Firefighter	
Nurse	Machinist	
Precision occupation	Programmer	
Professor	Government worker	
Salesman	Older man (in rape case)	
Social worker	Minority (if police on trial)	
Older woman (in rape case)		
Trucker		

Source: David Cromwell Johnson, "Voir Dire in the Criminal Case: A Primer," *Trial* 19 (October 1983): 62. Reprinted by permission.

prosecution? Without logic or data to support such assertions about favoritism, they seem highly suspect, as are many of the supposed correlates of jury bias.

Second, the information that lawyers have about members of the venire is limited. Judges frequently put severe limits on the scope of the voir dire, so it is often impossible to find out about the kinds of factors listed in Table 3-1. Moreover, prospective jurors give incomplete answers to judges' and lawyers' probings; they hold back many of their feelings or express them in subdued fashion, especially if they are eager to sit on the case.

A third obstacle to shrewd jury selection is that, in many states, peremptory challenges must be made at the time each member of the venire is questioned (the "sequential method"), rather than after all of them have been interviewed (the "struck jury" method). This makes it difficult, if not impossible, to make relative judgments about prospective jurors. Lawyers may eliminate someone who seems biased only to find that subsequent members of the venire look even worse. Peremptory challenges can thus be squandered on someone who, in retrospect, does not appear so bad.[35]

Opinions vary on how good all the lawyers' machinations and insights are. One assessment of jury selection processes is glowing in its praise: "Trial attorneys have developed a perceptiveness that enables them to detect the most minute traces of bias . . . ."[36] On the other hand, a defense lawyer who has written extensively about this topic is dubious: "[Jury selection] is so much witchcraft. It smacks of modern alchemy, full of jargon, superstition and mystification, but precious little real knowledge."[37]

The truth probably lies somewhere between these two extremes, as indicated by the results of a rather ingenious study done by Hans Zeisel and Shari Diamond.[38] With the cooperation of the federal district court of Northern Illinois, many of the jurors from twelve federal cases who had been eliminated from the juries through peremptory challenges were gathered to witness the trials and to decide the cases as if they were the empaneled jurors. Care was exercised to make their experiences similar to those of the real jurors: they were removed from the courtroom whenever the real jury was sent out, they handled the physical evidence, and so forth. Combining their verdict preferences with the first ballot preferences of the real jurors, revealed in post-trial interviews, enabled the researchers to reconstruct "juries without challenges" and to predict what their final verdict would likely have been. It was found that in seven of the twelve cases the effect of the challenges was minimal, but in the remaining five cases the probability of a guilty verdict increased by 13 percent when the inclinations of the excused jurors were substituted for those who replaced them. In one case in which the real jury acquitted, the reconstructed jury "almost certainly" would have convicted.[39]

However, the comparison of the individual excused jurors with their replacements suggested that the prosecutors made as many bad challenges as good ones and the defense attorneys fared only slightly better. Because the defense is allocated more peremptory challenges than the prosecution, however, even the mediocre judgments of defense attorneys sometimes resulted in juries that were somewhat more pro-defendant than juries without challenges would have been. All in all, the authors of the study concluded that although some of the lawyers used their challenges effectively, the "collective performance of the attorneys is not impressive."[40]

Thus, there does seem to be some skill entailed in the exercise of peremptory challenges. But there are no magic formulas or telltale signs divining jurors' predilections: the margin of error is great, mistaken predictions about jurors are commonplace, and juries often do not turn out as anticipated.

These failings have generated an interest in using social science to improve the chances of picking the right juror and avoiding the wrong juror. The politics of jury selection is too important to be left to guesswork.

"Scientific" Jury Selection

Dissatisfaction with the speculative nature of traditional approaches to jury selection have led to the use of behavioral sciences, especially psychology and sociology, to better ascertain the predilections of jurors. The aim is to replace lawyers' guesses and gut reactions to members of the venire with empirical studies that connect biases with the backgrounds, personalities, and courtroom behaviors of prospective jurors. The spirit of this approach is captured well by Alan Dershowitz, a Harvard law professor who often represents unpopular clients:

> Lawyers' instincts are often the *least* trustworthy basis on which to pick jurors. All those neat rules of thumb, but no feedback. Ten years of accumulated experiences may be 10 years of being wrong. I myself, even when I trust my instincts, like to have them scientifically confirmed.[41]

There are a number of specific systematic techniques used to try to tap juror biases. The cheapest, although probably the least reliable, is the psychological analysis of the *body language* of prospective jurors. Facial expressions and body movements sometimes reflect inner feelings, so careful observations of how people comport themselves in the courtroom are made. On the assumption that people's behavior sometimes reveals their prejudices better than their words, the slightest actions are recorded—facial expressions, yawns, head turns, twitches, fidgeting, and the like. Even psychics have been employed in an attempt to use extrasensory perceptions to reveal jurors' inner selves, although few would call this "science."

A case in which observation of body movements seemed to be fruitful was that of Angela Davis, a black, Communist professor of philosophy, who went on trial in 1971 for furnishing weapons to the murderer of a white judge. Because the district attorney was using his peremptory challenges to eliminate all the black members of the venire, the defense realized that it was going to have to make the best of an all-white jury. To try to find whites who were unprejudiced or even sympathetic toward blacks, one black defense lawyer conducted the voir dire while another member of the defense team noted the degree to which each person being questioned made eye contact with the black lawyer. Whites who averted the eyes of the black man interrogating them, or who glanced in another direction, were interpreted as uncomfortable relating to blacks—likely candidates for a peremptory challenge. Conversely, those who gazed intently into the black lawyer's eyes were thought to be more at ease with blacks and potential supporter's of Davis's cause. Just how effective this indirect method of getting at prejudice was we will never know, but after a several-month trial, Davis' all-white jury not only acquitted her in less than an hour but toasted her at a post-trial party given in her honor.[42]

A more elaborate and more expensive technique is the use of the *community survey*. Random samples of the community are polled before a trial to find out what kinds of people are inclined toward the prosecution and what kinds are partial to the defense. The voir dire is then used in an attempt to locate jurors who match the characteristics of those in the poll who were supportive or to eliminate those kinds of people who were found to be hostile.

The usefulness of such polling stems from the fact that sometimes the nature of supporters belies the expectations we would have had based on a general knowledge of attitudes and ideologies. For example, surveys by defenders of political dissidents tried in the 1960s and 1970s found all kinds of surprises: in Harrisburg, Pennsylvania, more young people than older people were opposed to individuals on trial for disruptive anti–Vietnam War protests; in New York more blue-collar workers than white-collar workers were favorable toward a female militant on trial for engaging in political bombing of buildings; and in Gainesville, Florida, more women than men were harsh toward political radicals on trial.[43] These sources of bias would not have been suspected by either seasoned lawyers or experts in public opinion; they could only be gleaned from original research.

Another approach is the use of *information networks*. All of the people on the venire are investigated outside of court in an attempt to get a better inkling of their biases than can be obtained through the voir dire. Neighbors, work associates, and others who know members of the venire are interviewed to determine the members' real beliefs. However, because it takes a great deal of time to track down solid information about people, this technique is only feasible when there is an extended period of jury selection. Morever, care must be exercised not to press the investigation too far, such as by talking directly to the prospective juror outside of court, lest one be accused of the criminal act of jury tampering.

Finally, research on *group dynamics* is sometimes brought to bear during jury selection. In the process of deciding who to exclude and who to keep, predictions are made about probable leadership roles within the jury. As we will see in Chapter 9, complex interactions among jurors occur in the process of reaching agreement on a verdict. It is important to keep jurors who will be biased against your side off the jury, and it is even more important to exclude antagonists who are capable of swaying others to their point of view. It is not just the direction of one's biases that must be taken into account but whether the person is likely to be active or passive during deliberations.

Expertise in group dynamics proved useful in defending the Vietnam Veterans Against the War against charges that they had conspired to disrupt the Republican National Convention in Miami during summer 1972. The defense team predicted that a very self-possessed, college-educated woman, who appeared to value fairness strongly, could emerge as the foreperson of the jury. The defense then used peremptory challenges to exclude high-status males who were likely to contest her leadership role and prevent her from using the influence she might otherwise wield over undecided jurors.[44]

There is much debate about how good these "high-tech" jury selection methods are, and whether they even deserve to be called "scientific" methods. Many of the practices deployed lack the rigor and precision associated with the scientific method. The meaning of body language is often unclear; the community surveys often suffer from excessive sampling error, and the impressive sounding "information network" is sometimes little more than gossip-mongering. Social science methodology requires time and money that is often unavailable in the fast-moving jury selection process, so participants in trials often must settle for rather crude studies with questionable validity.

A deeper issue is the question of juror predictability. One critic, dubious about attempts to determine jurors' biases in advance, has said, "Social scientists can't rig juries."[45] Correlations between demographic characteristics and juror behavior are not high: studies of former jurors and mock jury simulations have shown only modest differences between the sex, race, age, socioeconomic status, and education of jurors who vote to convict and those who vote to acquit.[46]

This is not to deny the significance of jurors' politics but to recognize that it is hard to pigeonhole jurors, with or without scientific information. Although we can and frequently do make relatively successful predictions about how politicians and judges will act in office on the basis of data about their backgrounds, the scant information obtainable about jurors gives us much less to go on. Can we really "put jurors on the couch," probing the core of their inner being, as one journalist, somewhat glorifying scientific jury selection, would have us think?[47] Probably not, but judicious use of social science may provide hints about the political tendencies of jurors that improve the odds of securing a jury helpful to one's cause.

A final concern about scientific jury selection is, even *if* it works, is it fair? Rarely will both sides in a case have the same resources available to them to finance quality research. According to one successful practitioner of jury research, the bare minimum for decent research is $50,000, and a "full-scale workup" can cost $500,000.[48] Ford Motor Company, defending itself on criminal charges arising from deaths caused by its defective Pinto automobile, paid $1,000 per day to one of the nation's top sociologists specializing in the jury.[49] A method that originated in the 1960s to help downtrodden defendants faced with potentially hostile juries is now more commonly used by affluent litigants in civil cases and is sometimes even employed by prosecutors in criminal cases. Perhaps it is all right for both sides to have access to similar weapons for fighting courtroom battles, but it is open to question whether it is ethically proper to permit those who already have the upper hand to extend their advantage by employing science for the purpose of stacking the jury.

57

Conclusion

The composition of juries remains decidedly skewed. While the expansion of the master wheel to include a broader cross section of the community has widened the representative political views on juries, it is sheer mythology to think that subsequent jury selection procedures remove jurors whose political views would impinge on their decision making.

First of all, that is an impossibility: everyone has political sentiments that, despite the best intentions, get entangled in the process of evaluating the evidence. It may be possible to eliminate extremists who are incapable of considering the evidence at all, but to purge the jury of people affected by values and prejudices is to create an empty jury box. A depoliticized jury is a contradiction in terms.

Second, as we have shown, jury selection mechanisms are only partially effective at exposing bias. The voir dire uncovers little about people, and what it does reveal is often wrong. The words of Judge Learned Hand are just as true today as when he wrote them in 1950:

> . . . any examination on the voir dire is a clumsy and imperfect way of detecting suppressed emotional commitments to which all of us are to some extent subject, unconsciously or subconsciously. It is of the nature of our deepest antipathies that often we do not admit them even to ourselves; but when that is so, nothing but an examination, utterly impracticable in a courtroom, will disclose them, an examination extending at times for months, and even then unsuccessful.[50]

Judge Hand may have overstated the point. It may well be that *probable* bias is more detectable than he thought, especially with the aid of modern methods of empirical research. But lawyers do not use this information to secure an impartial jury; what they want is one biased toward their side. The voir dire and peremptory challenges are employed to pack the jury with supporters or at the very least to cleanse it of opponents. How effectively this is done can certainly affect the balance of power in the jury room.

The jury selection process, then, leaves us with jurors who are anything but neutral. In the chapters to come, we shall see how their views of justice, attitudes toward the law, ideologies, and prejudices affect the rendering of verdicts. *Who* jurors are has an effect on *what* they decide.

Notes

1. *Taylor v. United States*, 419 U.S. 522, 528 (1975).
2. *Strauder v. Virginia*, 100 U.S. (10 Otto) 303 (1880).
3. *Holland v. Illinois*, No. 88-5050 (1990).
4. *Swain v. Alabama*, 380 U.S. 202 (1965).
5. Michael Finkelstein, "The Application of Statistical Decision Theory to the Jury Discrimination Cases," *Harvard Law Review*, 80 (December 1966): 338–376.

6. *Taylor* v. *United States*, 419 U.S. 522 (1975).
7. *Craven* v. *Carmical*, No. 71-1602, cert. denied (1972).
8. Quoted in John Vanderzell, "The Jury as a Community Cross-Section," *Western Political Quarterly*, 19 (March 1966): 136–139.
9. *Carter* v. *Jury Commissioner of Greene County*, 396 U.S. 320 (1970).
10. *Castaneda* v. *Partida*, 430 U.S. 482 (1977).
11. Haywood Alker, Carl Hosticka, and Michael Mitchell, "Jury Selection as a Biased Social Process," *Law and Society Review*, 11 (Fall 1976): 9–40.
12. Roger Durham, Geoffrey Alpert, and Darrell Conners, "Black Representation on Juries in Miami," *The Justice System Journal*, 11 (1986): 79–88; Lyle Knowles and Kenneth Hickman, "Selecting a Jury of Peers: How Close Do We Get?" *Journal of Police Science and Administration*, 12 (1984): 207–212.
13. G. Thomas Munsterman and Janice Munsterman, "The Search for Jury Representativeness," *The Justice System Journal*, 11 (Spring 1986): 68.
14. *Taylor* v. *United States*, 419 U.S. 522 (1975).
15. *United States* v. *Burr*, 4 Cr. 470 (1807).
16. *Ham* v. *South Carolina*, 409 U.S. 524 (1973); *Rastaino* v. *Ross*, 424 U.S. 589 (1976).
17. *Irwin* v. *Dowd*, 366 U.S. 717 (1961); *Murphy* v. *Florida*, 421 U.S. 794 (1975); *Patton* v. *Yount*, 467 U.S. 1025 (1984).
18. *Ham* v. *South Carolina*, 409 U.S. 524 (1973).
19. *Lockhart* v. *McCree*, 476 U.S. 162 (1986).
20. "In the Supreme Court of the United States: *Lockhart* v. *McCree*; Amicus Curiae Brief for the American Psychological Association," *American Psychologist*, 42 (January 1987): 59–68.
21. See Anne Rankin Mahoney, "American Jury Voir Dire and the Ideal of Equal Justice," *Journal of Applied Behavioral Science*, 18 (1982): 481–494.
22. Paula Di Perna, *Juries on Trial: Faces of American Justice* (New York: Dembner Books, 1984), p. 133.
23. Ann Fagan Ginger, *Minimizing Racism in Jury Trials* (Berkeley, California: National Lawyers Guild, 1969), p. 158.
24. Robert Balch, Curt Griffiths, Edwin Hall, and L. Thomas Winfree, "The Socialization of Jurors: The Voir Dire as a Right of Passage," *Journal of Criminal Justice* 4 (Winter 1976): 271–283.
25. "Arizona Ranchers' Jury Protested," *The New York Times* (June 27, 1980), p. A10.
26. *Batson* v. *Kentucky*, 476 U.S. 79 (1986). This holding was reaffirmed and broadened in April 1991 when the Supreme Court ruled that it was unconstitutional to use peremptory challenges to exclude blacks even when defendants were white. Said Justice Kennedy for the Court: "Race cannot be a proxy for determining juror bias or competence." *Powers* v. *Ohio*, No. 89-5011 (1991).
27. Sam Howe Verhovek, "New York Court Says Defendants Can't Reject Jurors Based on Race," *The New York Times* (March 30, 1990), p. A1.
28. The manual was reprinted in the Spring 1973 issue of the *Texas Observer*.
29. Quoted in "We, the Jury, Find the . . .," *Time* (September 28, 1981), p. 47.
30. Shari Diamond and Hans Zeisel, "Jury Behavior," in Sanford Kadish (ed.), *Encyclopedia of Criminal Justice III* (New York: Free Press, 1983), p. 929.
31. Reid Hastie, Steven Penrod, and Nancy Pennington, *Inside the Jury* (Cambridge, Mass.: Harvard University Press, 1983), p.122.
32. Fred Inbau *et al.*, *Cases and Comments on Criminal Procedure*, 2nd. ed. (Mineola, New York: Foundation Press, 1980), p. 1097.
33. Di Perna, *Juries on Trial*, p. 151.
34. L. Heller, *Do You Solemnly Swear?* (New York: Doubleday, 1968), pp. 120–121.
35. Steven Brams and Morton Davis discuss this problem in "Optimal Jury Selection: A Game-Theoretical Model for the Exercise of Peremptory Challenges," *Operations Research*, 26 (November-December 1978): 966–991.
36. R. G. Begam, "The Attorneys," *Judicature*, 61 (1977): 78.

59

37. Harold Price Fahringer is quoted in "Jury Choice to Be Difficult for Lennon Trial Defense," *The New York Times* (June 18, 1981), p. 33.
38. Hans Zeisel and Shari Seidman Diamond, "The Effect of Peremptory Challenges on Jury and Verdict: An Experiment in a Federal District Court," *Stanford Law Review*, 30 (February 1978): 491–531.
39. *Ibid.*, p. 508.
40. *Ibid.*, p. 517.
41. Quoted in Morton Hunt, "Putting Juries on the Couch," *The New York Times Magazine* (November 28, 1982), p. 82. Reprinted by permission.
42. James Levine, Michael Musheno, and Dennis Palumbo, *Criminal Justice in America: Law in Action* (New York: Wiley, 1986), pp. 405–406; Howard Moore, "Redressing the Balance," *Trial Magazine*, 10 (November-December 1974): 29–35.
43. Jay Schulman, Phillip Shaver, Robert Colman, Barbara Emrich, and Richard Christie, "Recipe for a Jury," *Psychology Today*, 37 (May 1973): 37–44; "Judging Jurors," *Time* (January 28, 1974), p. 60; Robert Buckhout, *Studies in Systematic Jury Selection: An Inside View* (Brooklyn, N.Y.: Center for Responsive Psychology, 1978).
44. R. Christie, "Probability v. Precedence: The Social Psychology of Jury Selection," in G. Bermant, C. Nemeth, and N. Vidmar (eds.), *Psychology and the Law* (Lexington, Mass.: Lexington Books, 1976), pp. 265–281.
45. Michael Saks, "Social Scientists Can't Rig Juries," *Psychology Today* (January 1976): 48. See also, John Berman and Bruce Sales, "A Critical Evaluation of the Systematic Approach to Jury Selection," *Criminal Justice and Behavior* 14 (September 1977): 219–229.
46. Gary Moran and John Craig Comfort, "Scientific Juror Selection: Sex as a Moderator of Demographic and Personality Predictors of Impaneled Felony Juror Behavior," *Journal of Personality and Social Psychology*, 43 (1982), 1052–1063. Carol Mills and Wayne Bohannon, "Juror Characteristics: To What Extent Are They Related to Jury Verdicts?" *Judicature* 64 (June-July 1980), 22–31; John Baldwin and Michael McConville, "Does the Composition of the English Jury Affect its Verdict?" *Judicature*, 64 (September 1980), 133–139. See J. Reed, "Jury Deliberations, Voting, and Verdict Trends," *Social Science Quarterly*, 45 (1965), 361–370.
47. Hunt, "Putting Juries on the Couch," 70–88.
48. *Ibid.*, p. 72.
49. Di Perna, *Juries on Trial*, p. 136.
50. *United States* v. *Dennis*, 183 F. 2d. 201, 227 (2d, cir., 1950), aff'd. 341 U.S. 491 (1951).

I n 1975, Joan Little, a 20-year-old black woman, was charged with using an ice pick to kill a 62-year-old white guard in the Beaufort County jail, located in a small backwoods town in eastern North Carolina. Ms. Little claimed it was an act of self-defense to ward off a sexual attack from the guard, during which she was forced to perform an act of oral sex. The prosecution argued that she had enticed the guard into a sexual liaison and then killed him as part of a successful attempt to break out of jail. The only physical evidence was the semen found on the thigh of the dead guard and the ice pick. There were no eyewitnesses.

Consider Ms. Little's plight. The case pitted the word of an apparently disreputable convict against that of a member of the criminal justice establishment. The defendant was a young black woman and the victim an older white man. The trial was to be held in a backwoods courthouse, before a jury likely to be dominated by conservatives and peppered with bigots. The defendant was too poor to hire a private lawyer and was up against an amply funded district attorney's office.

Ms. Little's image compounded her difficulties. She was in jail serving time for breaking and entering after a previous conviction for shoplifting. She had been sexually active as early as the age of fourteen, had contracted syphilis at age fifteen, and was widely rumored to be a prostitute. She had been sent to a reform school at age fifteen. While in jail, she spent considerable

4
· · · · · · ·
Influencing
Jurors
During Trials

time naked from the waist up. There were allegations that she had had previous sexual contact with her jailer.

How would you rate her chances? The odds would certainly seem to be against an acquittal. If advising her, most people would probably urge her to take any reasonable deal offered by the prosecutor rather than put her fate in the hands of a jury.

Joan Little's prospects looked grim, but she won her case. Not only did the jury acquit her, they did so after only one hour and eighteen minutes of deliberation. Belying initial predictions, the jury wound up on Joan Little's side.

It was not luck that caused this result; it was power. The defense was able to accomplish a tour de force in what has come to be a textbook example of how jurors can be legitimately influenced. What changed the odds immediately was money: when Joan Little's situation became public, more than $350,000 was raised by women's rights and black political groups to pay for her defense. A competent lawyer was hired, one who was able to devote himself full-time to her case for many months.

Lawyer Jerry Paul did a lot with the resources at his command. First, he assembled a team of lawyers to examine the evidence in painstaking fashion. They were able to obtain a change of venue, moving the trial from Beaufort County to the much more heterogeneous state capital of Raleigh. Intensive effort was directed at jury selection to get jurors with a pro-Little bias; three psychologists, a body language expert, and three statisticians helped Paul select the jury, which included six black jurors. Responses to a 70-item telephone survey of 952 local residents were analyzed by the complex statistical technique of factor analysis, which yielded a rather precise profile of the ideal juror. This effort paid off: several jurors were seen crying during the defense's summation, and one black man on the jury later said that he kept thinking of his own little girl in empathizing with Ms. Little's ordeal.[1]

Lawyer Paul used various strategies to get the jury on his side. First, in his own words, he "orchestrated" the press.[2] Events were constantly staged before and during the trial to enhance Ms. Little's reputation and dramatize her version of events in the jail. One photo, which was widely reproduced, showed her clutching a copy of *To Kill a Mockingbird*, with the title conspicuously showing.

The heart of the defense strategy was to prepare Ms. Little to testify in court. Paul spent days with the defendant going over every bit of the questioning he was going to engage in when she took the witness stand. Role-playing experts were brought in to help train the defendant as a witness and enable her to withstand the badgering by the prosecution expected during cross-examination. Ms. Little was instructed to be matter-of-fact when that was appropriate and to break down into tears at the opportune moment. Her courtroom performance got rave reviews; she appeared calm, intelligent, and absolutely compelling in her assertion that she had been the victim of sodomy and attempted rape.[3]

The jurors, as usual, disavowed having been "won over." The foreman blandly explained that the burden of proof was on the state and they didn't produce enough evidence. But as columnist Mike Royko pointed out later, "It was just as easy to believe that she had set up the old geezer for murder and escape as it was to believe that he forced her to defend herself."[4] Perhaps Ms. Little was really innocent, perhaps not; but it was her lawyer's handling of the trial that got the jury to see things her way.

Paul was the first to acknowledge that his scheming and plotting were instrumental in getting the not guilty verdict. Claiming to have "bought" an acquittal, he boasted that "given enough money, I can buy justice. I can win any case in the country, given enough money."[5] This is a gross overstatement, probably brought on by the thrill of his unexpected victory. But his comment has more than a grain of truth to it, and the Joan Little case has a powerful message: jurors are influenced and sometimes manipulated by a myriad of participants during the trial.

This chapter is about such influence. Trials are power struggles, with both sides trying to dominate the will of the jurors. If power is defined as X's ability to get Y to do what Y ordinarily would not do (the standard political science definition), lawyers are Xs and jurors are Ys. Lawyers resort to all kinds of strategies and use all kinds of gambits to control jurors. Other participants wield influence, too, although often unwittingly—the judges, the press, the spectators, and in rare instances, associates of those on trial. Judge Frank was again on target: trials are fights; verdicts are valuable prizes; the fighting to control the jurors, who are in charge, can be intense; and there are no guarantees that the truth emerges.[6] The powerful are not always right.

The Role of Lawyers

Satirist Jonathan Swift once said that lawyers are "a society of men among us, bred up from their youth in the art of proving by words multiplied for that purpose that *white* is *black* and *black* is *white*."[7] This is an unkind and probably unfair blow: lawyers are *supposed* to do everything they can within the limits of legal ethics to fight for their cause.

Lawyers use a host of strategies and tactics in their attempts to prevail. The layperson, perhaps enamored with the argumentative skills of television lawyers like Perry Mason, may think that the key to success is glowing oratory and sharp repartees with witnesses. But hard work and methodical preparation before trials usually pay off more. Building solid cases is crucial for winning over juries, especially given situations like that of Joan Little in which jurors may be unsympathetic to the lawyer's side.

Case Preparation

Tediously digging out facts helpful to one's cause is one of the most important steps in putting together a persuasive case for the jury. Clients must be interviewed assiduously, both to get clues for further research and to figure out the strengths and weaknesses of their testimony in case they should testify. Other witnesses must be tracked down and interrogated, sometimes by securing a sworn statement called a *deposition*. Physical evidence such as blood stains, bullet shells, and ripped clothing must be scrutinized, which sometimes requires painstaking scientific analysis.

The law too must be studied. The penal code and any relevant legal precedents must be scoured in order to present a favorable set of instructions to the jury. The nuances of legal procedure must be examined in the hopes of finding ways to get harmful evidence or testimony excluded from the trial. Remember, both the substantive and the procedural law are ambiguous, and part of the lawyer's role is to get interpretations from the judge that are beneficial to the client's cause.

These old-fashioned research activities remain important means of building a persuasive case. Jurors do take their mandate to base verdicts on facts and the law seriously, so anything that can be done to bolster the legally relevant features of a case can be instrumental in winning. When lawyers fail to meet these responsibilities adequately, disaster may result for their clients.

Ordinary research can be decisive, but lawyers are increasingly supplementing standard approaches with more sophisticated methods of scoring points with jurors. The time-tested device of rehearsing witnesses before trial has been improved through the use of videotapes. Lawyers can view tapes of themselves handling witnesses to see how both the substance of their questions and their style of questioning can be improved. Just as politicians and actors can enhance their performances through self-criticism, so can lawyers, and modern technology can help them do so more effectively.

Getting the juror's pespective can be even more enlightening. Some lawyers representing defendants in retrials have questioned jurors from the earlier trial about what influenced their decision and what did not. However, using surrogate juries is a more professionally acceptable method of "tuning in" to jurors' thinking and can be employed at original trials as well. In surrogate juries, people are hired to play the roles of jurors so lawyers can observe the effectiveness of their methods of communication and can make adjustments to correct for any shortcomings.[8]

One type of surrogate jury is the *shadow jury,* a group of people demographically similar to the real jury who are hired to sit in the courtroom each day and report their impressions of the evidence to the lawyers. The shadow jury was used successfully by the International Business Machines Corporation (IBM) in defending itself against antitrust charges in the 1970s.

64

Nicholas deB. Katzenbach, IBM's general counsel, explained the rationale: "The purpose was to see whether what was being said was being communicated. Every now and then we would find a person with a total misconception. The lawyers could clear things up."[9]

This approach has the advantage of the authenticity of the real trial, but it can be quite expensive and logistically difficult to herd a shadow jury in and out of the courtroom every day. A more economical approach is to use a *mock jury*, a group of surrogates who hear abbreviated versions of a case before the trial and then engage in mock deliberations, which are videotaped or observed by attorneys through one-way mirrors. The most noted example of this method in action was in the $900 million suit by MCI Communications against the American Telephone and Telegraph Company (AT&T). Lawyers discovered that the mock jury had taken the mention of MCI's $100 million in lost profit due to AT&T's monopolistic practices and used that figure as the basis for their damage award. Thereafter in the actual trial, no mention was made of any dollar figure, and the real jury returned a verdict of $600 million. Without the elucidation provided by watching the mock jury, even the sharpest of lawyers probably would have made the costly blunder of triggering a lower damage award by placing an amount in the jurors' minds.

Courtroom Tactics

It is often claimed that it is the quality of lawyers' courtroom presentations that sways the jury. Balzac once characterized the jury as "twelve men chosen to decide who has the better lawyer."[10] Lawyers are fond of exchanging "tricks of the trade" with each other, musing about everything from what color of clothing to wear to whether it is better to attack opposition witnesses sharply or mildly. There are endless little schemes that are thought to be useful; one tale told is of turn-of-the-century lawyer William Jennings Bryan, who, just as the opposition's star witness was testifying, would keep the jury's attention riveted on the steadily growing ash of his cigar, ready to fall onto his protruding belly. Apart from such gimmickry, many trial lawyers think that their adeptness at interrogating witnesses and the rhetorical skills in addressing the jury can carry the day.

How effective are all these courtroom machinations of lawyers? A few mock jury studies suggest that proper handling of technical details, such as phrasing of questions to witnesses, can make a difference,[11] but there is no evidence that dazzling courtroom displays by lawyers spell the difference between victory and defeat. The importance of the lawyer's "golden tongue" is probably overrated; it is the witnesses that the lawyer presents before the jury who do the most persuasive talking. The lawyer's most decisive role is therefore in building a solid case.

The Role of Money

Earlier in this chapter lawyer Jerry Paul was quoted as saying that with sufficient money *any* case can be won. This was an exaggeration, of course. There are plenty of instances of people hiring high-priced legal talent and losing; the Melvin Bellis and Percy Foremans don't always win.

But there is also little doubt that even a mediocre lawyer can significantly improve the chances of success before the jury given sufficient resources to build as solid a case as possible. The State of California spent $5 million retrying Juan Corona in 1982 for the slaying of 25 farm workers; Corona was convicted. The Police Benevolent Association spent $300,000 in defense of the New York City police officers accused of killing graffiti scrawler Michael Stewart after a confrontation; the police were acquitted. John Hinckley's father spent more than $400,000 on legal and related fees to help defend him against charges of the attempted murder of Ronald Reagan; Hinckley was found not guilty by reason of insanity.

It is impossible to determine that in these cases it was the money that made the difference; sorting out the relative contribution to jury verdicts of the law, the evidence, juror sentiments, and lawyers' work cannot be done. But this much is certain: money buys research; research digs up facts; and facts can overpower jurors. If a case is tight enough, it is very difficult for all but the most fanatical jurors to decide the other way. Lawyers cannot do much to change jurors' politics, but they can go a long way in influencing their conceptions of reality.

Many of the strategies and techniques aimed at augmenting power that we just discussed are not utilized in the average case. Rather, they are confined to celebrated criminal cases or civil cases entailing large damage claims, in which one side or both sides have ample resources to devote to the courtroom battle. Lawyers handling "garden variety" robbery or burglary cases generally lack the means necessary to engage in such high-powered activities. The routine case simply involves the presentation of a modicum of evidence and a sprinkling of witnesses. Use of manipulative devices by attorneys is at a minimum, and it is the people who take the witness stand who have much greater sway over jury verdicts.

The Impact of Witnesses

Jurors, as we have constantly reiterated, try very hard to get at the facts. Consequently, what goes on at the trial can have a decisive impact. If both adversaries argue equally plausible cases, the potential for jury politics to resolve matters is greatest. But if one side presents evidence that is far more persuasive, it has the upper hand in winning the jury over.

There are three major categories of evidence introduced at trials. *Real evidence* are physical objects, called *exhibits*, such as guns or drugs. *Direct*

66

evidence are the recollections of eyewitnesses who viewed a crime. *Circumstantial evidence* is the testimony from people privy to information relevant to proving or disproving facts that are germane to determining a defendant's culpability. All three kinds of evidence are perfectly legitimate, although all are limited by a complex set of legal rules largely specified in appellate court opinions and enforced by trial court judges. For example, there are severe restrictions on the introduction of certain types of evidence, such as facsimiles of documents, results of polygraph tests, testimony of spouses against each other, and "hearsay"—a witness' recollections of comments made previously by a person not present in court.

Judges spend much effort screening what jurors hear and shielding them from inadmissible evidence, but it is up to the jurors themselves to decide how seriously to take the exhibits and the testimony. The persuasiveness of witnesses depends not only on whether what they say makes sense but on their credibility, their demeanor, and their ability to relate positively to jurors. In other words, how jurors receive information aired at the trial depends on the inherent power of the testimony (the message) and how powerfully it is communicated (the medium). In the next few sections we shall see that the impression that witnesses make on jurors depends on *who* they are, *what* they are saying, and *how* they are saying it.

Defendants

Defendants know whether they actually did what they are accused of doing. Jurors are therefore eager to get the defendant's side of the story: as in the Joan Little case, a defendant's good performance on the witness stand can offset other damaging evidence, whereas an unbelievable alibi or poor accounting of events can be devastating. Jurors are inordinately attentive to defendants' testimony, and some studies have suggested that the credibility of defendants is often the pivotal factor in close cases.[12]

Defendants who testify on their own behalf may well be treated skeptically by the jury. If the defendants are facing serious charges, they have a compelling incentive to lie—and jurors know it. Although all defendants take an oath to tell the truth and can face perjury charges if they do not, it is commonly assumed that most people wouldn't hesitate to lie if a prison sentence or even death were at stake. Defendants' self-interest in making themselves look good is therefore an inherent obstacle to their credibility, a problem that Frankel and Morris call "the ingratiator's dilemma."[13]

The defendants' plight is compounded by several other factors. The deepest problem is that there are no foolproof methods for distinguishing honest people from liars. Jurors sometimes take into account such unreliable indicators as the defendant's bearing on the witness stand. One mock jury study has shown that testifying in a fidgety or tense manner rather than appearing calm and relaxed can be the undoing of defendants, especially where the evidence against them is weak.[14] Yet many honest people might well be nervous testifying in public with so much at stake; so the demeanor test of jurors would seem to penalize many unfairly.

A second problem defendants encounter in testifying is that unflattering elements of their backgrounds may be brought up under cross-examination as the prosecution's means of impeaching defendant's veracity. Revelation of a defendant's previous criminal record often sows doubts in the jurors' minds. "Once a scoundrel, always a scoundrel" is not an uncommon assumption. On the other hand, a clean past augurs well for the defendant, as Kalven and Zeisel report: "The jury's broad rule of thumb . . . is that . . it is especially unlikely that a person with no prior record will commit a serious crime, and that this is relevant to evaluating his testimony when he denies his guilt on the stand."[15]

Still another problem facing defendants is that assessing a person's truthfulness requires, to some degree, an assessment of his or her character. Such character judgments are sometimes informed by jurors' biases and stereotypes, as Chapter 8 will fully explain. "Sizing up people" is a guessing game, and the guesswork in which jurors engage may at times be unwittingly grounded in their political views about race, ethnicity, class, or other legally irrelevant matters.

If defendants rely on the Fifth Amendment's privilege against self-incrimination and choose *not* to testify, they can be going out of the frying pan and into the fire. Although judges routinely and sometimes adamantly lecture jurors that refusal to testify creates no inferences about guilt or innocence whatsoever, it is hard to put aside the nagging question, What does the defendant have to hide? There is a substantial body of experimental evidence indicating that criminal defendants appearing to withhold evidence are more likely to be deemed guilty than those who are forthcoming.[16] Not testifying at all puts a defendant particularly at risk of being presumed guilty.[17]

Thus, defendants appear to be damned if they do testify and damned if they don't; they are in an unenviable situation. However, their position improves immeasurably if they are fortunate enough to have a more liberal jury devoted to the presumption of innocence. The ideologies of the jurors affect their judgments, as will be shown in Chapter 7, and one way it creeps into the juror's thinking is through their interpretation of what it means for defendants to remain silent.

Character Witnesses

One strategy for countering jurors' negative perceptions of defendants is for the defense to introduce character witnesses—people who, on the basis of personal dealings with the defendant, can attest to his or her honesty. Members of the clergy, employers, teachers, and neighbors are the kinds of people typically brought in to vouch for the defendant's decency and honor.

"He's just not that type of person"; "She's hard-working and conscientious"; "A prince of a guy"; these are the kind of comments that such witnesses are apt to make to back up the defendant's denial of wrongdoing.

It takes little reflection to recognize why this type of testimony ordinarily falls on deaf ears. It is often biased, because of the particular nature of the relationship between the character witness and the defendant. It is occasionally self-serving, because the character witness will often suffer a certain degree of grief if the defendant is convicted. And it has little to do with the issue that is all-consuming for jurors: What really happened?

Nonetheless, there are times when character witnesses help. When witnesses themselves are held in high esteem, their reputations reflect well on the defendant. In a strange twist of the scourge of "guilt by association," defendants may be deemed innocent by association. Praising a defendant's character is not the kind of testimony likely to exculpate those who are deeply implicated by the evidence, but it can indeed rescue those on the borderline—especially if the jury for political reasons is inclined to acquit them.

Child Witnesses

Another suspect category of witnesses are children. Historically, children under the age of seven were not allowed to testify because of doubts about their understanding of the concept of truthfulness; but rigid age barriers have now been dropped. It is up to the judge in pretrial hearings to determine if the child is sufficiently competent to remember the past and to disentangle real events from imaginary ones. Where children have been crime victims or are the only witnesses to crime, there is a growing tendency to let them take the stand. To spare the child the trauma of confronting his or her accuser in court and to prevent the courtroom immobilization that occurs when a child becomes tongue-tied by such ordeals, some courts have allowed a child's testimony to be videotaped out of court.

Children now testify, but they are not necessarily believed. Recall the McMartin case from Chapter 1: the jury refused to convict in large part because it was thought that some of the children were fantasizing and others were confused. This case was no exception: jurors consider child witnesses to be less trustworthy than adults. Although empirical research has discovered that children remember more and forget less than previously had been assumed, the laypersons on the jury remain dubious.[18]

Eyewitnesses

One kind of witness the jury *does* listen to is the eyewitness. The accounts of bystanders and victims who purport to have seen the crime take place make for powerful courtroom testimony. Despite the fact that voluminous research has demonstrated that much eyewitness testimony is unreliable and that eyewitnesses often err in identifying persons committing crimes,[19] mock jury research suggests that this type of evidence is nonetheless very influential.[20]

Inaccurate eyewitness testimony tends to be accepted just as readily as sound testimony from others and has quite an incriminating effect.[21] Mock juries convicted much more frequently when an eyewitness was added to the circumstantial evidence making up the prosecution's case, even in one case in which the eyewitness had an uncorrected visual handicap at the time of the crime.[22] Other experiments have shown that when eyewitnesses can recount trivial details and present a confident manner of expression, it bolsters juror acceptance of their testimony and compensates for the poor conditions under which the observations were made.[23] In the minds of two reviewers, all the studies taken together "clearly indicate that jurors are insensitive to eyewitness evidence,"[24] meaning that they fail to differentiate between sound and unsound eyewitness observations.

Consequently, eyewitness testimony can be a devastating adversarial resource at the trial. Rebutting such evidence requires patient and careful probing by attorneys to undermine the appearance of accuracy and certainty. This brings us back to one theme of this chapter: the ability to influence jurors depends in part on the legal resources available to each side. In addition to persistent cross-examination, another weapon to combat questionable eyewitness identification is available to the defendant fortunate enough to be able to afford it or secure it for free—the expert on eyewitness testimony. A good number of psychologists with expertise on perception and memory have applied their knowledge to the issue of eyewitness identification, and most jurisdictions permit them to alert jurors to the factors impinging on witness accuracy. Mock jury research has consistently revealed that the introduction of such expert testimony reduces jurors' faith in the prosecution's eyewitnesses and results in fewer convictions.[25]

70

Expert Witnesses

There are many professionals other than psychologists dealing with eyewitness observations who are called in to interpret factual evidence during trials: psychiatrists will proffer opinions on insanity; biochemists will analyze blood stains; geneticists will try to decode the DNA in semen; coroners discuss causes of death; ballistic experts trace bullet trajectories. The list goes on: magazines like *Trial* that are intended for practicing lawyers are full of advertisements for specialists willing to give expert opinions on a whole range of matters.

It is unclear just how successful the experts are. There are cases, like that of socialite Claus von Bülow, in which expert testimony seems to have been decisive. In 1982, a Providence, Rhode Island, jury convicted von Bülow of trying to kill his multimillionaire wife by injecting her with insulin, which left her in an irreversible coma. The jury concluded that he had a powerful motive—wanting to keep his mistress while he got his wife's inheritance—and convicted him on the basis of circumstantial evidence; the defense called almost no witnesses. That verdict was overturned because of procedural errors, and during the retrial von Bülow's lawyer, in his own words, "presented a medical case."[26] *All nine of the defense witnesses were doctors*; they testified that the cause of Mrs. von Bülow's coma was not insulin but the destructive interactive effect of the various drugs she routinely abused. The jury acquitted.

It is unclear whether this was a fluke or whether experts regularly do convince jurors. One mock jury experiment discovered that monetary awards in civil cases were significantly higher when experts testified about future wages plaintiffs lost as a result of their injuries.[27] Another study collated the various research efforts assessing the impact of *social framework testimony*—how jurors respond to the presentation of information on phenomena such as battered women's syndrome, "brainwashed" defendants, and racial discrimination. It was found that although jurors listen to such testimony and bring it to bear on the facts of the case, they are not overwhelmed by it.[28]

A good example of just such a skeptical jury was the one in Rochester, New York, which in 1990 convicted Arthur Shawcross of killing and mutilating eleven women over a period of twenty-one months. Shawcross relied on an insanity defense, and his main witness was a nationally known psychiatry professor at New York University Medical Center. Although she testified for nine days during the course of the trial, jurors later said that they were unpersuaded by her lengthy and complicated answers to lawyers' questions. Said the jury foreman, "If she could have kept her feet out of her mouth, she would have been okay. The more she talked, the worse it got. It's just too bad she didn't leave after she read her qualifications."[29]

Where both sides come to the trial armed with convincing experts, the jury is sometimes left wondering what to believe. Such was the plight of the New York jury that dealt with the murder trial of Robert Chambers. Chambers was accused of strangling his sometimes-lover Jennifer Levin during a middle-of-the-night sexual tryst in Central Park. Chambers claimed that he acted in self-defense to ward off Ms. Levin's sexual aggression, and the case turned into a battle of the experts concerning the cause of death. The Detroit medical examiner, testifying for the prosecution, and the Los Angeles medical examiner, testifying for the defense, agreed on virtually nothing— the type of strangulation, the time it took the victim to die, or the cause of other wounds and bruises discovered on her body. Pity the poor jury: it flip-flopped back and forth in the jury room, apparently going from 8 to 4 for acquittal to 9 to 3 for conviction to 9 to 3 for acquittal to 7 to 5 for acquittal; the case was finally plea-bargained while the jury was still struggling in the jury room.[30] Clearly then, experts who contradict each other can cancel out each other's influence, requiring the jury to resort to its own devices—which are often their own political viewpoints.

Cuing by Judges

Judges are supposed to be neutral referees during jury trials. Judges take a backseat role, intervening primarily to prevent procedural errors and to maintain courtroom decorum. In explaining the law to jurors, judges theoretically are just transmitting established legal norms and principles. They keep their opinions about who should win to themselves and leave the jurors to their fact-finding business. Judges stand above the fray—so it is said.

Actually, judges do influence jurors. First of all, judges can make one or another verdict more likely by the way they give the jurors instructions about their task, how they present the standard of proof necessary to convict, and how they define the laws in question. Even if jurors do not quite fathom the legal terminology given to them, they may be affected by the manner in which the instructions are given.

Second, judges often handicap one side or the other through their many rulings on what evidence and testimony are permissible. Even if their decisions are made wholly on the basis of the formal law, a relentless series of sustained or overruled objections can prejudice jurors in a particular direction. They may be more likely to think that someone is guilty if his or her lawyer is constantly being rebuffed.

Legal rulings do affect outcomes, but ideally they emerge from the laws and not sheerly from judges' personal opinions. However, there is a third source of influence that judges have over jurors—their own inclinations about who should win as expressed through cues transmitted in an oblique manner. Laughter, nods, expressions of anger, and the like can intentionally or unintentionally communicate what the judge thinks. Jurors who are baffled by conflicting and confusing evidence may well seek guidance from judges, who can use both words and mannerisms to indicate their feelings.

The influential role of judges on jurors has been demonstrated. Research published in the *Stanford Law Review* correlated the verbal and body language of California Municipal Court judges with jury verdicts. Negative messages about defendants, often derived from the fact that the judge knew of defendants' prior records, resulted in substantially more guilty verdicts. In other words, judges managed to "leak" their opinions to jurors, jurors were able to ascertain the judges' leanings, and jurors responded accordingly. As the authors of the study put it, "judges' behavior alone can predict the verdicts returned by juries" in many cases.[31]

A concrete example illustrates how judges can use their position of authority to influence jurors. In 1968, a federal jury was hearing criminal charges against Dr. Benjamin Spock, whose book on child care had been a ready reference source for millions of parents. He was accused of being part of a group that had illegally urged young people to resist the draft in protest against the Vietnam War. Here is how one reporter present at the trial described Judge Frances Ford's conduct of the case, so extreme in its anti–Spock orientation that a higher court later reversed the jury's conviction:

The official transcript does not convey the skeptical tone that the judge employed in addressing defendants when they denied government allegations. Nor does anything in its nineteen volumes describe the elaborate shuffling of papers and ordering about of clerks and marshals when defense attorneys were scoring points—though the transcript does show that he sometimes capped such points by admonishing the jury to keep an open mind. In reading the transcript, one cannot hear his hectoring tone as he urged defense lawyers to "get on" or "go forward" on numerous occasions—something he rarely did to the prosecution.[32]

Judge Ford's influence on the jury was particularly blatant. More typical is the behavior of the presiding judge handling corruption charges against Newark Mayor Kenneth Gibson in 1982. During the trial, the judge repeatedly criticized the prosecution's case whenever the jury was not present in the courtroom. One member of the jury that acquitted Gibson of the major charge said she was unaware of the criticisms the judge had directed against the prosecution.[33] But in light of the findings in the *Stanford Law Review* discussed earlier, it seems likely that the judge's opinion did not remain outside the jury's ken.

The judges' cues to the jury are normally sufficiently guarded that the jurors are unaware of being influenced; judges themselves may be oblivious to engaging in such indirect prejudicial communications. Judge Marvin Frankel commented, "The jury is likely to discern hints, a point of view, a suggested direction, even if none is intended and quite without regard to the judge's effort to modulate and minimize his role."[34] Because such body language and verbal innuendoes are generally done in an offhand, seemingly harmless way, they are not normally grounds for appeal. With rare exceptions, like the case of Dr. Spock, judges can influence jurors with impunity.

The Role of the Press

Ordinary crimes and lawsuits, while critically important to the participants, rarely get much press coverage. Even if the event engendering a trial is newsworthy, coverage usually fades quickly. The trial doesn't occur until months or years later, prompting only brief media coverage when the trial first gets under way and then again when a verdict is reached. Under these circumstances, the role of the press in influencing jurors is negligible. Input to the jury comes from what they hear, see, and sense in the courtroom, not what they read in the papers or watch on television.

However, terrible crimes and cases involving celebrities are an altogether different matter. The news media are often saturated with the day-to-day unfolding of events prior to trials, and the reporting is rarely neutral. Although jurors are routinely asked during voir dire whether they have followed the case at hand in the press, a positive answer does not automatically disqualify them. It hardly could in some cases: virtually no one, no matter how indifferent to current events, could fail to have seen the videotapes of President Reagan being shot by John Hinckley. So courts satisfy themselves by getting assurances from potential jurors that they could put aside any intimations of guilt or innocence that such exposure might have generated. But, like other aspects of the voir dire discussed in chapter 3, the search for bias stemming from pretrial publicity is rather superficial.

So when defendants like Hinckley, Oliver North, or Bernhard Goetz go on trial, most jurors have to some extent already been influenced. The Supreme Court has struck down attempts to "gag" the press through court orders barring publication of pretrial revelations damaging to the defendant,[35] so there is no way to avoid the problem of jurors having previous information about the trial they will be hearing.

However, the impact of such exposure is unclear. There is considerable empirical evidence suggesting that people can and do shed much of their prior impressions when they are sworn in as jurors. When he was a practicing lawyer, law professor John Kaplan took an informal post-trial survey of a number of jurors, which revealed that they had forgotten most of what they had read in the newspapers and had a general mistrust of the press anyway. This led Kaplan to conclude that newspaper publicity has "virtually no impact upon the jury trying the case."[36] Results from jury simulations, are mixed: after reviewing the literature on jury simulations, sociologist Rita Simon concluded that jurors are able to withstand pretrial publicity,[37] but there are other findings to the contrary.[38] Only recently, Kramer, Kerr, and Carroll's intricate experiment exposing mock jurors to damaging pretrial publicity showed that this exposure tended to increase convictions, a bias that was not mitigated by judges' admonitions to disregard such publicity.[39]

There have been occasions when the media's presence during a trial was so pronounced that convictions have been overturned, as happened when the Supreme Court declared that Dr. Sam Sheppard's murder trial in Ohio had turned into a "carnival atmosphere" and a "Roman holiday for the news media."[40] Out of concern for such negative effects, trial judges now are usually quite careful in establishing ground rules that keep the media as unobtrusive as possible. Although the Supreme Court has ruled that an absolute ban of television from the courtroom is unconstitutional[41] and some states now permit live television coverage of trials, judges try to keep camera people and their equipment inconspicuous.

There is another problem with media coverage. Juries are rarely sequestered during trials because of the expense and the inconvenience to jurors caused by keeping them in seclusion; so jurors are subject to all sorts of influences when they go home from the courthouse. One is press coverage; it is the rare juror who scrupulously avoids all news stories having a bearing on the case being tried. A month-long federal trial of people purported to be part of an international heroin-smuggling ring ended in a mistrial in 1981; eleven jurors admitted to the judge that they had watched an installment of the CBS program "60 Minutes" that dealt with smugglers who used the same Asia–Sicily–New York route allegedly used by the defendants on trial. One can only conjecture how often the fact that jurors watch potentially biasing programs germane to their trials simply fails to come to light.

Even if jurors try diligently to insulate themselves from such exposure, they may inadvertently come across information about the trial—including damaging headlines or partisan commentary. A juror may hear a music station broadcast a news item about the trial on the car radio while driving home from court. Someone on a bus may hold up the front page of a newspaper featuring a big story about the case two feet from a juror's face. Some local television stations and newspapers practice sensationalism in reporting crime news, and jurors can't always avoid coming across pejorative media accounts with disparaging references to defendants. It is doubtful that jurors can excise such adverse allusions to defendants from their psyches when they go back to court.

One final note should be made. Even though, when press coverage before and during trials has an impact, it is generally adverse to defendants, it can also be helpful. It is commonly thought that John Gotti, accused of being the nation's top Mafia boss, received acquittals in three successive trials in part because of positive portrayals by the New York City media. The press focused on his dapper appearance and neighborhood ties, not on the criminal deeds that he was alleged to have committed or instigated. As one lawyer familiar with the Gotti cases put it, "He's depicted as a charming rogue rather than a corrupt thug."[42] One frustrated FBI official lamented that the media had turned a "flat out" criminal who surrounded himself with ruthless killers into a "folk hero."[43] As usual, jurors who acquitted Gotti in 1990 said the verdict was simply a response to insufficient evidence.[44] But who can say that Gotti's glorification in the press did not at the very least reduce the stigma that normally goes along with a reputation for being a major figure in organized crime? Juror prejudices sometimes play a role in outcomes (as chapter 8 will explain), and on occasion the press may have the effect of changing a person's image from bad to good.

Jury Tampering

One justification for giving juries so much power is that jurors have nothing to gain or lose as a result of their verdicts, unlike many other participants in the criminal justice system. However, occasionally someone will cater to the self-interests of jurors either by offering them a reward if they vote a certain way or by threatening to punish them if they do not. Such bribery and intimidation are against the law; they constitute the crime of jury tampering, which carries substantial penalties.

Actual threats to jurors are rare, but the fear of physical retaliation that jurors sometimes experience is not. In cases in which defendants are on trial for acts of violence, it cannot help but enter jurors' minds that they could become targets for retaliation if they convict. This is all the more a source of anxiety if the defendant is linked to collaborators still at large, as is normally the case in organized crime cases. Jurors' worries about personal repercussions can be compounded if the person on trial has associates sitting in the spectator gallery–perhaps glaring intently at the jury box or sporadically mouthing angry curses.

This does not mean that jurors "knuckle under" if they happen to experience a few tinges of fear. People who are terrified usually are able to get excused from serving on cases that are particularly scary, and jurors who become empaneled usually manage to take their feelings of uneasiness in stride. However, people do succumb to their fears; there is an occasional case where a juror is so worried that he or she goes to great lengths to figure out ways to exculpate defendants.

Judges sometimes take steps to assuage jurors' worries. Some states permit "anonymous juries" when there is just cause for concern about retaliation; nothing about jurors is revealed, not even their names. But this makes effective use of peremptory challenges difficult, so less severe measures are sometimes utilized. These include refusing to read jurors' names in open court, transporting jurors from their homes to the courthouse, and providing police protection to jurors who feel threatened.

Relatives, friends, neighbors, and associates of the victims of crime are another group of bystanders who may on occasion make an impression on jurors. It is not uncommon for aggrieved persons to show up at court every day and observe trials avidly; and there are formal court monitoring projects that mobilize enraged community residents to turn out in droves. Police officer associations have also sent large contingents to witness court proceedings when an officer is on trial or was the victim of a crime. Jurors cannot help but be aware of the charged atmosphere created by such outpourings, and at times they may experience it as pressure on them to return verdicts favorable to the pressure group.

Conclusion

Many courtroom participants influence jurors, witnesses first and foremost. Sometimes attempts at persuasion are open; at other times they are covert. Lawyers play a prominent role in trying to win jurors over, but they seem to be more influential in their roles as orchestrators of a case than as virtuoso performers in the court. Judges and the press can wittingly or unwittingly affect jurors' judgments through their own lines of communication. Controlling jurors by buying them or frightening them, although rare, is not unknown.

When trials are over, sometimes the evidence is overwhelmingly clear, and jurors usually return verdicts consistent with it. But in the many cases that end inconclusively, jurors' values come into play. As they unravel the facts, jurors apply common sense—not only in determining what happened but in deciding what is just. It is to these political judgments—deciding issues of moral culpability—that we now turn our attention.

Notes

1. "It was the People," *Newsweek* (August 25, 1975), p. 29.
2. Wayne King, "Joan Little's Lawyer Scorns Legal system and Says He 'Bought' an Acquittal," *The New York Times* (October 20, 1975), p. 23.
3. James Reston, *The Innocence of Joan Little: A Southern Mystery* (New York: Times Books, 1977).
4. Quoted in King, "Joan Little's Lawyer," p. 23.
5. *Ibid.*
6. Jerome Frank, *Courts on Trial: Myth and Reality in American Justice* (New York: Atheneum, 1967), pp. 80–102.
7. Quoted in Lori Andrews, "Exhibit A: Language," *Psychology Today*, 18 (February 1984): 28.
8. For a discussion of the virtues of surrogate juries, as well as some illustrations of how they have been used, see David Gidmark, "The Verdict on Surrogate Jury Research," *ABA Journal*, 74 (March 1988): 82–86.
9. Quoted in Aric Press and Donna Foote, "Trials by Jury Trial," *Newsweek* (March 9, 1981): 84.
10. Quoted in Warren Burger, "A Judge Is Better," in Sidney Ulmer (ed.), *Courts, Law and Judicial Process* (New York: Freed Press, 1981), p. 176.
11. Jack Lipton, "On the Psychology of Eyewitness Testimony," *Journal of Applied Psychology*, 62 (1977): 90–95; Jeffrey Frederick, *The Psychology of the American Jury* (Charlottesville, Va: Michie, 1987), chap. 6.
12. Harry Kalven and Hans Zeisel, *The American Jury* (Boston: Little Brown, 1966), pp. 177–181.
13. Arthur Frankel and William Morris, "Testifying in One's Own Defense: The Ingratiator's Dilemma," *Journal of Personality and Social Psychology*, 34 (1976): 475–480.
14. Sarah Hendry, David Shaffer, and Dina Peacock, "On Testifying in One's Own Behalf: Interactive Effects of Evidential Strength and Defendant's Testimonial Demeanor on Mock Jurors' Decisions," *Journal of Applied Psychology*, 74 (1989): 539–545.
15. Kalven and Zeisel, *The American Jury*, p. 179.
16. C. Hendrick and David Shaffer, "Effect of Pleading the Fifth Amendment on Perceptions of Guilt and Morality," *Bulletin of the Psychonomic Society*, 6 (1975): 449–452; David Shaffer, C. Sadowski, and C. Hendrick, "Effects of Withheld Evidence on Juridic Decisions," *Psychological Reports*, 42 (1978): 1235–1242.
17. David Shaffer and Thomas Case, "On the Decision to Testify in One's Own Behalf: Effects of Withheld Evidence, Defendant's Sexual Preferences, and Juror Dogmatism on Juridic Decisions," *Journal of Personality and Social Psychology*, 42 (1982): 335–346.
18. For an extended discussion of the effects of child testimony on jurors, see Lawrence Wrightsman, *Psychology and the Legal System* (Pacific Grove, Calif.: Brooks/Cole, 1987), pp. 326–329.
19. Robert Buckhout, "Eyewitness Testimony," *Scientific American*, 231 (December 1974): 22–31; Steven Penrod, Elizabeth Loftus, and John Winkler, "The Reliability of Eyewitness Testimony," in N. Kerr and R. Bray (eds.), *The Psychology of the Courtroom* (New York: Academic Press, 1982), pp. 119–168.
20. Frederick, *The Psychology of the American Jury*, p. 260.
21. Gary Wells, R. C. L. Lindsay, and Tamara Ferguson, "Accuracy, Confidence, and Juror Perceptions in Eyewitness Testimony," *Journal of Applied Psychology*, 64 (1979): 440–448.
22. Elizabeth Loftus, "Reconstructing Memory: The Incredible Eyewitness," *Psychology Today*, 1974 (December): 116–119.

23. Steven Penrod and Brian Cutler, "Eyewitness Expert Testimony and Jury Decisionmaking," *Law and Contemporary Problems*, 52 (Autumn 1989): 61; Brad Bell and Elizabeth Loftus, "Degree of Detail of Eyewitness Testimony and Mock Juror Judgments," *Journal of Applied Social Psychology*, 18 (1988): 1171–1192; Brad Bell and Elizabeth Loftus, "Trivial Persuasion in the Courtroom: The Power of (a Few) Minor Details," *Journal of Personality and Social Psychology*, 56 (1989): 669–679.

24. Penrod and Culter, ''Eyewitness Expert Testimony and Jury Decisionmaking'': 62.

25. *Ibid.*, p. 68.

26. Jonathan Friendly, "Von Bulow Jury Issues Acquittal on All Charges," *The New York Times* (June 11, 1985), p. A1.

27. Allan Raitz, Edith Greene, Jane Goodman, and Elizabeth Loftus, "The Influence of Expert Testimony on Jurors' Decision Making," *Law and Human Behavior*, 14 (August 1990): 385.

28. Neil Vidmar and Regina Schuller, "Juries and Expert Evidence: Social Framework Testimony," *Law and Contemporary Problems*, 52 (Autumn 1989): 166, 173.

29. William Glaberson, "Defense Witness Assails Lawyers in Rochester Serial Murder Case," *The New York Times* (December 8, 1990), p. 32.

30. Stuart Marques, "Flip-Flops by Jurors," *New York Daily News* (March 26, 1988), p. 43.

31. Peter David Blanck, Robert Rosenthal, and LaDoris Hazard Cordell, "The Appearance of Justice: Judges' Verbal and Nonverbal Behavior in Criminal Jury Trials," *Stanford Law Review*, 38 (November 1985): 136.

32. Daniel Long, "The Trial of Dr. Spock," in Theodore Becker and Vernon Murray (eds.), *Government Lawlessness in America* (New York: Oxford University Press, 1971): 176–180.

33. Alfonso Narvaez, "Gibson Acquitted of a Conspiracy in 'No Show' Case," *The New York Times* (October 22, 1982), p. A1.

34. Marvin Frankel, "The Search for Truth: An Umpireal View," *University of Pennsylvania Law Review*, 123 (1975): 1042.

35. *Nebraska Press Association* v. *Stuart*, 477 U.S. 539 (1976).

36. John Kaplan, "Afterword—of Babies and Bathwater," *Stanford Law Review*, 29 (February 1977): 243.

37. Rita Simon, "Does the Court's Decision in *Nebraska Press Association* Fit the Research Evidence on the Impact of Jurors of News Coverage?" *Stanford Law Review*, 29 (February 1977): 528. In a more recent review of research, psychologist Edith Greene reached a similar conclusion. See "Media Effects on Jurors," *Law and Human Behavior* 14 (October): 448.

38. Stanley Sue, Ronald Smith, and George Pedroza, "Authoritarianism, Pretrial Publicity, and Awareness of Bias in Simulated Jurors," *Psychological Reports*, 37 (1975): 1299–1302; Stanley Sue, Ronald Smith, and R. Gilbert, "Biasing Effects of Pretrial Publicity on Judicial Decisions," *Journal of Criminal Justice*, 2 (1974): 163–172.

39. Geoffrey Kramer, Norbert Kerr, and John Carroll, "Pretrial Publicity, Judicial Remedies, and Jury Bias," *Law and Human Behavior*, 14 (October): 409–438.

40. *Sheppard* v. *Maxwell*, 384 U.S. 333 (1966).

41. *Chandler* v. *Florida*, 449 U.S. 560 (1981).

42. David Margolick, "Catch Is More Prized and Elusive with Each Miss," *The New York Times* (February 10, 1990), p. 28.

43. Selwyn Raab, "Gotti and Fame: Dapper Folk Hero or Ruthless Mob Boss?" *The New York Times* (February 19, 1990), p. B1.

44. Jim Nolan, Sonia Reyes, and Ann Bollinger, "Juror Tells Why They Cleared Mob Boss," *New York Post* (February 10, 1990), p. 4.

A remarkable event occurred on April 8, 1986. A videotape of jury deliberations in a real criminal case was aired nationally on the public television documentary series FRONTLINE. The producer had secured the permission of the Wisconsin trial judge, the prosecutor, the defendant, and the jurors to record not only the trial but what took place in the jury room. The public got a rare glimpse of a jury doing its work, and the nature of the discussion reveals an important dimension of jury decision making.

The case of the *State of Wisconsin* v. *Leroy Reed* entailed charges that the defendant had violated the law prohibiting convicted felons from possessing a firearm. Reed had been hanging around the courthouse in Milwaukee when a detective asked him for identification. Reed produced a sales receipt with his name on it for the purchase of a gun from a sporting goods store. When asked about his reason for buying the gun, Reed said he was planning to become a private investigator and would be required to carry a gun. The detective told him to go home and get the gun, and when Reed returned with it, he was arrested.

The law that Reed was charged with breaking had three elements that had to be satisfied in order for Reed to be found guilty. It had to be shown that: (1) the defendant was a convicted felon; (2) the defendant had a gun; and (3) the defendant *knew* he had a gun. The prosecution argued that there was a very sound reason for keeping guns out of the hands of ex-felons and that the jury's only job was to determine whether the law had been violated.

5

· · · · · · ·

The Search
for Justice

The defense's case was that Reed was a harmless person of borderline intelligence who bought the gun after having signed up for a mail-order detective course. The 42-year-old Reed had been out of prison for nine years, during which time his record was clean. The defense argued that the slow-witted Reed was unaware that he was violating the law.

What is particularly interesting about this case is how the jury handled its mission. The following excerpts from their dialogue show that jury thinking is hardly the simple mechanical function of applying the law to the facts at hand:[1]

> *Juror Boly:* I really don't know which way to fall on this. It makes me extremely uneasy because I think it is a good law. . . . And there's no question but that this man is a felon and there's no question but that he purchased a firearm, and . . . I'm not sure.

> *Juror Collins:* I would be really hard-pressed to say that he was absolutely guilty in light of . . . all the evidence that has been turned in. His educational level and his ability to even know the law. . . if someone would have said, "Anyone who's a convicted felon cannot own a firearm," he still might not have understood that, and still went ahead and purchased a firearm. So I would have to lean more towards him not being guilty. . . .

> *Juror Arvin:* Technically, the man is guilty, guilty as sin. But I want to acquit Leroy because I don't think he was fully aware of the rules of—of parole, and secondarily, I don't think convicting him of this charge . . . would do the general public any good.

> *Juror Buetow:* I just don't—there's entirely too much sympathy for the man, which is what is very hard to rule out. But we're not here to be sympathetic to him for what may or may not have happened. It's—it's the three points of law. Mr. Reed, to me, is not a violent person, and I'm sure he did not buy this gun with the intent of doing anything violent with it. He was swayed by a magazine article. The same person who has a . . . problem that he has, could read another article and, if he has a gun in his house, that could trigger him off into who-knows-what. That's why the law is there; why felons cannot own guns.

> *Juror Savage:* I'm trying to decide in my own mind—has justice been done here? I don't care what the law says. Has justice been done? And in my mind, I'm still trying to decide that.

> *Juror Boly:* I think this is a good law. And I don't want to say or do anything that suggests that I don't take the law seriously. So, I mean, I want to do my civic duty—I've got a lot of other things to do—I come down to the courthouse, and the D.A. gives me this. And in spite of . . . these very serious people, and in spite of . . . the legal rigmarole, I'm sort of thinking, this is "Mickey Mouse."

Eventually the jurors acquitted Leroy Reed. No one, not even the hard-liners, really wanted to see Reed go back to jail. So they found a way out—that the defendant really didn't "know" he had a gun, because his mental disability prevented him from knowing much of anything. Therefore one of the elements of the crime was not satisfied, and Reed was not guilty.

From the moment the jury began deliberations, it was engaged in a search for justice. Ultimately all twelve jurors became convinced that Leroy Reed should go free, and what they managed to do was twist the fact about his knowledge of the gun in order to justify a verdict of acquittal. This jury was far more outspoken than most about the issue of justice; rarely do jurors get into such heady matters. But even people unschooled in law are quite adept at figuring out ways to interpret the laws and the evidence to reach verdicts that they can support. As jurors go about their tasks, they are as concerned about meting out justice as they are about finding the truth.

This was the central finding of Kalven and Zeisel's classic work on the American jury, published in 1966. They discovered that while juries generally agreed with the law on the books, they were ever attentive to the issue of applicability of the laws and were often moved to make exceptions *based on the specific circumstances of the case at hand*: "[the jury] is non-rule minded; it will move where the equities are."[2]

Years later, sociologist Zeisel was much more emphatic in articulating this theme: "When the facts are halfway uncertain, the jury will decide the case in terms of what they think is just—which is what they should do."[3] But recall from Chapter 1 that uncertainty is inherent in the trial process and the truth is never absolutely clear. Because facts are so hard to pin down, the justice motif often enters the picture when juries reflect about verdicts. The Leroy Reed case is *not* an oddity.

Juror's Intuitions about Justice

What *is* justice? It is a profound concept, an age-old concern that has defied precise definition. Even scholars have been baffled. One defines it as "the decision the jury believes to be best and right for the community,"[4] but this only begs the question, What, after all, is "best and right"? Asking jurors themselves what they mean by justice generally produces blank stares; they too will be hard-pressed to put its meaning into words. However, jurors do have an intuitive sense of this noble ideal, which basically boils down to giving people what they deserve. People who do things that are very wrong should pay a stiff price, whereas those who violate the law for good reason are entitled to leniency.

A civil case that on one level looks like nothing more than a contest among three giant corporations engaged in complex financial machinations may well have been perceived by jurors as an issue of simple justice. Getty, Inc., had agreed in 1984 to merge with the Pennzoil Company—a not uncommon happening in an era of constant corporate restructuring. Soon thereafter Texaco made a better offer for the purchase of Getty, which Getty promptly accepted. Having been outdone in the corporate marketplace,

Pennzoil sought redress in the Texas courts, suing Texaco for wresting Getty from Pennzoil's grasp.

The legal issue came down to whether Pennzoil had really entered into a binding contract with Getty before Texaco made its offer—even though the final details of the intricate Getty–Pennzoil merger had not been put into writing. But it has been conjectured that the jury looked past legal technicalities and reduced the case to simpler dimensions. And in awarding $10.53 *billion* to Pennzoil, thereby putting Texaco on the brink of bankruptcy, the jury's sense of justice was that people and businesses need to keep their word: a deal is a deal. What was at stake was trust, and, according to this theory, the jury decided that the untrustworthy should pay—dearly. As columnist William Safire put it, "In a Texas courtroom, 12 simplistic, vindictive, normal souls said 'That ain't right, hang [them]. . . . '"[5]

The law itself directs jurors to considerations of justice; most criminal laws require that the offender have a criminal intent. Technically known as *mens rea*, this requirement impels jurors to determine moral culpability as well as the sheer commission of some illegal action. Furthermore, a particular act may entail violation of any one of a number of laws—some serious, some not so serious, and some minor. In selecting among these possibilities, jurors almost inescapably must weigh the gravity of the wrongdoing and the malevolence of the wrongdoer—which means taking into account the circumstances of the crime.

82 These delicate judgments require the balancing of conflicting interests. Justice is not always a black-and-white issue; the "right" verdict in the jurors' minds is often the one that takes both sides of a moral question into consideration. People should not steal, but what if someone was impoverished and took a few apples from a fruit stand? Murder is a horrible crime, but what if the killer did it in retaliation for years of violence suffered at the hands of the victim? "A deal is a deal," but what if a slick real estate agent conned an uneducated person into using his or her life savings to buy a house for a price that is double or triple its market value?

In the quest for justice, difficult cases arise all the time. Values conflict, and in choosing between them, jurors act politically. Take, for example, the aggravated assault charges brought against members of the Christ Miracle Healing Center and Church in Miracle Valley, Arizona. The controversial religious group, which, among other things, believes in faith healing rather than medical care, was being probed by a local television station news crew. When the crew began filming the church's premises, members flung hammers at them.

The issue at hand was freedom of the press versus freedom of religion. The jury's verdict? Five defendants were exonerated of all charges and two were found guilty of simple assault only—a misdemeanor. The reason? According to the jury foreman, the news team had been provocative and should not have been filming the church at all; "the crew was guilty of invasion of privacy."[6] Certainly people should not throw hammers at newspeople; but neither should newspeople snoop into people's private affairs and places of worship. For this jury, justice dictated that people protecting themselves from newspaper harassment should be spared.

Sometimes jurors have to make more agonizing value choices. Jurors tend to be lenient in dealing with defendants who may have used excessive force in repelling attempted crimes against them, as in the Goetz case described in Chapter 1. In another case, a deaf and dumb thirteen-year-old, who for the sake of a little adventure was wandering around the rooftops of some apartment buildings, was taken to be a burglar and shot to death by the owner of one of the buildings. Imagine hearing as testimony the following exchange between the police officer who arrived on the scene and the slayer of the boy (who was charged with murder):

> *Defendant*: "I shot a burglar."
>
> *Police officer* (with tears in his eyes): "You shot a little boy."[7]

The jury found the defendant guilty of second-degree manslaughter rather than murder. In effect, the jury said: Yes, the shooting was premeditated; yes, the victim was innocent of any crimes except the minor offense of trespass; yes, it is a tragedy that a young life was snuffed out; but defending oneself against presumed criminals is an understandable act in a crime-plagued society; and the man on trial *is* in almost all respects a hard-working, honorable citizen. "Yes, but . . ." is a stock-in-trade of juror thinking; the pursuit of justice is the wrenching business of deciding when and how to make exceptions. There are no magic formulas, which in a point well expressed a half-century ago by Judge Learned Hand: "Justice, I think, is the tolerable accommodation of the conflicting interests of society, and I don't believe there is any royal road to attain such accommodations concretely."[8]

As we shall see in the rest of this chapter, although jurors have strong views about right and wrong, they often realize that blame assessment is a subtle business. Determining what the equities are requires taking many things into account—whether the law permits this or not. And sometimes the only fair, just thing to do is to "split the difference"—to come up with some middle ground between total exculpation and complete condemnation. Jurors pit mitigating circumstances against aggravating circumstances, and at times their verdicts represent a balance between these competing forces.

Mitigating Circumstances

It has been said that "the jury system brings a pot-au-feu approach to justice,"[9] in reference to the French stew comprised of all kinds of meats and vegetables. The jury considers a hodgepodge of factors in assessing moral culpability, some factors that are relevant to the legal issues before them and some that are totally extraneous. What follows is a brief survey of some conditions that tend to make the defendant's lawbreaking seem less reprehensible. Juries are not given a checklist of possible mitigating circumstances, but these factors, if at all compelling, make themselves known by pulling at the jurors' heartstrings. And according to one mock jury study, appreciation of these circumstances encourages greater leniency.[10]

Good Intentions

It is said that the road to hell is paved with good intentions. That may be true, but jurors sometimes will absolve defendants whose alleged crimes were done in the interest of helping rather than hurting someone. Noble motives can sometimes atone for ghastly deeds.

Consider the case of *Massachusetts* v. *Anne Capute*. The defendant, a nurse, was accused of murder by illegally dispensing huge doses of morphine. She had administered the drugs for the purpose of easing a terminal cancer patient out of her misery. Ms. Capute told the jury that she loved her patient and was only trying to end the pain and suffering of a woman for whom surgery had failed to remove a malignant spinal tumor only twelve days earlier. The dead woman's daughter, hoping for a conviction, said while awaiting the verdict, "I just want to see justice come out of it."[11] But the jury apparently had a different view of justice: not only did it acquit the nurse of murder and manslaughter, but it absolved her of the charge of illegally dispensing drugs. On the basis of good intentions, taking a human life was tolerated.

Provocation

The mirror image of good intentions of the accused is wrongdoing on the part of the victim. Juries are sometimes more lenient toward defendants if the person injured was in some way responsible for his or her own undoing. The civil law actually builds this notion into the legal norms: at one time most states operated under the *contributory negligence* rule, whereby plaintiffs were excluded from collecting damages if they themselves were simultaneously negligent. Today most states have switched to a *comparative negligence* rule, which allocates blame and damages according to the degree to which both the plaintiff's and the defendant's negligence contributed to the harm the defendant suffered. Beyond and above these norms, juries are reluctant to treat defendants harshly if the plaintiff came into court with "dirty hands."

The criminal law takes less account of the victim's illicit or improper behavior, but juries by all means consider such moral culpability in meting out justice. One of the most common grounds for exoneration is provocation by the victim. Jurers are rather ingenious in coming up with ways to absolve people who have committed violence if they conclude that the victims themselves had acted inappropriately. Jurors will stretch the right to self-defense, expand the definition of insanity, and close their eyes to the defendant's criminal intent—if they think the victim's fate was deserved. Defendants who respond illegally but understandably to the victim's reprehensible behavior are often spared by juries.

For example, in 1981 a Texas jury hearing a civil assault suit brought by a fan of the San Antonio Spurs basketball team against Boston Celtic star Larry Bird ruled for the defendant. Bird admitted hitting the plaintiff with a heavy gym bag, but the jury found he had acted in self-defense. Bird had been provoked when the fan had spit in Bird's face as the Celtics were leaving the basketball arena. Because Bird was in no physical danger, his response was probably excessive according to the nuances of tort law, but the jury no doubt thought he had been subjected to a disgusting indignity, and so they exonerated him. This verdict is in keeping with Kalven and Zeisel's finding that "under some circumstances the jury, in a marked departure from the formal rule of law, will recognize an insult as sufficient aggression to privilege violence."[12]

The Bird case, although a nice illustration of the juror's tendency to turn their backs on nasty people who feel victimized, is rather petty. This is in stark contrast to a devastating form of provocation often treated as a mitigating circumstance: the many cases of battered women who go after their abusers. Jury after jury in recent years has been acquitting women or convicting them of lesser charges, even when the evidence pretty clearly revealed that the woman committed premeditated murder—if the facts also showed that the slain person had been brutalizing the defendant.

It is the details of abuse suffered by those who strike back that jurors can find so gripping. An excellent example is the case of Karen Straw, who stabbed her ex-husband to death with a six-inch kitchen knife at the culmination of years of abuse at his hands. She testified that she tried to protect herself by leaving her husband, by repeatedly calling the police to report his continued attacks, and by securing an order of protection against him— all to no avail. He kept returning to inflict more abuse, and on the night of the slaying, Ms. Straw was raped in front of her young chidren by her crack-smoking ex-husband. The prosecutor argued that the defendant was the aggressor on the fateful night of the slaying, or in any event she could have fled unscathed. But the jury was not persuaded and later acknowledged being on the defendant's side from the beginning. As one juror said after the verdict, "The justification was there—the intent wasn't."[13] A more honest restatement might have been, "Because the justification for the slaying was there, we refused to find an intent to kill."

Children who retaliate against parents who have molested them are sometimes the beneficiaries of similar juror empathy. Consider the case of sixteen-year-old Richard Jahnke, who admitted killing his father with a 12-gauge shotgun. The boy and his younger sister had laid in wait to ambush

85

their father on his return from an anniversary dinner with his wife. The prosecutor appeared on solid ground: this certainly seemed to be a case of cold-blooded, first-degree murder. But after hearing uncontradicted testimony that both children had been methodically brutalized over the course of fourteen years, a Wyoming jury convicted Jahnke only of manslaughter. The jury may have sensed that justice lay in finding a middle ground between a first-degree murder conviction and a complete acquittal on the basis of self-defense, as argued by the defense. The seemingly illogical verdict recalls a bit of wisdom offered by an oft-quoted anonymous juror: "We threw away the facts and decided the case on its merits."

Revenge

Another mitigating circumstance closely akin to provocation is revenge—breaking the law to get even for past misdeeds of one's victim. In this situation there is no danger to the defendant at the time the crime is committed; but the jury feels that the defendant is justified in seeking his or her own brand of justice for prior harm done. Reprisal for unavenged harms that have been previously inflicted on oneself or someone dear is sometimes seen as legitimate.

86

The case of Mark Cauchi is a very straightforward illustration of jury tolerance toward those who strike back. While serving time at San Quentin prison, Cauchi saw the television news report of his wife's body being wheeled out of their house after she had been bound, gagged, and stabbed. Four years later James Dance, the prime suspect in the case but who had never been charged, was sent to San Quentin for an unrelated crime. When Dance began bragging to other inmates about his murder of the woman, Cauchi confronted Dance and stabbed him to death. The Marin County jury trying Cauchi for murder cleared him of all charges, ruling it a "justifiable homicide" committed in self-defense. This was clearly an act of retaliation, *not* self-defense; but the jury thought Dance "had it coming."

Entrapment

Just as juries will acquit if the victim has done something wrong, they will sometimes do likewise if the government has acted improperly. A form of government malfeasance particularly scorned by jurors is entrapment—actively encouraging defendants to engage in a crime and then prosecuting them for it. Even though the defendant intended to commit the crime and actually carried it out, he or she is absolved because it is thought improper for government authorities to lure people into criminal acts. The criminal justice system is supposed to be preventing crime, not inciting it.

Why is this a mitigating circumstance? Because juries recognize that decent, law-abiding people are susceptible to being tempted into committing crime, especially if cunning is used to prey on normal human weakness. The classic case illustrating the jury's reaction to entrapment is the acquittal of automobile manufacturer John DeLorean. He was prosecuted for entering a scheme to help distribute $5 million worth of cocaine in order to raise money for his nearly bankrupt company, DeLorean Motor Company. Although FBI agents videotaped DeLorean receiving a suitcase containing fifty-five pounds of cocaine and then toasting that it was "better than gold," several jurors were convinced that DeLorean had been enticed into the operation by undercover agents who took advantage of his precarious financial situation. Jurors said later that DeLorean was acquitted not because he was thought to be innocent of drug trafficking but because of the impropriety of law enforcement officials. Famed California lawyer Melvin Belli got to the heart of the verdict: "The jury felt that this guy was guilty as hell, but felt the worse crime is what was done by the FBI."[14] Justice required letting DeLorean off, because the government had exploited the weaknesses to which almost everyone is vulnerable.[15]

It is an altogether different story if the government merely provides the opportunity for a defendant to carry out criminal intentions that he or she already has. Jurors are unsympathetic to entrapment pleas when they sense that they are dealing with scoundrels who happened to be caught as a result of some ruse or ploy engaged in by authorities. "Sting" operations wherein undercover police officers "set up shop," such as by running a business where stolen merchandise is purchased, normally result in convictions—as long as the people who get stung were in trouble to begin with. In the juror view, it is not wrong to outsmart genuine criminals; it is wrong to turn decent people into criminals.

Thus, *all seven* members of Congress charged in the 1980 ABSCAM scandal were convicted after seven separate trials heard by seven different juries. "ABSCAM" was a code name used by the FBI that stood for "Arab scam"—a deceptive operation that successfully caught the politicians taking huge sums of money from Arab sheiks in exchange for help with the Arabs' immigration problems. The "sheiks" were FBI agents in disguise who contacted lawmakers thought to be "on the take"—eager to take bribes. Juries rejected entrapment defenses in all cases because they were convinced that all seven men were rogues open to bribery solicitations rather than honorable lawmakers tempted to act out of character.

Hardships

Defendants whose crimes stem from troubled lives sometimes get mercy from jurors. Desperation or torment are very rarely legal defenses to crime, but people who are victims of life's misfortunes are sometimes treated more leniently than those who have fared better. Defendants who are destitute, sick, enfeebled, or suffering from serious mistreatment are to some extent seen as being out of control and therefore less blameworthy; some of them will reap the benefit of the "yes, but" juror response. On the other hand, toughness may be in store for the well-situated person who commits an identical crime.

The jury's verdict in the Jack Abbott case illustrates this point. Abbott was convicted of manslaughter instead of murder in the fatal stabbing of a waiter, despite the fact that he had coaxed the waiter with whom he was arguing to go outside, where the deadly encounter took place. This is not a crime that initially engendered much sympathy. Abbott was out of jail on a work-release program when the crime took place and had previously been convicted for bank robbery and the murder of a fellow inmate. But the jury also considered Abbott's life: when he went on trial at the age of 37, he had already spent 24 years in reform schools and prisons, where he was exposed to unremitting violence at the hands of guards and other inmates. The jury concluded that his crime was mitigated by "extreme emotional disturbance" caused by a near-lifetime of incarceration, and one juror told reporters after the verdict that it was Abbott's tragic history that resulted in the leniency.[16]

Insanity

A particular form of hardship that the law explicitly allows as a defense for those charged with crime is insanity. The rules about insanity vary from state to state, but the gist of the concept is that people who commit crimes as a result of mental illness ought not to be treated as harshly as people who are in their right mind. Indeed, most states still stipulate that defendants acquitted by virtue of insanity are to be spared any punishment. Defendants who are considered dangerous can be confined to a psychiatric hospital, however, but only until they are no longer a threat to society.

The logic behind the much maligned insanity defense can be appreciated through the following analogy. Imagine two situations in which children soil their parent's new white sofa. In the first, the child gets angry about being prohibited from watching television and proceeds to stomp on the couch with his or her messy shoes; in the second, the child lying on the sofa suddenly gets sick and vomits on the sofa. Most parents would punish the child who muddied the sofa, whereas very few parents would punish the child who got sick, even though vomiting may have caused greater damage. The two children are treated differently because the first was presumably able to exercise self-control whereas the second was not. We do not consider it just to hold people responsible for acts that they cannot prevent.

Just as our bodies are sometimes beyond our control, so too can our minds malfunction, leaving us helpless to stop criminal behavior. As early as 1724, lunatic defendants were absolved when they acted like "wild beasts";

it was thought barbaric to punish people who were functioning on a subhuman level. In the mid-eighteenth century, the "wild beast" test was replaced by the "right–wrong" test: was the defendant capable of knowing the difference between right and wrong? Since then, advances in psychology have led to further expansions of the definition of insanity, acknowledging that diseases such as schizophrenia permit those who have it to engage in both rational and irrational behavior. Thus, in many states the law simply says that a person whose criminal acts are the product of a diseased mind must be acquitted. Someone can hold a job, participate in neighborhood activities, raise a family, and function normally and still be subject to pathological mental disturbances that result in crime.

That brings us to the jurors' dilemma. In the words of Hans and Vidmar, jurors must decide whether the defendant is "mad or bad."[17] Jurors have ample discretion in considering insanity defenses because legal definitions are vague, medical terms are perplexing, and there is almost always conflicting testimony from psychiatrists. In the Hinckley case involving the attempt on President Reagan's life, eighteen out of the forty-one witnesses were psychiatrists or doctors whose testimony consumed twenty-four of the trial's thirty-two days.

In general, jurors are reluctant to acquit by reason of insanity because they share with the general public the sense that it is often used as a gimmick by defendants to avoid suffering the consequences of their harmful acts.[18] The law has changed to accord with modern knowledge about mental disorders, but jurors are loathe to acquit unless the defendants are clearly psychotic and it was clearly their psychosis that caused their criminal behavior. One study found that out of about 2 million criminal cases dealt with in American criminal courts in a single year, only 1,625 produced verdicts of not guilty on the basis of insanity.[19] The value being respected by juries is individual responsibility—the idea that under all but the most extreme circumstances people should be considered autonomous beings capable of exercising free will and moral judgment. Justice dictates that truly sick people be spared, but the presumption is that the great majority of people are sane.

What circumstances, then, do lead to a successful insanity defense? Generally, jurors want to see evidence of either organic brain damage or some devastating life event that very understandably might bring about a mental disorder. The 1982 case of Charles Heads was a perfect example in this regard: he was acquitted of killing his brother-in-law after a complex family feud. The prosecution characterized this as a standard case of domestic violence, but the jury was influenced by a special fact: Heads was a Vietnam veteran who suffered intensely from post-traumatic stress disorder (PTSD). While in Vietnam at the age of twenty, Heads was part of a reconnaissance unit that went on twenty-six missions deep into enemy territory; he killed at least six people and was himself wounded in an ambush. After the war he married, had children, kept a steady job, and bought a house, but this semblance of normality cloaked a turbulent internal life that included constant nightmares

89

and fears. The jury, which heard much testimony about the psychological stress plaguing many veterans, thought it unjust to punish Heads for criminal actions that were beyond his control and that stemmed from injuries to his mind sustained while serving his country.

Intoxication

Years ago, juries considered intoxication a mitigating circumstance even though it was not a legal defense if the defendant had voluntarily consumed alcohol.[20] No longer: the rise of concern about drunk driving and other alcohol-related crimes, spurred in part by organizations such as Mothers Against Drunk Driving (MADD), has resulted in a harder line being taken by juries. Although drinking is firmly embedded in American culture, the notion of "drinking responsibly" has caught hold. Thus, Michael Deaver, who was a high White House aide in the Reagan administration, was unable to win over the jury that convicted him of perjuring himself before a House subcommittee and a grand jury. His claim that he was drunk so often that he could not remember what he had said was unpersuasive, although the presiding judge took it into account in sparing him a jail sentence.

Somewhat ironically, those who are pathologically addicted to alcohol or other drugs fare a little better in the courts. Juries sometimes show leniency even when adjudicating gruesome crimes if defendants have been so ravished by substance abuse that their minds are obliterated; they are truly out of control. This is the reason a jury in 1985 acquitted Christopher Thomas of murdering ten people, including seven children between the ages of three and fourteen, when he stormed into their Brooklyn apartment furious about his suspicions that one of the victims was having an affair with his wife. In convicting Thomas only of manslaughter, the jurors took into account that he had been free-basing cocaine for two years and relied on testimony that he was "completely spaced out" earlier in the day of the crime.[21] Those who are so disturbed because of their addiction that they act in subhuman ways sometimes become the beneficiaries of their pathology.

Repentance

It has long been conjectured that defendants who appear repentant in court are treated more leniently than those who accept no responsibility for the crimes of which they are accused. The accused's words of regret, mournful expressions, and tears shed in court are said to temper the jury's normal insistence on retribution. In the 1960s, Kalven and Zeisel reported ten cases from their massive study in which the presiding judge thought that the defendant's remorse in court was what moved jurors to acquit those who looked guilty on the basis of the evidence.[22]

A more recent example is the December 1990 case against one of the teenagers accused of brutally raping and almost killing a jogger in a gang attack in New York's Central Park. A member of the jury in that case said that the panel acquitted the youth of the most serious charges (including rape and attempted murder) in part because he was remorseful about his role in the tragic events. The videotaped statement to police the defendant made after he was arrested and which was introduced into evidence included the following: "I guess we got to pay for what we did. We went to the park for trouble, and we got trouble."[23] Such atonement for wrongdoing can somewhat tip the balance of the scales of justice and move the jury toward leniency.

Relative Culpability

The Oliver North case exemplifies another kind of mitigating circumstance. North was the Reagan administration official who admitted to secretly selling arms to Iran and using the cash to support the Contras who were fighting the Communist government in Nicaragua, in violation of a federal law banning such support. In convicting North of three counts—including shredding documents and accepting an illegal gratuity—but acquitting him of nine more serious charges, the jury treated him too sternly for conservatives and too leniently for liberals. This was an equivocal verdict that seemed to leave North's culpability up in the air.

Unsatisfying as the outcome was for some, it nicely illustrates the concept of relative culpability: the person may be guilty but seems *less* guilty than someone else. Jurors are not prone to come down hard on defendants if they feel that others who were even more deeply implicated may be getting preferential treatment.

R. W. Apple, Jr., writing for *The New York Times*, called the North verdict a "measured judgment."[24] That it was, a somewhat typical case, in the jury's opinion of justice lying somewhere between the extremes. But what is striking is not the finding of middle ground but the reasons for it—that North had been pursuing a policy approved if not instigated by those above him, including President Ronald Reagan, who had referred repeatedly to the Contras as "freedom fighters" embarked on a noble mission.

Some of the jurors were quite explicit in explaining the verdict after the trial. Said the foreman, "North was the subordinate. He wasn't the boss. He wasn't running the show. . . . He was used and abused." Another juror said, "He was just the low man on the totem pole." A third juror, furious at Reagan, lashed out: "I think Reagan should stand up and give an account of what he did. No man is above the law. . . . He knew a lot of things going on." In still another juror's view, "I think there were people higher up who gave him the authority to do a lot of things, and then when he got caught out there high and dry, no one came to help him."[25]

91

It is not that the jurors were enamored with North but that they were resisting the unfair penalizing of the underling in a large scale operation. Not surprisingly, National Security Adviser John Poindexter, who was North's boss and was very close to the president, was convicted on all charges by a subsequent jury. In both the North and the Poindexter cases, the juries' interest was justice—seeing to it that those with the greatest responsibility for a crime paid the dearest price.

Whenever more than one person is involved in a crime, a nagging concern in the back of jurors' minds is whether he or she is getting a "fair shake" in comparison with others. Evenhandedness is implicit in the concept of justice, and jurors on occasion will give defendants a break because they are being treated worse than others who are equally if not more guilty. It is beyond the control of jurors to bring to justice those who seem to be escaping punishment, but what they can do is see to it that no single person appearing before them at the moment "takes the rap" for the wrongdoing of others.

Aggravating Circumstances

Most crimes and civil suits that wind up being considered in jury trials are serious; trifling matters are usually resolved earlier. However, there are gradations in the gravity of even serious offenses; some instances of murder, rape, robbery, or recklessness are more heinous than others. Certain characteristics of the crime or the criminal can create aggravating circumstances that may incline the jury to opt for conviction on the most serious charges.

Extreme cruelty is one such circumstance; inflicting injury over and above what is necessary to satisfy one's immediate needs can bring on the wrath of jurors. It is one thing to commit an armed robbery, a bad enough offense; it is another to needlessly assault the victim if he or she has given the robber what was demanded. Killing someone is the worst imaginable crime, but it is compounded if the victim is tortured before being slain. Jurors will be tough dealing with any crimes against the person, but they may come down especially hard where excessive pain and suffering are imposed.

Jurors may thus respond to a defendant's depravity by denying defense claims that might otherwise have been heeded. The case of Steven Smith is apropos. While living inconspicuously in a storage area in New York City's huge Bellevue Hospital, Smith was alleged to have beaten, raped, and fatally strangled a pregnant doctor, who had gone to the hospital on a weekend to do some extra laboratory work. The defense pleaded insanity and presented evidence showing that the twenty-three-year-old defendant had had psychiatric problems since the age of fourteen, had been committed to a South Carolina mental institution, and had tried to commit himself to a psychiatric hospital only a few weeks before the doctor was murdered. But the jury convicted Smith after a mere two hours' deliberation, apparently mindful of the prosecutor's request: "If you have any sympathy for the defendant, I ask that you think just for a moment how Kathryn Hinnant spent the last few moments of her life. She is entitled to one final measure of justice."[26] The jury disregarded fairly compelling psychological evidence in the face of horrendous aggravating circumstances.

Proportionality of Punishment

Assessing how blameworthy people are is one facet of the jury's search for justice. It is also necessary to contemplate what punishment, if any, is deserved. This brings up the concept of "commensurate deserts"—the notion that somehow the severity of the punishment should be proportionate to the gravity of the offense.

This principle has deep historical and cultural roots, long antedating the founding of the United States. The Old Testament is explicit, stating the idea of proportionality in very concrete terms:

> When one man strikes another and kills him he shall be put to death. Whoever strikes a beast and kills it shall make restitution, life for life. When one man injures and disfigures his fellow countryman, it shall be done to him as he has done; fracture for fracture, eye for eye, tooth for tooth; the injury and disfigurement that he has inflicted upon another shall in turn be inflicted upon him.[27]

93

American criminal law has incorporated the concept of proportionality inherent in the biblical precept. Legislatures have graduated levels of punishment according to the seriousness of the crime: petty theft can bring a few days in jail; burglary can result in a few years in prison; rape and murder can call for life imprisonment. The United States Supreme Court has given constitutional status to this idea, holding "as a matter of principle that a criminal sentence must be proportionate to the crime for which the defendant is convicted."[28] Disproportionate sentences are said to violate the Eighth Amendment's prohibition of cruel and unusual punishment.

This principle is not the least bit controversial. What *is* debated is its application: what sentences are proper for what kinds of crimes? Almost no one now takes the biblical injunction literally, but there are big differences in people's opinions about when imprisonment is justified and, when it is, what length of time is appropriate. The Supreme Court, while endorsing the principle of proportionality, has said that, with rare exceptions, working out the details is the province of legislative bodies and trial judges. Thus, in 1982, it upheld a forty-year sentence imposed by a Virginia judge for the offense of possession of nine ounces of marijuana having a street value of $200.[29]

Now we come to the role of juries. As explained in Chapter 2, the law by and large leaves juries out of the sentencing phase of the trial, and judges will sometimes warn them not to consider the sentence when rendering their verdicts. But because the idea of proportionality is so tied to the rendering of justice, juries do not always abdicate their role in pondering the ultimate fate of defendants. There are times when they will acquit defendants of some or all charges because they are worried that the sentence would be excessive otherwise.

Jurors may well have had this worry in the back of their minds in returning a manslaughter verdict against Luis Bonilla instead of finding him guilty of murder in 1979. Bonilla was a thirteen-year-old tried as an adult under a New York state law that permits such a practice when youths are accused of committing certain serious crimes. The crime was a hideous one: a boy out walking his dog was fatally shot in the back when he refused to give up his radio during an attempted robbery. There was not one iota of doubt: if Bonilla did the shooting, *this* was premeditated murder. But a murder conviction would have required a mandatory sentence of life imprisonment, which the jury was reluctant to impose on someone so young, no matter how ghastly the crime. So the facts were either disregarded or twisted beyond recognition to permit the imposition of a sentence of no more than three years in prison.[30]

Other examples abound. Juries confronted with death or injuries arising from automobile accidents may hesitate to convict on charges as serious as manslaughter if they harbor doubts about whether the speeding that caused the accident is a bad enough offense to warrant possible imprisonment. Young drug offenders may be acquitted if jurors are worried about stigmatizing them for life for a youthful mistake in judgment. The point is that juries to some degree preserve for themselves the responsibility of teasing out just deserts by arriving at verdicts that guard against punishments that are disproportionate to the offense.

Imposing the Death Penalty

There is one area of sentencing in which jurors play a straightforward role—determining who gets the death penalty. The Supreme Court has insisted that, in states that allow capital punishment, juries must be given this discretion, striking down as unconstitutional laws that make the death penalty mandatory in certain kinds of cases. Because of the grievous nature of this punishment and its difference in kind rather than degree from other sentences, it was held in *Woodson* v. *North Carolina* that juries must be given an opportunity to search for "compassionate or mitigating factors stemming from the diverse frailties of humankind."[31] To treat all convicted murderers "not as uniquely individual human beings, but as members of a faceless, undifferentiated mass" automatically deserving death is so unjust that it violates the Constitution.

With that, the Supreme Court threw the onerous job of deciding who deserves to die and who deserves to live into the laps of the jurors. But jurors were not allowed unfettered discretion; in *Gregg* v. *Georgia,* handed down the same day as the *Woodson* case, the Court ruled that death penalty statutes must provide guidance to jurors by listing sets of mitigating and aggravating factors to be considered in reaching a verdict about life or death.[32] Jurors must be told to look for the following kinds of things: Was the crime committed in the course of another capital offense? Was it committed on a peace officer? Was it committed in a particularly heinous way? Did it endanger many people? Was it committed for money? Has the defendant been convicted of other capital offenses? How young was the defendant? What was the defendant's emotional state at the time of the crime? And so forth and so on.

The Supreme Court was satisfied that by requiring consideration of explicit criteria, it was reducing if not eliminating the potential for arbitrariness. But in fact the application of these criteria has been anything but evenhanded, and in looking at the record of jury verdicts concerning death, one searches in vain for some uniform conception of justice underlying them. Out of thousands of people convicted of murder annually in the 1980s, fewer than 300 people were sentenced to death in the thirty-eight states that have the death penalty.

This is quite a paradox. About 75 percent of the public supports capital punishment for people convicted of murder,[33] and the percentage of jurors in capital cases who favor the death penalty is much higher because avowed opponents of capital punishment are excluded from juries in those cases. However, when presented the opportunity to send murderers to their death, these very jurors do so in a relatively small minority of cases. They are tough in the abstract, but concerns about justice soften them up when deciding the fate of specific individuals. The death penalty is reserved for the very worst of murderers.

The problem is determining who the very worst are. It all comes back to the most profound issue—who, among all the awful criminals who have committed dreadful crimes, deserves to die. The guidelines provided by the law and interpreted by the judge provide jurors precious little help in making this critical decision, and the inconsistent results are therefore not surprising.

As of now we know very little about how jurors make capital decisions.[34] Prosecutors demanding death dwell on the theme of justice in their final argument,[35] yet we do not know how these arguments are received and processed by jurors. Deciding whether to impose capital punishment is a decidedly political question, but how jurors go about getting answers must await further research.

Rendering Justice in Civil Cases

Civil cases also involve the rendering of justice, although the consequences of verdicts are not nearly so weighty as in death penalty decisions or even in noncapital criminal cases. Recall that jurors adjudicating civil law have two or three tasks: (1) determining if defendants are liable for the injuries done to plaintiffs; (2) figuring out compensatory damages the plaintiff is due;

and, in appropriate cases, (3) considering punitive damages. Theoretically, the jury is simply supposed to determine if defendants acted in a legally improper way and, if so, convert the plaintiff's losses into monetary compensation. In reality, the search for justice is again at work; conceptions about which defendants deserve to pay more are put into the decision crucible.

In figuring out blameworthiness and compensation in civil cases, juries not only look at the amount of expense, pain, and suffering sustained by plaintiffs as the law impels them to do but also consider the defendants' financial resources. This is a peculiar form of proportionality: damages are allocated according to the presumed wealth of defendants. Distributive aspects of justice come into play when jurors use damage awards as a mechanism for redressing some of the massive inequalities in American life.

This is not mere conjecture. A sophisticated study of 9,000 civil cases tried before juries in Cook County, Illinois, between 1969 and 1979 demonstrated the "deep pockets" effect.[36] Table 5-1 shows the differences in treatment afforded corporations and nonprofit organizations in comparison with government and individual defendants. To some degree, the large averages paid by corporations in comparison with individuals reflects a few huge awards which pulled the averages up. But even the median figures, which are not affected by these extraordinary damages awards, show a fourfold difference between the amount paid by corporations who have more resources and that paid by individuals who have less.

Refinements in the analysis of the data in the Cook County study show even more strikingly the "ability to pay" factors at work in juries' assessments. The "deep pockets" effect was still evident when the cases were broken down according to type (i.e., product liability, automobile negligence, work injury). Moreover, harsher treatment of presumably well-endowed corporations was even stronger when the plaintiffs were seriously injured; corporations paid 4.4 times as much as individuals in such cases. And if we include the cases in which plaintiffs were not awarded damages because the jury found for the defendant, the expected award confronting corporations was 6.5 times that facing individuals.

The discrimination against corporations shown in the following data is supported by the findings of experimental data produced by Hans and Ermann: students asked to judge the action of dumping toxic waste that subsequently made people ill were more likely to consider the behavior reckless and immoral when it was done by corporations than when the *identical activities* were done by individuals.[37] We can only guess the reasons for differential treatment of defendants by jurors and mock jurors: they may feel that corporations have special social responsibilities because of their privileged position; they may feel that corporations are in a better position to bear the burden of paying; or they may be discounting awards when the defendant is an individual out of concern for the undue burden that huge awards would impose. Whatever the reasoning, jurors' punishment depends on who the defendants are and what they have rather than on what they

Type of defendant	Average award	Median award	Median award in cases of severe injuries*	TABLE 5-1
Corporation	$120,000	$24,500	$161,000	Jury awards against defendants in civil cases in Cook County, Illinois
Nonprofit**	97,000	25,000	n.a.	
Government	37,600	11,000	98,000	
Individual	18,500	5,800	37,000	

*These are the medians in cases of white plaintiffs, 20 to 39 years old in injury-on-property cases.
**Nonprofit organizations are mainly hospitals.
Source: Audry Chin and Mark Peterson, *Deep Pockets, Empty Pockets: Who Wins in Cook County Jury Trials* (Santa Monica, Calif.: The Rand Corporation Institute for Civil Justice, 1985), pp. 28, 43. Reprinted by permission.

did. Jury justice in civil cases, reduced to an axiom, comes down to this: those who have more should pay more. This is politics par excellence—application of a theory of justice based on the ability to pay to the adjudication of civil law.

But jurors' political sentiments are more refined than simply cracking down on those with big money. The norm of corporate responsibility conflicts with other values, so the jury's search for justice involves endless attempts to balance the values. Hence, some kinds of corporate malfeasance are sharply condemned while other harmful practices are more or less shrugged off by juries.

Litigation involving tobacco companies is a case in point: before 1988, tobacco companies had not lost one lawsuit out of three hundred filed against them. Surveys of ex-jurors in such cases reflect the strong impact of the ethic of individual responsibility, summed up by one juror: "People are responsible for their own smoking, whether tobacco companies advertise or not. A person with any common sense is going to recognize that smoking is bad for you. I don't believe the companies can be held responsible."[38]

Thus, Valerie Hans is correct when she notes that "juries in business cases play an important political role. . . . [They] are in a position to reflect in their verdicts contemporary norms about business standards and responsibilities."[39] Many of society's most acute conflicts come to a head before the civil jury: business versus consumers, doctors versus patients, government agencies versus citizens, employers versus employees. Jurors take sides, thus dispensing their special brand of justice.

Conclusion

Jurors rely on common sense as they grope for justice. They want to "do the right thing," but it is no simple matter to figure out what the right thing is. The primary considerations are blameworthiness, mitigating circumstances, aggravating circumstances, and proportionality. But these are generalities, and the focus on *concrete details of cases* is the essence of the search for justice in order to place the defendant's behavior in its proper context. Dispensing justice requires looking at the whole picture—the defendant, the victim, and the setting in which critical events occurred.

As jurors sort out the facts and the legal issues, the most fundamental question in applying justice looms large: who deserves what? There are no eternal verities or simple formulas for arriving at just results, so jurors do what all government decision makers do when faced with matters of great complexity: they muddle through.

Notes

1. The jury deliberations are taken from a transcript of the program entitled *Inside the Jury Room*, which was part of the "Frontline" series. The transcript was provided by WGBH Transcripts, Boston, Massachusetts. Reprinted by permission.
2. Harry Kalven, Jr., and Hans Zeisel, *The American Jury* (Boston: Little, Brown, 1966), p. 495.
3. Quoted in Otto Friedrich, "We, the Jury, Find the . . ." *Time* (September 28, 1981): 48.
4. John Call, "Psychology in Litigation," *Trial,* 21 (March 1985): 48.
5. William Safire, "A Deal Is a Deal," *The New York Times* (January 19, 1986), p. E23.
6. Gene Varn, "Women Acquitted of Felony Charges in Hammer Attack," *Arizona Republic* (February 5, 1983), p. A1.
7. Lee Daniels, "Guilty Verdict in Deaf Boy's Slaying," *The New York Times* (May 3, 1980), p. 26.
8. Learned Hand, *Philip Hamburger, The Great Judge,* quoted in John Bartlett, *Familiar Quotations,* 15th ed., edited by Emily Beck (Boston: Little Brown, 1980), p. 737.
9. Paula DiPerna, *Juries on Trial: Faces of American Justice* (New York: Dembner Books, 1984), p. 2.
10. David Suggs and John Berman, "Factors Affecting Testimony about Mitigating Circumstances and the Fixing of Punishment," *Law and Human Behavior,* 3 (1979): 251–260.
11. Gloria Negri, "Capute Jury Still Deciding," *Boston Globe* (October 23, 1981), p. 17.
12. Kalven and Zeisel, *The American Jury,* p. 229.
13. Ellen Tumpowsky and Ruth Landa, "Straw Acquitted," *New York Daily News* (October 1, 1987), p. 4.
14. Charles Lachman, "Top Lawyer Hails Decision," *The New York Post* (August 17, 1984), p. 17.
15. For a detailed analysis of the DeLorean case, including reports of interviews with jurors, see Steven Brill, *Trial by Jury* (New York: American Lawyer Books/Touchstone, 1989), pp. 201–265.
16. Mike Pearl, Cynthia Fagen, and Philip Messing, "Inside the Bitter Jury Room," *The New York Post* (January 22, 1982), p. 5.
17. Valerie Hans and Neil Vidmar, *Judging the Jury* (New York: Plenum, 1986), chap. 12.
18. *Ibid.,* pp. 189–190.
19. Henry Steadman, John Monahan, Sharon Davis, and Pamela Robbins, "Mentally Disordered Offenders: National Survey of Patients and Facilities," *Law and Human Behavior,* 6 (1982): 31–38.
20. Kalven and Zeisel, *The American Jury,* p. 335.
21. Jesus Rangel, "Defendant in the Killing of 10 Is Guilty of Reduced Charge," *The New York Times* (July 20, 1985), p. 1.
22. Kalven and Zeisel, *The American Jury,* p. 209.
23. William Glaberson, "Juror Says Wise's 'Remorse' Helpful," *The New York Times* (December 12, 1990), p. B6.
24. R. W. Apple, Jr., "Measured Judgment," *The New York Times* (May 5, 1989), p. A18.
25. The quotations from jurors in this and the next paragraph are from Larry Martz with Robert Parry, "The Hero's Clay Feet," *Newsweek* (May 15, 1989): 32–38; Richard Lacayo, "A Partial

Vindication,'' *Time* (May 15, 1989), pp. 34–35; David Rosenbaum, ''Jurors See North as a Scapegoat for His Superiors,'' *The New York Times* (May 6, 1989), p. 1.

26. Larry Sutton, ''Quick Verdict: Guilty,'' *New York Daily News* (October 31, 1989), p. 3.
27. *Lev.* 24: 17–22.
28. *Solem* v. *Helm,* 463 U.S. 277 (1983).
29. *Hutto* v. *Davis,* 454 U.S. 370 (1982).
30. Robert McFadden, ''Boy, 14, Tried as Adult, Found Guilty of Manslaughter,'' *The New York Times* (July 28, 1979), p. 19.
31. *Woodson* v. *North Carolina,* 428 U. S. 280 (1976).
32. *Gregg* v. *Georgia,* 428 U.S. 153 (1976).
33. United States Department of Justice, *Sourcebook of Criminal Justice Statistics—1989* (Washington, D.C.: U.S. Department of Justice, Office of Justice Programs, Bureau of Justice Statistics, 1990), p. 171.
34. Valerie Hans, ''Death by Jury'' in Kenneth Haas and James Inciardi (eds.), *Challenging Capital Punishment: Legal and Social Science Approaches* (Newbury Park, Calif.: Sage, 1988), p. 171.
35. D. D. Logan, ''Why You Should Not Kill This Man,'' presented at the British Psychological Society's International Conference on Psychology and Law, Swansea, Wales, 1982.
36. Audrin Chin and Mark Peterson, *Deep Pockets, Empty Pockets: Who Wins in Cook County Jury Trials* (Santa Monica, Calif.: The Rand Corporation Institute for Civil Justice, 1985).
37. Valerie Hans and M. David Ermann, ''Responses to Corporate Versus Individual Wrongdoing,'' *Law and Human Behavior,* 13 (1989): 151–166.
38. David Gidmark, ''The Tobacco Juries—An In-Depth Study,'' *Trial Diplomacy Journal,* 10 (1987): 26.
39. Valerie Hans, ''The Jury's Response to Business and Corporate Wrongdoing,'' *Law and Contemporary Problems,* 52 (Autumn 1989): 203.

99

6
. . . .
Jury
Nullification

I n December, 1988, Dr. Peter Rossier went on trial before a St. Petersburg, Florida, jury for the crime of first-degree murder. The facts were straightforward: after his wife of twenty-two years, who was terminally ill with cancer, tried unsuccessfully to kill herself with sleeping pills, Rossier gave her morphine in an attempt to kill her. When the morphine dosage also failed to end her life, the woman's stepfather used his hands to suffocate her.

After Rossier publicly admitted his role in the suicide plan that resulted in his wife's death, he was charged with murder for his part in the fatal plan. His defense was that this was a mercy killing, an act of compassion to end futile pain and suffering. The defense maintained that people who commit or help carry out euthanasia against loved ones who want to die should *not* be convicted of homicide—even when they may have intentionally and with premeditation taken someone's life. Said his lawyer: "When the people of the state of Florida wrote these laws, they were thinking of Charles Manson [a cult leader convicted of mass murder], not people like Peter Rossier."[1]

The prosecution admonished the jury to stick to the letter of the law and to ignore philosophical and moral arguments. The prosecution's stand was that there is never a right to take someone's life except in cases of self-defense. But the jury thought otherwise: they acquitted him. After the verdict was rendered, Dr. Rossier said, "The love of my life was vindicated."

The Rossier case illustrates how juries judge laws as well as people. Although judges instruct jurors to follow the law as it is explained to them and to set aside any personal feelings they may have about the wisdom of the law in question, jurors nonetheless implicitly or explicitly make exactly such judgments. Their willingness to convict depends in some measure on their approval of the law or of particular applications of the law. Jury verdicts are thus to some degree referenda on the penal code—the expression of popular sentiment about political issues and public policy. What the English jurist Patrick Devlin said of the British jury is true of the American jury as well: "Every jury is a little parliament. The jury sense is the parliamentary sense."[2]

The Florida jury that acquitted Dr. Rossier was like a little state legislature. It apparently felt that some forms of euthanasia are legitimate or at least forgivable and that people who perform it should not be punished. If many juries act in like fashion in similar cases, the law in effect gets repealed or amended. Oliver Wendell Holmes once said, "The prophecies of what the courts will do in fact, and nothing more pretentious, are what I mean by the law."[3] The law on the books may say one thing, but the jury may say another. In that case, the jury's word *is* the law.

The Legislative Role of Juries

Nullification

Jury nullification takes place when juries refuse to convict because they dislike a law or the use to which the law is being put; in effect, they nullify the law. This is a practice with deep roots in the Anglo-American legal system.[4] As long ago as the fourteenth century, British jurors refused to convict many murderers because they thought that the law did not take mitigating circumstances into account and so the mandatory death penalty was improper.[5] The same unwillingness to convict was widespread in England in the eighteenth and nineteenth centuries in response to the "Bloody Code," which prescribed death for more than 200 offenses, including forgery and pickpocketing. The jurors nullified the harshness of Parliament by absolving many persons who were clearly guilty, thus in effect rewriting the criminal law.

Instances of jury nullification in the United States can be traced to colonial days. The classic case is that of Peter Zenger, the publisher of *The New York Weekly Journal*, who in 1735 was charged with committing seditious libel for printing many articles critical of the British colonial government. The judge instructed the jury that as a matter of law the articles in question were indisputably libelous, so their only job was to decide whether Zenger had in fact printed the articles. A verdict against Zenger seemed assured, but after deliberating no more than a few minutes, the jury rendered a verdict of not guilty. Apparently responding to the urging of Zenger's lawyer that "jurors make use of their own conscience and understandings" in rendering verdicts, the jury upset a British law that the jury thought to be repressive and undemocratic.[6]

This proved not to be an isolated case, and by the time of independence, jury nullification was an accepted practice. It continued after 1776: nineteenth-century juries in the North exonerated a good number of escaped slaves and white accomplices accused of violating fugitive slave laws that the juries thought were unjust.[7] In the early twentieth century, jurors revolted against the puritanical restrictiveness of Prohibition laws by refusing to convict many who had in fact engaged in the manufacture or purchase of alcoholic beverages.[8]

The right of jury nullification was supported by most of the Founding Fathers, although the Constitution itself makes no mention of it. At any rate, throughout much of the nineteenth century, both federal and state judges routinely instructed jurors that they could decide issues of law as well as of fact. This practice, however, was struck down by the United States Supreme Court in 1896 in *Sparf and Hansen* v. *United States*,[9] and most states thereafter abolished it.

Most courts today remain firm in their opposition to advising jurors that they have the right to nullify laws, as indicated by the words of the United States Court of Appeals for the District of Columbia:

> What makes for health as an occasional medicine would be disastrous as a daily diet. . . . An explicit instruction to the jury [of their right to set laws aside] conveys an implied approval [of such a practice] that runs the risk of degrading the legal structure requisite for true freedom.[10]

Curiously, the jury's right to engage in nullification still remains in Maryland and Indiana, where state constitutions require judges to inform jurors that the instructions judges give about the law are only advisory. This is what Maryland judges tell jurors:

> Members of the jury, under the Constitution of Maryland, the jury in a criminal case is the Judge of the law as well as the facts. Therefore, anything which I may say about the law, including any instructions which I may give you, is merely advisory and you are not in any way bound by it. You may feel free to reject any advice on the law and to arrive at your own independent conclusions.[11]

However, many of the judges in Maryland and Indiana manage to soft-pedal this message, and it appears that most jurors are inclined to follow the judge's interpretation of the law in any event.[12] A study of mock juries showed that advisory-type instructions were no more likely to produce acquittals than "normal" instructions were.[13]

Although juries now are almost never given the right to nullify the law, they sometimes exercise this power anyway; they exercise "de facto" nullification. This process can occur because jurors are permitted to base their decisions on any factors they deem important without having to divulge the grounds for their verdicts. Most verdicts are general verdicts, conclusions about the guilt or liability of defendants rather than answers to specific factual questions (called *special verdicts*). Consequently, in practice, jurors can assess the law in question to their hearts' content as a part of their decision making without any repercussions. Jurors can do as they please, and refusing to apply a law sometimes pleases them.

Clearly that is what happened when a Massachusetts jury acquitted Amy Carter, the daughter of former president Jimmy Carter, and acquitted longtime radical activist Abbie Hoffman (among others) on charges of trespassing and disorderly conduct at an anti-CIA demonstration at the University of Massachusetts. There was little question that demonstrators illegally occupied a college building and later blocked buses trying to carry away arrested persons. But the defendants successfully convinced the jury to focus on the alleged crimes committed by the CIA in Latin American countries as a justification for the defendants' behavior. The prosecutor urged the jury to abide by the law in question: "We're talking about crimes that were committed in Amherst, Massachusetts, just down the road, in Hampshire County. We're not talking about illegal activities of the CIA in Central America or elsewhere." But this argument was to no avail, as reflected in the comments of one of the jurors after the trial: "These young people are doing what most of us should be doing."[14] Political issues concerning national security and Latin America infused the courtroom and the verdict—and the criminal law went by the wayside.

In some cases, jurors confront the issue of jury nullification directly, as was the case in regard to Seattle protesters tried for blocking munitions trains carrying bombs destined for Vietnam. Said one juror: "They were all guilty of violating the law. But, you know, this war is a nasty situation. If it weren't so nasty, we probably wouldn't have made the decision we did."[15]

However, when juries do broach the issue of nullification directly, they usually choose to adhere to the law. Blatant disregard of the law does not sit well with jurors, who see such a practice as an invitation to anarchy. One juror, highly sympathetic to the cause of defendants accused in 1985 of illegally smuggling politically persecuted Salvadorans and Guatemalans into the United States, nevertheless stated: "I thought about it a lot. I came to the conclusion that if every jury went in and decided that they didn't like the laws and didn't go with them, it wouldn't be a very good system. I kind of decided in my mind that we had to follow the instructions."[16]

Thus, forthright refusal to apply a law is atypical. More commonly, jurors who have reservations about applying a law simply construe the facts in a manner advantageous to the defendant. Jury nullification, like most aspects of jury politics, is a subconscious phenomenon.

Redefinition of Laws

Sometimes jury legislating takes the form of rewriting terms of the law, a process that can be called *jury redefinition*. Because so many legal concepts are quite ambiguous, there is ample opportunity for the jury to provide its own meaning of a law. Although judges go to great lengths in their instructions to pinpoint meanings of words such as *"force"* in the robbery statutes and *"premeditation"* in the homicide laws, some vagueness always remains. So jurors often have much leeway in giving meaning to the law, and in the process they may give a decidedly different coloration to the law than lawmakers or presiding judges intended.

Juries may in effect add to a law, enlarging the set of situations to which it applies. Thus, a Fort Lauderdale, Florida, jury convicted Theresa Jackson of child abuse for contributing to her seventeen-year-old daughter's suicide by forcing her to work as a nude dancer in bars. Child abuse laws normally apply to physical harm inflicted on a child, but the jury apparently accepted the testimony of a Harvard psychiatrist that the exploitation of the girl by her mother was akin to physical violence in its devastating effects.[17] To the extent that subsequent juries act similarly, they are defining as "criminal" behavior that previously had not been illegal, however immoral it may have been. In essence, a new category of crime is created: psychological torment of a child that leads to suicide.

The opposite side of legal redefinition is qualification of a law, in which juries make exceptions that are not permitted or implied by the law itself. In recent years, for example, juries have been exonerating women who kill their husbands or lovers after suffering from long-term brutality committed against them. Even when the slayings are clearly premeditated, juries will seize on some loophole in the law to absolve the killers. In doing so, the juries are not nullifying the murder laws but specifying a narrow set of circumstances under which homicide is thought to be justifiable. They are coming to the rescue of battered women who felt that they had no way out of their plight but to use violence against their male assailants. Juries are in effect amending the criminal law by carving out exceptions to it.

Fortification of Laws

Jury evaluations of laws can work against defendants as well as for them. When jurors are passionately in favor of a law, they may inject their feelings into a case by prejudging guilt and then giving short shrift to exonerating evidence. This allegedly occurred in the trial of many World War I sedition cases, according to federal Judge Amidon who presided over several of them:

> I have tried war cases before jurymen who were candid, sober, intelligent business men, whom I have known for thirty years, and who under ordinary circum-

104

stances would have had the highest respect for my declarations of law, but during that period they looked back into my eyes with the savagery of wild animals, saying by their manner, "away with this twiddling, let us get at him." Men believed that during that period that the only verdict in a war case, which could show loyalty, was a verdict of guilty.[18]

This is an example of jury fortification—reinforcing a well-liked law by convicting on the basis of what may be insufficient evidence. The jury gives its stamp of approval to the law by taking a dim view of the arguments and proof presented by the defendant. This form of jury legislating is almost never done straightforwardly, because it runs so counter to the presumption of innocence to which virtually all jurors subscribe. Rather, it takes the form of a tough-minded bias in favor of the prosecution that works to the disadvantage of defendants.

The Uses of Jury Nullification

Although there are many opportunities for jury legislating, what Kalven and Zeisel found in their classic 1950s study remains true three decades later: there is no major war between the jury and the law. The reason is rather simple: by and large the jury agrees with the law and feels comfortable applying it to concrete cases. But jurors do not follow the law rigidly and automatically; one study of Indianapolis juries concluded that the jury engaged in "substantial rule departures."[19] We now look at some of the circumstances in which juries engage in such nullification.

Unpopular Laws

Jurors have very few quarrels with laws that protect people and their property, such as laws against murder, rape, robbery, and assault. It is in regard to crimes entailing less direct or less serious harms that questions arise. Certain economic crimes are of this nature, such as price-fixing and violations of security laws, and conviction rates in these areas have been relatively low.

Instances of nullification are most notable in the area of so-called victimless crimes. There is substantial evidence that jurors have often been disinclined to convict defendants accused of violating "sumptuary" laws—attempts to regulate personal expenditures or activities for moral reasons.[20] Jurors are hesitant to convict people for engaging in such vices as gambling and prostitution when those providing and partaking of illegal goods and services do so willingly. In an era of relatively high social permissiveness, it is commonly thought that the parties involved should accept the risks and bear the burdens of consensual activities. Hence, acquittals, in such cases are often rendered even in the face of compelling evidence.

Drug crime trials, on the other hand, have a high conviction rate. One study of jury trials in Tennessee showed a drug conviction rate of 85 percent—higher than the conviction rate of 71 percent for all other felonies, and even higher than the 75 percent conviction rate for murder.[21] Although there may be evidentiary disparities in the different types of cases, there is little doubt that Tennessee drug laws are *not* being nullified. The furor about drugs that has escalated the problem to the top of the national political agenda apparently is also taking place in the jury room, where there is strong approval of stern drug laws.

Juries thus differentiate among vices, overlooking some and cracking down on others. They are inclined to nullify laws that seem needlessly puritanical and antiquated. But when vices pose a frightful national problem, juries legislate the other way—fortifying the law by their toughness.

Unpopular Policies

Wayne Cryts flagrantly violated the law in Missouri, but he became an instantaneous hero as a result, and a federal district court jury took only thirty minutes to acquit him. What had Cryts done? He and 2,000 other desperate Missouri farmers broke into a sealed grain elevator and took thousands of bushels of soybeans that had been impounded by a federal bankruptcy judge, who had ordered the grain sold to pay for the grain elevator's debts. Farmers saw Cryts' actions as a rebellion against unfair federal bankruptcy laws, but a federal judge had Cryts jailed for contempt of court for selling his illegally seized crop in violation of a court order. Jurors took the farmers' perspective, and the jury foreman said the jury voted 100 percent for acquittal on the first ballot.[22]

Jurors were in effect nullifying a particular application of the law rather than the law itself. Farmers are generally a fairly conservative group, quite committed to the ideal of obeying the law and protecting property rights. But in this situation, they saw family farms being devastated by national agricultural policy, and they were not about to lend a hand in pursuit of such a policy. Their actions illustrate a particular kind of jury nullification: acquittal as a protest against unpopular policies backed up by the law, rather than a condemnation of the law per se.

This verdict is akin to the Amy Carter case described earlier, in which jurors registered their disapproval of national security policy by *temporarily* withdrawing their usual support for trespass and disorderly conduct laws. Nullification of the variety exercised by the Carter and Cryts juries arises when cases get politicized by the intrusion of current social controversies. Jurors do not remain on the sidelines of debates about such questions, and they may choose to sanction violations of a law they would otherwise support as a means of expressing opposition to a current policy. They use their short-lived positions of authority to have a say in the working out of controversial political issues.

De Minimus

Another situation that at times engenders nullification is *de minimus,* which is a shorthand expression for the Roman legal maxim *de minimus non curat lex*—the law does not concern itself with trifles. This concept enters into all stages of criminal justice decision making, from the police officer who ignores people who drive five miles over the speed limit to the prosecutor who dismisses the charge of marijuana possession against someone caught with one or two joints. Similarly, jurors are disinclined to convict when the harm is minor.

This tendency was noted by television newscaster Daniel Schorr, who served on several juries during a two-week stint of jury duty in Washington, D.C. Schorr said afterward that he and his co-jurors were more willing to find reasonable doubt in a case involving the sale of a prescribed dose of methadone than in another case dealing with large-scale heroin peddling. In published post-trial reflections, Schorr was quite candid about the jury's role: "Let me . . . reveal the jury-room secret that despite judges' instructions to the contrary we engaged in a certain amount of 'jury revisionism' of the law."[23] The jury's pro-defendant bias in dealing with a relatively minor infraction by a young addict under medical treatment is a cardinal example of the *de minimus* idea in action.

What is really in operation is a double standard, indeed a triple or quadruple standard, applied to defendants accused of crimes of different degrees of seriousness. Jurors employ a kind of gravity scale, distinguishing between crimes perceived to cause substantial personal harms to victims and those in which consequences are remote or attenuated. What is convincing evidence in serious cases may often be insufficient in minor ones.

This dilution of the law when less damage has been done seemed apparent from Kalven and Zeisel's mid-1950s data. Their findings showed great variations in conviction rates depending on crime categories, from a high of 90 percent for alleged drug violations to only 53 percent for possession of stolen property. Defendants charged with murder were convicted twice as often as those charged with rape. Those charged with robbery and burglary were found guilty 50 percent more often than those accused of fraud and embezzlement.[24] The worse the crime, the greater the number of convictions.

Data collected more recently has produced similar findings. Whereas only about one out of three people tried for misdemeanors in Florida between 1978 and 1980 was convicted, 62 percent of those on trial for felonies were convicted. In Tennessee, 75 percent of those charged with assault, burglary, kidnaping, robbery, rape, and drug violations were convicted in 1979, whereas the conviction rate was only 64 percent in other felony cases.[25]

Some of the differences in the conviction proneness of juries could be the result of prosecutors' choices of which cases to take to trial, but it seems unlikely that prosecutors would expend time and money trying less serious cases unless they had fairly strong evidence. It seems more plausible to conclude that juries are more dubious about convicting when the alleged misconduct is less offensive, so they insist on a much stronger showing of culpability.

Federal jurors dealing with regulatory crimes also seem to have kept the nature of the offense in the back of their minds. Conviction rates in the 1960s and 1970s ranged from a high of 82 percent in national defense cases to a low of 36 percent in cases involving killing of migratory birds.[26] The latter crimes probably seemed trivial in a period when conservation and ecology had yet to reach national consciousness.

In a sense, what jurors seem to be doing is prioritizing. Well aware that there may be considerable overcriminalization in our legal system and concerned about wasting scarce resources such as prison space on people who do not threaten public safety, the jury is more lenient toward less serious offenders. Judges can temper convictions in *de minimus* cases with light sentences, but because jurors lack this option in all but a few states, their only recourse for keeping priorities straight is to raise the standard of doubt in minor cases. By insisting on a very high level of proof to convict, they are in effect nullifying the law.

Folk Crimes

Jurors will sometimes turn their backs on the law if they feel that the crime committed is a common occurrence, often called a *folk crime.* Thus, the conviction rate in drunk driving cases has been well below average,[27] in part because many jurors have themselves driven while intoxicated and can empathize with the defendant. This is different from *de minimus*: most jurors would agree that the law makes sense and no doubt recognize that drunk drivers are a social menace, but they have trouble convicting for behavior that has been part of their own experience. Their skepticism of breathalyzer test results, police observations of defendants' erratic behavior, and other incriminating evidence has made it difficult to convict, thus partially nullifying laws against driving while intoxicated.

Another commonplace crime that jurors are prone to overlook is income tax evasion, unless it is done on a massive scale. "There but for the grace of God go I" becomes the rationale for finding a way to acquit. To jurors, it may seem unfair and hypocritical to convict the few hapless defendants who were prosecuted for "folk crimes"—illegalities that are a part of everyday behavior.

Local Sentiments about Laws

We have seen that jurors do play a legislative role: they nullify the law, redefine the law, and sometimes fortify the law. But is each jury a unique collage of political sentiments, or does jury law bending reflect the prevailing political atmosphere? To what extent can verdicts by juries be seen as the voice of the people, populism in action? Is the jury an instrument of democracy?

Prevailing views of local communities are more or less reflected in jury behavior, depending on the representativeness of the jury. Sometimes the law requires the jury to rely on local norms, as when jurors in child brutality cases must determine the boundaries of "normal" corporal punishment. Such judgments invariably take local customs and views into account as jurors wrestle with the applicable standards.

It is not only in regard to defining and redefining ambiguous parts of the law that local views are brought to bear by jurors. Outright jury nullification of relatively clear-cut statutes also normally reflects local feelings about laws.

Rural communities have historically been loathe to convict in game law cases because of their disaffection for restrictions on hunting rights.[28] This tendency to protect hunters was taken to an extreme by a Bangor, Maine, jury, which in October 1990 acquitted a hunter of manslaughter in the killing of a woman mistaken for a deer while standing in her own back yard, adjacent to the woods. The defendant had mistaken the woman's white mittens for a deer's tail and had fired several shots at her. The jury, according to one commentator, reflected the prevailing view that there is "an inalienable right to hunt anywhere."[29] The manslaughter law was interpreted by the standard of the local pro-hunting political culture.

Urban jurors also mirror the pulse of their environment. This is starkly illustrated by a Detroit arson case in which jurors consciously absolved two men who burned down a "crack house"—the scene of constant drug dealing and more than occasional gunplay. The defendants, frustrated by the inability of police to handle this neighborhood menace, admitted to dousing every floor with gasoline, setting them on fire, and watching the house burn to the ground. The jury had no trouble accepting the defendants' peculiar legal arguments based on self-defense and duress, and so it distinguished between "good" arson and "bad" arson.

This was a jury uninterested in legal niceties; politics was more important than law. The foreman said the verdict was a message to city officials to do more to fight drugs. Another juror was even more outspoken, saying: "I would have done the same thing. . . . No, I would have been more violent." This jury was perfectly in tune with local feelings; the defendants' neighbors said they were grateful to the two men and a poll of the city conducted by the *Detroit Free Press* found that 87 percent of readers thought the burning of the crack house was justified.[30] In carving out an exception to the law of arson, the jury was—rightly or wrongly—speaking for the community.

Changing Attitudes Toward Laws

Public sentiments about laws fluctuate, and the jury's inclinations sometimes move accordingly. These changes in juror perspective often occur independently of alterations in the law itself, so the "law in action" applied by jurors has a life of its own. This susceptibility of juries to changing norms and mores is markedly revealed by trends in the disposition of rape cases, civil rights cases, and draft evasion cases.

Verdict Trends in Rape Cases

Historically, the conviction rate for rape has been notoriously low. Indeed, one of Kalven and Zeisel's most striking findings is that, in their national sample of jury cases in 1954 and 1955, only three defendants (out of forty-two) were convicted of rape when either (1) the victim was an acquaintance of the alleged assailant or (2) the defendant and victim were strangers to each other but additional violence was absent.[31] This can be interpreted as a rewriting of the law of rape in two ways: first, it implicitly gives men the right to have sex with women who choose to associate with them, whether the women agree to intercourse or not; second, it requires women to fight off their attackers even at the risk of serious assault or death. This qualification of the law of rape at the hands of juries surely stemmed in part from the sexist assumption that women who are victimized are themselves to blame for their own fate because they are either seductive or unresisting.

By the early 1960s, very little had changed, as is shown by an analysis of rape cases decided by federal juries illustrated in Figure 6-1.[32] In the first half of that decade (before the women's movement had gained much national momentum), juries were very lenient toward rape defendants, and in 1964 only 27 percent of those tried were convicted. In fact, in the five-year period between 1961 and 1965, only two types of federal prosecutions resulted in lower conviction rates—alleged violations of migratory bird statutes and antitrust laws. Only 38 percent of defendants in rape cases were convicted, in contrast to an overall federal jury conviction rate of 70 percent during that same period.

These low conviction rates materialized despite the fact that most rape cases before juries are strengthened by the longer-than-average duration of the crime and the better-than-average identification of assailants by victims. So it is hard not to conclude that the normally male-dominated juries of years past, which absolved so many defendants, reflected the widely held judgment that sexual domination of women by men was legitimate under many circumstances. During this period, the law itself permitted husbands to force sex on their wives, and juries in a sense extended this prerogative to other male aggressors. At best, rape was not taken seriously; at worst, it was seen as permissible.

But change was in the wind in the 1960s. Guilty verdicts increased continuously (with some normal year-to-year fluctuations), rising to 74 percent between 1976 and 1978, which was only 3 percent lower than the conviction rate in all federal cases before juries. The percentage of convictions inexplicably dropped off in the early 1980s, but it climbed back up to 73 percent

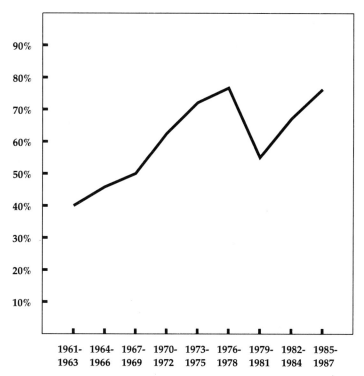

FIGURE 6-1

Federal jury
conviction rates
in rape cases

| | 1961-1963 | 1964-1966 | 1967-1969 | 1970-1972 | 1973-1975 | 1976-1978 | 1979-1981 | 1982-1984 | 1985-1987 |

Source: Administrative Office of the United States Courts, *Annual Report of the Director,* 1961 through 1987 (Washington, D.C.: U.S. Government Printing Office).

between 1985 and 1987. In short, almost twice as many defendants are being convicted now as was the case thirty years ago.

Why the turnabout? There are no doubt many reasons, but one factor is unmistakable: the substantial increase in public support for women's rights in the contemporary era that carries over into the jury room. Other elements were also at work, such as the rise in the number of women jurors, more sympathetic handling of rape cases by police and prosecutors, a greater willingness of rape victims to testify about the details of their ordeal, and reform of rape laws to bar certain prejudicial evidence, such as the victim's previous sexual activities. But experimental research suggests that jurors' personal attitudes toward rape are one of the most significant influences on their decision making.[33] Similarly, Michigan judges, interviewed in the aftermath of legal changes in that state that made it easier to convict in rape cases, contended that it was the change in juror attitudes more than changes in the law that was responsible for the surge in convictions that we have witnessed.[34] Although sexism is still quite rampant, the right of women to control their own sexuality and to have legal protection from uninvited male advances has surely won greater social acceptance. Jurors have responded to these changes by

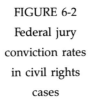

FIGURE 6-2

Federal jury
conviction rates
in civil rights
cases

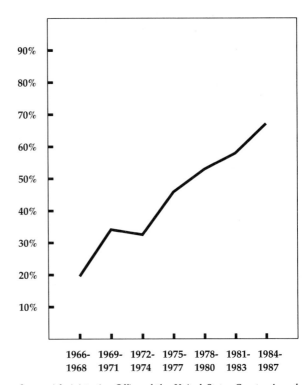

90%

80%

70%

60%

50%

40%

30%

20%

10%

| 1966- | 1969- | 1972- | 1975- | 1978- | 1981- | 1984- |
| 1968 | 1971 | 1974 | 1977 | 1980 | 1983 | 1987 |

Source: Administrative Office of the United States Courts, *Annual Report of the Director,* 1966 through 1987 (Washington, D.C.: U.S. Government Printing Office).

taking a tougher posture in rape cases and thereby making the law as applied more commensurate with the tough penal law on the books.

Verdict Trends in Civil Rights Cases

The effect of changing norms is even more dramatically illustrated by trends in the way federal juries have handled civil rights cases. In 1964, 1965, and 1968, Congress passed a series of laws banning racial discrimination in education, voting, employment, public accommodations, and housing. Although such discrimination was and is a nationwide problem, the primary target of the original laws was the South—which was also the locus of the most strident resistance to the laws. Most of the early prosecutions under the civil rights laws arose in the Southern jurisdictions, and juries in these areas had the responsibility of putting the laws into practice.[35]

Figure 6-2 indicates that the first juries to hear cases under these laws were anything but enthusiastic about enforcing them. In fact, the low conviction rates in the early years are unprecedented and unsurpassed in the annals of federal judicial statistics—lower even than the abysmally low conviction rate in rape cases just reported.[36] In the first three years, only 19 percent of defendants tried before juries were found guilty, despite the fact that federal prosecutors, who were themselves tied into local racist traditions, generally limited the cases coming before juries to blatant acts of discrimination in which the incriminating evidence was strong. The juries, many if not most of which were all-white, clearly opposed the upsetting of established cultural traditions based on the premise of racial inequality and resented the federal government's intrusion into local affairs. The South of the 1960s had lost the power in Congress to stop civil rights laws from being enacted, but its juries were able to retard implementation by systematically refusing to convict alleged lawbreakers. This was a classic case of jury nullification.

As time passed, the prosecution of civil rights violations became a national phenomenon. Conviction rates crept upward but still remained quite low—hovering around 50 percent by the end of the 1970s. The Kerner Report, authored by some of the nation's top leaders in 1968, focused on racial problems in the North and concluded that discrimination and segregation "permeated much of American life."[37] This finding was mirrored in jury rooms throughout the country as jury leniency emasculated the laws intended to protect minorities from wrongful treatment.

However, crosscurrents also were at work. The civil rights movement ultimately did have a moderating impact on white racism: thousands of schools *were* desegregated; millions of voters *were* registered; most public accommodations *were* opened to blacks; and some historic barriers to employment *were* surmounted. These events were accompanied by a marked decline in overt racial prejudice.

Juries followed suit; conviction rates in civil rights cases continued to rise, reaching 65 percent by the mid-1980s. What is especially striking is that cases adjudicated more recently have usually involved more subtle forms of discrimination, which are harder to prove. The growing willingness of juries to convict stems in part from the inclusion of more black jurors, but it surely also represents the effect of liberalization on racial issues among white jurors. The almost continuous rise in convictions shown in figure 6-2 and the fourfold increase in the percentage of cases resulting in conviction over a twenty-year period are not chance events. The jury reflects changes in the national pulse.

Verdict Trends in Selective Service Cases

Results of selective service cases tried before federal juries are one of the best examples of conviction rates that depend on the popularity of government policies. During the four major wars Americans fought in this century, a draft was imposed on young men and tough criminal sanctions of up to five years imprisonment have been employed to back it up. However, the law has always exempted some from serving, such as the physically handicapped and conscientious objectors who do not believe in fighting. The task for juries in selective service cases is to determine whether those who were denied such exemptions by their draft boards were improperly turned down.

A study of jury decision making in such cases decided between 1945 and 1974 indicates that fluctuations in jury verdicts correspond to shifts in public support for the wars requiring the draft.[38] It was shown that the rise and fall of jury conviction rates roughly corresponds to the vicissitudes of public approval of the wars from which selective service cases stem. The "rally-around-the-flag" spirit that usually engulfs nations at the onset of wars was accompanied by an abnormally high conviction level, 93 percent in the first year of the Korean War and 96 percent in the first two years of the Vietnam War. But as national doubts about the wisdom of continued involvement in the two wars grew and support for the war efforts diminished, conviction rates dropped sharply, reaching a level of around 70 percent in the last full years of both wars.

The correlation between war popularity and jury behavior was especially notable in the Vietnam War, as is shown in Figure 6-3. At the beginning of the war, the public registered a bit of opposition; but as the war popularity gained momentum, a broad consensus in favor of continuation arose reaching its zenith in 1967—which has been called "the year of the hawk." In that year, jury acquittals became almost nonexistent, dropping to an incredible 3 percent in 1967. But by 1968, as American troops got bogged down during the famous "Tet offensive" and dissent swelled within the United States, the public was starting to turn against the war. "Dovish" sentiment surged, with more and more people supporting American troop withdrawal and opposing further escalation of the war. At the same time, the number of acquittals in selective service cases went up, reaching 32 percent in 1973, when the United States exited from the war. In that year, 79 percent of those responding to a Gallup poll opposed reintervention of American troops, even if it meant that South Vietnam would be taken over by the communist North Vietnam regime (which eventually happened). Jurors were echoing what the public was saying.

Interpreting jury verdicts in the aggregate is tricky business, as was discussed in the brief methodology section in Chapter 1. There may be other factors that account for shifting verdicts, such as changes in the strength of the evidence, fluctuations in prosecutors' pretrial case-selection practices, or amendments of the law. But in fact, the decline in convictions over the course of the Vietnam War occurred in the face of *stronger* prosecutions and changes in selective service law that made it *more* difficult to secure exemptions, including a Supreme Court decision ruling that moral objections to specific wars were insufficient to qualify one for conscientious objector status.[39] After all kinds of alternative explanations of jury verdicts were ruled out, the author of the study concluded that in selective service cases verdicts become means

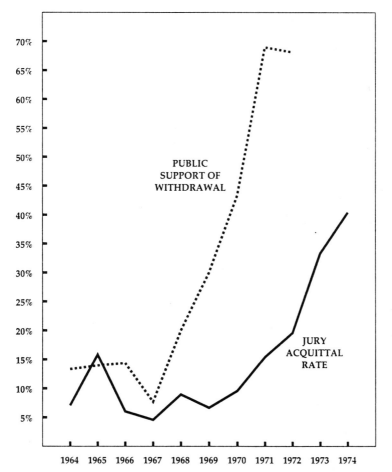

Source: James P. Levine, "The Legislative Role of Juries," *American Bar Foundation Research Journal,* 1984 (Summer): 619.

by which jurors make political statements about the military policy of their government. Juries judge wars as well as defendants.

Conclusion

In his dissent in *United States* v. *Dougherty* (cited above), Judge Bazelon eloquently argued that juries *should* be given the explicit right to nullify laws. It was a populist dissent: the judge emphasized the role of the jury "as spokesman for the community's sense of values" and affirmed "trust in the jury . . . [as] one of the cornerstones of our entire criminal jurisprudence."[40] The evidence produced in this chapter shows that Judge Bazelon's disappointment with the majority's antinullification decision was needless; in practice, the jury maintains a robust willingness to amend or totally ignore laws that displease them. At times the jurors in effect become legislators—infusing their responses to trials with their political beliefs about the proper direction of public policy.

However, most of the time juries do *not* legislate; they take the law as is. Relatively few legal norms are in disrepute, so jury nullification is not normally on jurors' minds or in their hearts. Although jurors are uneasy about convicting for trivial crimes or folk crimes, much of the jury's workload deals with offenses considered to be quite serious. The jury has few qualms about laws dealing with murder, robbery, rape, and assault—offenses that endanger people's lives and property.

We have seen that the nullification issue takes place in the context of public sentiment about laws and their application. The political milieu in which juries function is an omnipresent phenomenon, affecting jury decisions even when jurors are in full accord with the law. It is to a consideration of how the political climate affects the way the jury handles its ordinary business that we turn our attention in the next chapter.

Notes

1. "Doctor Freed in Wife's Death," *The New York Times* (December 2, 1988), p. A20.
2. Patrick Devlin, *Trial by Jury* (London: Stevens & Sons, 1956), p. 114.
3. Oliver Wendell Holmes, *Collected Legal Papers* (New York: Harcourt, Brace, 1920), p. 237.
4. For a brief history of jury nullification, see Steven Barkan, "Jury Nullification in Political Trials," *Social Problems*, 31 (October 1983): 28–44.
5. Thomas Green, "The Jury and the English Law of Homicide, 1200–1600," *Michigan Law Review* 74 (1976): 413.
6. The Zenger case is described in detail in Valerie Hans and Neil Vidmar, *Judging the Jury* (New York: Plenum, 1986), pp. 32–35.
7. Harold Hyman and Catherine Tarrant, "Aspects of American Trial Jury History," in Rita Simon (ed.), *The Jury System in America: A Critical Overview* (Newbury Park, Calif.: Sage, 1975), pp. 23–44.
8. Harry Kalven and Hans Zeisel, *The American Jury* (Chicago: University of Chicago Press, 1971), p. 286.
9. *Sparf and Hansen* v. *United States*, 156 U.S. 151 (1896).
10. *United States* v. *Dougherty*, 473 F.2d 1113 (D.C. cir. 1972).
11. Quoted in David Aaronson (ed.), *Maryland Criminal Jury Instructions and Commentary* (Charlottesville, Va.: Michie, 1975), p. 3.
12. Gary Jacobsohn, "The Right to Disagree: Judges, Jurors, and the Administration of Justice in Maryland," *Washington University Law Quarterly* (1976): 571–607.
13. Irwin Horowitz, "The Effect of Jury Nullification Instruction on Verdicts and Jury Functioning in Criminal Trials," *Law and Human Behavior,* 9 (1985): 25–36.
14. The prosecutor's remarks are taken from Mathew Wald, "Amy Carter Is Acquitted over Protest," *The New York Times* (April 16, 1987), p. A17. The juror's comment is from "Not Guilty by Necessity," *Time,* April 27, 1987, p. 71.
15. Quoted in Barkan, "Jury Nullification in Political Trials": 36–37.
16. Steven Brill, *Trial by Jury* (New York: American Lawyer Brooks/Touchstone, 1989), p. 462.

17. "Mother Convicted of Abuse in Daughter's Suicide," *The New York Times* (November 31, 1987), p. 28.
18. Quoted in William Chambliss and Robert Seidman, *Law, Order, and Power* (Reading, Mass.: Addison-Wesley, 1971), p. 439.
19. Martha Myers, "Rule Departures and Making Law: Juries and Their Verdicts," *Law and Society Review,* 13 (1979): 781–797.
20. Kalven and Zeisel, *The American Jury,* pp. 286–297.
21. James Levine, "Using Jury Verdict Forecasts in Criminal Defense Strategy," *Judicature,* 66 (1983): 452.
22. "Arkansas Farmer Who Defied Court Found Innocent," *Rocky Mountain News* (June 3, 1983), p. 47; Lynda Schuster, "A Missouri Farmer Gets His Beans Back and Becomes a Hero," *The Wall Street Journal* (May 12, 1982): 1; Jury Acquits Farmer in Seizure of Soybeans," *The New York Times* (June 3, 1983), p. A16.
23. Daniel Schorr, "Thoughts on Serving in a Seat of Judgment," *The New York Times* (April 25, 1974), p. 39.
24. Kalven and Zeisel, *The American Jury,* p. 42.
25. Levine, "Using Jury Verdict Forecasts in Criminal Defense Strategy": 458; James Levine, "The Impact of Crime Seriousness on Jury Verdicts," unpublished manuscript, Department of Political Science, Brooklyn College (1983).
26. Levine, "Using Jury Verdict Forecasts in Criminal Defense Strategy": 451.
27. An analysis of 209 jury trials for drunk driving in Boston, Denver, and Los Angeles revealed a conviction rate of 55 percent, well below the average in criminal cases. And in cases where the evidence showed a blood alcohol content level of less than .20, the conviction rate of juries was only 50 percent. See John Snortum, Paul Riva, and Dale Berger, "Police Documentation of Drunk-Driving Arrests: Jury Verdicts and Guilty Pleas as a Function of Quantity and Quality of Evidence," *Journal of Criminal Justice,* 18 (1990): 99–116.
28. Kalven and Zeisel, *The American Jury,* pp. 287–289.
29. "Death and Hunter's Trial Pose Tough Questions," *The New York Times* (October 22, 1990), p. A12.
30. "2 in Detroit Acquitted of Arson in Fires at House Tied to Drug Deals," *The New York Times* (October 8, 1988), p. 1; Isabel Wilkerson, " 'Crack House' Fire: Justice or Vigilantism?" *The New York Times* (October 22, 1988), p. 1.
31. Kalven and Zeisel, *The American Jury,* p. 251.
32. The rape conviction data through 1980 was reported in Levine, "Using Jury Verdict Forecasts in Criminal Defense Strategy": 455; subsequent data was obtained from successive volumes of the *Annual Report of the Director of the Administrative Offices of the U.S. Courts* (Washington, D.C.: U.S. Government Printing Office).
33. Hubert Field and Leigh Bienen, *Jurors and Rape: A Study of Psychology and Law* (Lexington, Mass.: Lexington Books, 1980), p. 121; Julie Weir and Lawrence Wrightsman, "The Determinants of Mock Jurors' Verdicts in a Rape Case," *Journal of Applied Social Psychology,* 20, part 2 (June 1990): 901–919.
34. J. Marsh, A. Geist, and N. Caplan, *Rape and the Limits of Law Reform* (Boston: Auburn House, 1982), pp. 56–57.
35. For a discussion of the civil rights laws of the 1960s and their implementation, see John Hope Franklin, *From Slavery to Freedom: A History of Negro Americans,* 5th ed. (New York: Knopf, 1980), pp. 473–498.
36. Data on civil rights verdicts were obtained from the *Annual Report of the Director of the Administrative Office of the U.S. Courts.*
37. *Report of the National Advisory Commission on Civil Disorders* (New York: Bantam Books, 1968), p. 1.
38. James Levine, "The Legislative Role of Juries," *American Bar Foundation Research Journal,* 1984 (Summer): 605–634.
39. *Gillette* v. *United States,* 401 U. S. 437 (1971).
40. *United States* v. *Dougherty,* 473 F2d. 1113 (D.C. cir. 1972).

7

. . . .

The Political

Climate

In the mid-1970s, I was part of a Brooklyn jury that convicted a man of aggravated assault for punching a subway passenger and causing him to lose the sight of one eye. It was a fairly cut-and-dried case in which the only questions were whether police had arrested the right man and whether he intended to cause serious bodily harm. Most of my co-jurors were absolutely certain of guilt before we even started deliberations, but two of us insisted on several hours of discussion before returning a guilty verdict and going our separate ways.

Several years later, I was again called for jury duty and, strangely enough, ran into two members of the earlier jury as we assembled in the central jury hall. As I approached them, I overheard one (Vinny) say to the other: "Eli, how are you? Who are we going to fry this time?" Eli responded, "I don't know, Vinny, but I'm drooling!" On one level, it was a meaningless joke between two jurors briefly reestablishing a bit of camaraderie; on another level, it was a deadly serious revelation about the way jurors often behave. Vinny and Eli were sharing deep-seated feelings about crime and revealing their zeal to make guilty people pay.

In this chapter we shall see that Vinny and Eli are not atypical; *all* jurors bring to bear their own distinctive ideologies as they engage in the process of reaching verdicts. It is the community that provides jurors, and it is the political climate of the community that influences where the jury will stand on key issues. Dominant ideologies affect the making of verdicts.

The Liberal–Conservative Schism

Ideologies, general views about the nature of society and feelings about how government should act, are an inevitable element in the functioning of the criminal justice system. It has been said that they are the "permanent hidden agenda" that affects the day-to-day decision making of police, prosecutors, judges, and corrections personnel.[1] These sentiments about the appropriate way to deal with the crime problem certainly help determine how discretion is exercised at all stages of case processing, including adjudication by jurors.

Attitudes toward crime and criminals are complex, but differences often boil down to the clash between liberalism and conservatism. It is the split between an ideology emphasizing the rights of the accused (the liberals) and an ideology focusing on the harm that criminals do to victims and to the society (the conservatives). What is at stake are the competing demands of two intrinsically conflicting value systems—the due process ideal of protecting the innocent and the norm of crime control geared to maintaining social order. This profound value conflict, which greatly affects the ballot-box decisions of voters and the actions of politicians, influences jurors as well.

This choice process pivots around a central criterion in the jury decision-making process: how convincing must the evidence be in order to convict? For centuries, English and American courts have said that the applicable legal standard in criminal cases is that guilt must be established beyond a reasonable doubt. Furthermore, the Supreme Court ruled in *In re Winship*[2] that use of this traditional standard is a constitutional requirement grounded on the assumption that it is far worse to convict an innocent man than to let a guilty man go free. But a moment's reflection shows that the word "reasonable" is fraught with ambiguity: how much evidence is enough evidence and how much doubt is too much doubt?

Judges' instructions do very little to clarify the meaning of reasonable doubt, a point confirmed by experimental research that shows subjects are quite confused by the concept.[3] Consider the attempt of the California Penal Code to define the term, borrowing the words of an 1850 Massachusetts court decision:

> Reasonable doubt is . . . not a mere possible doubt; because everything relating to human affairs and depending on moral evidence, is open to some possible or imaginary doubt. It is that state of the case, which, after the entire comparison and consideration of all the evidence, leaves the minds of jurors in that condition that they cannot say they feel an abiding conviction, to a moral certainty, of the truth of the charge.[4]

That's an important point: you don't need absolute certainty to convict, you need "moral" certainty. But what is moral certainty?

The obscurity of this notion has led a number of jurisdictions to abandon the quest for definition and simply leave jurors on their own to figure out the proper threshold. This is the policy announced by the Illinois Supreme

THE POLITICAL CLIMATE

Court: "Reasonable doubt is a term which needs no elaboration and we have so frequently discussed the futility of attempting to define it that we might expect the practice to be discontinued."[5] So whether courts try to explain reasonable doubt or leave it undefined, a semantic gap remains, and it is ideology that helps jurors give meaning to this inherently uncertain standard.

Extreme liberals need overwhelming proof in order to convict. They are devoutly committed to the presumption of innocence and quite worried about mistakenly convicting truly innocent defendants. Many liberals are concerned about an apparent inequality in the legal system that seems to put the poor in more jeopardy than the affluent. The liberal version of justice often includes considerable compassion toward the accused, who are seen as having led hard lives not completely of their own making. And liberals are concerned about overcriminalization, the broad reach of the law that penalizes and stigmatizes defendants whose transgressions may not have been all that bad. Put all these perspectives together, and you have jurors who are disinclined to convict and therefore very demanding in evaluating the strength of the prosecution's case.

On the opposite side are the extreme conservatives who will convict without hesitation. They are angry about the breakdown in "law and order"—the erosion of public safety, the damage done to victims' lives, and the depravity of the criminals who did it. Most conservatives are very troubled about the prospects of letting truly guilty people free to walk the streets, possibly to repeat their crimes. Many believe that the courts are too lenient and that procedural rights often become loopholes for letting criminals off the hook. Their heavy emphasis on individual responsibility for one's actions makes conservatives indisposed to consider mitigating circumstances. Theirs is an Old Testament brand of justice: an eye for an eye and a tooth for a tooth. In some cases, these are people with authoritarian personalities who have deep-seated psychological needs to control and punish.[6] All in all, extreme conservatives are a tough-minded lot whose rancor toward the accused makes them conviction-oriented.

We have just described two ends of a broad spectrum; most people and most jurors fall somewhere in between. There is a liberal–conservative scale, from far left (extreme liberalism) to far right (extreme conservatism) rather than a polarization of two camps 180 degrees apart. But make no mistake about it: there are very real differences in the way jurors with different ideological bents assess the evidence and reach conclusions. Where a juror stands on the scale, how he or she weighs the conflicting goals of due process and crime control, has a strong bearing on the propensity to convict.

Empirical research has shown substantial variation in the way individuals interpret the reasonable doubt guideline. When student respondents in a survey were asked to compare the undesirability of convicting a person who was really innocent with the undesirability of acquitting a person who was actually guilty, substantial differences emerged.[7] Virtually everyone was more upset by the prospect of a wrongful conviction, but almost no one was as

120

demanding as the great jurist William Blackstone, who once said it was *ten times* as bad to convict an innocent defendant as to acquit a guilty one. Whereas some respondents thought that an erroneous conviction was many times more harmful than an erroneous acquittal, others thought the two unfortunate outcomes were much closer in harmfulness.

Real jurors display the same kind of differences when probed about reasonable doubt. When Illinois jurors were asked what probability of guilt they could put up with and still convict, the answers ranged from none, meaning they required absolute certainty, to less than 50 percent, meaning they would convict even if the odds were less than 50–50 that the person was truly guilty.[8] There are jurors like Eli and Vinny, mentioned at the beginning of this chapter, for whom virtually *any* incriminating evidence is good enough, even if substantial doubt remained; they might convict on the basis of perceiving a defendant's "evil eye." On the other hand, there are those who insist that no doubt whatsoever remain; one Detroit juror said after an acquittal that he would never convict unless there was a motion picture of the event.[9] And then there are the mass of middle-of-the-roaders who fall somewhere in between.

These are not minor quibbles; they often spell the difference between guilty and not guilty verdicts. This was demonstrated in a sample survey of the Yolo County, California, jurors who were asked their opinions about three pending criminal cases in which defense attorneys had requested a change of venue. Among other things, potential jurors were asked about their general attitudes toward crime and punishment. Those jurors who manifested conservative values were substantially more predisposed to prejudge guilt than liberal respondents,[10] a finding confirmed by other research.[11]

Thus, jurors carry their ideological viewpoints and disagreements about the proper way to cope with crime into the courtroom and into the jury room. To understand jury decision making, we must look at the political climate that may be reflected in the ideological composition of the jury. Jury politics in part entails struggles between liberal and conservative perspectives, and the fate of defendants is to some degree dependent on which of these conflicting viewpoints holds sway.

The Legacy of Jury Leniency

Part of the folklore about the American and British legal systems is that juries are a source of leniency. It is commonly thought that there is an ingrained liberalism within the jury, a tendency to give defendants the benefit of the doubt and to insist on very compelling evidence before convicting. Blackstone certainly thought so, commenting that trial by jury was the "grand bulwark of [our] liberties" and "the most transcendent privilege which a subject can enjoy."[12] This notion, that juries are by nature a protection against unfair or erroneous prosecutions, is certainly one reason that the right to trial by jury in federal courts was put into the Constitution and later made binding in states courts as part of the Fourteenth Amendment's due process requirement. Indeed, Supreme Court opinions have glorified the jury as a protection "against the corrupt or overzealous prosecutor and against the compliant, biased, or eccentric judge."[13]

The idea of jury leniency is plausible enough. First, perceiving a David-and-Goliath aspect in trials, juries may sympathize with the "little person" being unfairly treated by a too-powerful criminal justice system. Second, because jurors don't routinely deal with criminals, they may be less hardened and perhaps more believing than police, prosecutors, and judges, who are continuously seeing the worst side of human nature. Third, juries may function as a "safety valve," humanizing the law by permitting deviations from it for the sake of justice. Fourth, jurors may have doubts about the soundness of the laws in question and therefore may be reluctant to convict people of violating them. And finally, as outsiders to the legal system, jurors have no organizational or political interests at stake in securing lots of convictions.

Systematic data have been gathered over the years to substantiate the notion of jury leniency. In 1922, the Cleveland trial courts were studied by the great legal scholars Roscoe Pound and Felix Frankfurter (Frankfurter later became a justice on the Supreme Court). After noting the 600 percent rise in acquittals since 1914, Pound and Frankfurter concluded that "the average jury errs much more on the side of leniency than severity."[14] To drive the point home, they quoted the words of an outraged trial court judge after receiving a verdict of acquittal: "It is apparently now lawful to attack a man with an axe, provided the blunt side only is used."[15] Their portrait of the jury is an assemblage of "bleeding hearts" and gullible fools.

This report can be discounted as unscientific because it relies heavily on anecdotes and opinions. But the overall thrust of it supports the central finding of Kalven and Zeisel's comprehensive study of the jury done in the mid-1950s. Judges presiding over 3,576 jury trials throughout the country disagreed with the verdicts of the jury in 22 percent of the cases, and in 86 percent of the cases in which the judge and the jury were at odds, the judge would have convicted defendants the jury actually acquitted.[16] Massive analysis of the data, taking into account hung juries and multiple charges, led the authors to conclude that there was a "marked imbalance" in favor of the defendant.[17]

A study of the outcomes of bench trials and jury trials in federal district courts validates the results obtained by Kalven and Zeisel.[18] Inspection of Figure 7-1 shows that actually juries were more lenient than judges in the 1950s, when Kalven and Zeisel did their study (assuming that judges and juries heard a relatively similar mix of cases). In fact, juries acquitted more frequently in sixteen out of the eighteen years between 1945 and 1962.

But careful readers of the Kalven and Zeisel study noted a major caveat in their results. As the researchers themselves cautioned, there was no inherent directionality to the jury's decision. In their words: "[The jury] is not

122

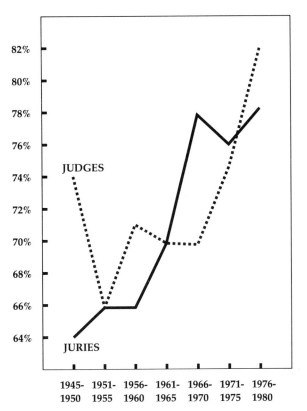

FIGURE 7-1

Conviction rates
by federal juries
and judges,
1945–1980

Source: James P. Levine, "Jury Toughness: The Impact of Conservatism on Criminal Court Verdicts," *Crime and Delinquency* 29 (January 1983): 84. Reprinted by permission.

fundamentally defendant-prone, rather it is non–rule minded; it will move where the equities are. And where the equities are at any given time will depend on both the state of the law and the climate of public opinion."[19] Further scrutiny of Figure 7-1 shows their words to be prophetic, as jury leniency seemed to disappear in the 1960s and early 1970s. This turnabout in jury decision making is not surprising, as the jury's behavior is always a product of the times and a manifestation of ongoing political currents. American society underwent tremendous changes in the last generation, and as we shall now see, the jury responded accordingly.

The Trend toward Jury Toughness

The late 1950s and especially the 1960s witnessed an explosion of concern for those accused of crime, but there was a national change of heart in the 1970s and 1980s. The tide turned against the accused almost everywhere; the

Supreme Court became more cautious in expanding defendants' rights, legislatures made criminal penalties more severe, judges imposed longer sentences, and the death penalty returned after a decade of constitutional challenge and nonuse. Jury behavior was no exception, as juries forsook their traditional leniency and cracked down.

There is considerable evidence in support of this notion. A further perusal of Figure 7-1 shows that jury conviction rates in federal courts shot up abruptly in the 1960s. In the 1940s, only about 60 percent of defendants were convicted, and the conviction rate hovered around the two-thirds mark in the 1950s; but in the next two decades, juries convicted more than three-fourths of the defendants before them. Indeed, juries became *more* stringent than judges for about ten years, until 1977, when bench trial convictions also catapulted, perhaps owing to the appointment of so many conservative judges by Presidents Nixon and Ford. Approaching the 1980s, toughness characterized jury decision making.

The transformation of the jury is demonstrated by state and local court data from the 1970s as well. An examination of criminal trial verdicts in felony cases rendered by judges and juries in six states, a large county of a seventh state, and the District of Columbia by and large supports the federal district court data. The results are reported in Table 7-1: in all but one of these jurisdictions, jury conviction rates were higher than those of the judges.

Jury severity is pervasive, persistent, and pronounced. The results reported in Table 7-1 are from all over the nation—East, West, Midwest, and South. In states and local courts where crimes involving attacks on persons or property dominate the docket, the jury convicted more often than the judges in *twenty out of twenty-one* years for which data were available. Jury conviction rates rose five years in succession in California and three years in a row in both Florida and Connecticut. In fact, totaling the findings from the separate jurisdictions reveals that juries convicted in 74 percent of 44,886 cases, whereas judges convicted only in 64 percent of the 13,450 bench trials.

These results are consistent with the findings of Roper and Flango, who looked at 22,812 verdicts in felony trials rendered in 1978 in a set of somewhat different jurisdictions. Juries convicted 72 percent of the time; judges presiding in trials without juries convicted in 58 percent of the cases.[20] The 1970s were not a decade of jury leniency.

An update of some of the findings reported in Figure 7-1 and Table 7-1 done for this book shows that juries remained tough in the 1980s.[21] In the federal district courts, the trend toward greater toughness continued as the jury conviction rate soared to 80 percent between 1981 and 1987. The jury "outconvicted" the judges during this period by two percentage points, even though the federal bench was filled with Reagan appointees not known for their softness.

Analysis of recent verdict data from the California courts produces results strikingly similar to the federal court results.[22] Between 1982 and 1988, juries in that state convicted at a rate of 82 percent to the judges' 80 percent conviction

125

TABLE 7-1

Verdicts of juries and judges in felony cases

Jurisdiction	Time period	Length of time (years)	Jury conviction rate (%)	Number of jury trials	Judge conviction rate (%)	Number of bench trials	Number of years juries harsher than judges
California	1976–80	5	82.8	21,314	78.4	6,005	5 of 5
Connecticut	1975, 77, 79	3	63.8	337	18.3	115	3 of 3
District of Columbia Superior Court	1974–75	1	79.2	1,060	51.4	331	1 of 1
Federal District Courts	1961–80	20	75.3	79,969	74.7	37,142	11 of 20
Florida	1978–80	3	62.2	7,375	55.6	2,767	3 of 3
Illinois	1978	1	70.6	1,237	52.8	2,103	1 of 1
Massachusetts (Middlesex County)	1978–80	3	60.2	398	64.2	187	2 of 3
New Jersey	1978–79	2	61.4	4,914	41.4	755	2 of 2
New York	1977–79	3	70.6	8,251	60.6	1,287	3 of 3

Source: James P. Levine, "Jury Toughness: The Impact of Conservatism on Criminal Court Verdicts," *Crime and Delinquency,* 29 (January 1983): 78. Reprinted by permission.

rate. The federal court percentages for the 1980s are based on nearly 45,000 trials and the California findings emerge from over 31,000 trials, so the tough-mindedness of the jury is surely no fluke occurrence.

The reader may be uneasy about the judge–jury comparisons we have just made. After all, it might be asked, how do we know that the types of cases heard with and without juries are similar? Although scrutiny of large numbers of cases makes it likely that the two groups of cases involve a roughly equal proportion of strong and weak prosecutions, it could well be that more guilty-appearing defendants chose the jury trial, believing jurors to be more lenient than judges. In other words, the cases before judges and juries could be differentially strong: defendants with more damaging evidence against them may be more likely to select juries. The appearance of jury harshness in all the verdict data could be an illusion.

Martha Myers' study of verdicts in the District of Columbia Superior Court goes far to eliminate this possibility.[23] Her analysis, too, showed juries to be tougher than judges, but by analyzing the characteristics of individual cases, she was able to conclude that there was virtually no difference be-tween the two caseloads. Judges and juries dealt with a similar mix of charges; there was the same ratio of acquaintance crimes to stranger crimes; the amount of harm done to victims was about the same; the average amount of incriminating evidence was more or less equal; and the numbers of defen-dants with prior records varied little. All in all, these results add credibility to the other findings reported in this section and reinforce the idea that the jury of today has a penchant for conviction.

Why the jury has become so tough is no mystery. Nationwide crime rose dramatically in the 1960s: reported robberies per capita *tripled* between 1965 and 1970, and murders went up 53 percent. The inaccuracies of crime data and the distortions about crime rendered by the media notwithstanding, there *was* a "crime wave."[24] Moreover, although crime rates leveled off in the mid-1970s, they leveled off at a very high plateau, leaving many communities in the grip of serious crime problems. Juries, like judges, are buffeted by events, and one of the central realities of our time is the onslaught of crime.

Jurors have responded like the public at large; they have embraced con-servatism when it comes to criminal justice issues. Although Republican Barry Goldwater was beaten badly when he ran for president in 1964, his message decrying lawlessness and violence took hold. Four years later, Richard Nixon made the breakdown of law and order a centerpiece of his successful cam-paign for the presidency, and a number of ex-police chiefs like Rizzo of Philadelphia and Stenvig of Minneapolis won mayoralties in the 1960s and 1970s by their hard-line views on crime. Ed Koch was not a former police official, but he won the first of his three four-year terms as mayor of New York City in 1977 by lashing out at crime and urging the resumption of capital punishment. In the words of political scientist Stuart Scheingold, who an-alyzed such political developments into the early 1980s: "In local as well as national politics, there has been a tendency for political leaders to call our attention to the danger of crime and promise us a crackdown."[25]

The mid to late 1980s saw no let-up in the political appeal of the "law and order" theme. In the 1988 presidential election campaign, Michael Dukakis lost his lead in the polls and the presidency to George Bush when Bush made Dukakis appear too permissive in dealing with crime. The turning point may well have been the widespread dissemination of the famous Willie Horton commercials, which included vivid pictures of a convicted murderer who committed a brutal rape while on furlough from a prison in Dukakis's home state of Massachusetts. The crime was a tragic event that Bush managed to convert into a symbol of Dukakis's alleged softness toward criminals.

Survey research bears out the nation's drift toward conservatism: in the span of only fifteen years, the percentage of people identifying themselves as liberals fell from 31 to 27 percent, whereas the number of those calling themselves conservative swelled from 29 to 34 percent.[26] Polls on capital punishment show that the gradual decline in public support for the death penalty, which fell to 42 percent in 1966, reversed itself, reaching 76 percent in 1985.[27] When the California Supreme Court overturned the death penalty in that state on the grounds that it violated the California Constitution, the voters by a 2-to-1 margin changed the constitution to restore the death penalty. And when Chief Judge Rose Bird, who authored the court's opinion, came up for reelection, she was voted out of office.

In a like vein, national surveys show that the percentage of persons who believe the courts are insufficiently harsh on criminals rose from 66 percent in 1972 to 85 percent in 1978; and in annual surveys asking the same question in the 1980s, an average of 83 percent of respondents thought the courts were too lax.[28] Moreover, there is very little variation among different groups in the population on this issue: rich and poor, black and white, male and female, young and old *all agree*.[29] There is broad public dismay and anger about the alleged coddling of criminals, and even many people who have remained faithful to liberalism in regard to economic and social welfare matters have adopted hard-nosed attitudes toward crime.

If people vote for "get-tough" candidates and favor "get-tough" policies, it isn't surprising that they act tough when they become jurors and get a chance to do something about crime. In the midst of what is perceived to be a crime siege, the jurors use their temporary power to strike back. Defendants to some degree become the targets of a quite conservative brand of jury politics.

The Local Political Culture

Up to this point we have been speaking of the United States as if it were one undifferentiated mass of like-minded people; it is not. Local political cultures vary enormously from somewhat liberal to conservative to very conservative. Jury behavior reflects these differences.

Referring back to Table 7-1, out of a variety of jurisdictions studied, the only one in which juries were more lenient than judges was Middlesex

County, Massachusetts. This is no accident: Middlesex County is one of the most liberal parts of what has become in recent decades the most liberal state in the nation. Thus, the bucking of the trend toward jury toughness in this county is a reflection of the persistence of a pocket of liberalism in a nation that has headed in the opposite direction. Jury behavior may have echoed the election returns.

The Bronx in New York City is another locale tremendously at odds with the rest of the nation. Bronx juries, overwhelmingly black and Hispanic, are as liberal as you can get in this country; their verdicts reflect this fact.[30] Plaintiffs in civil cases are disproportionately favored, winning 73 percent of jury trials (as compared with a 57 percent national average) and receiving damage awards of over $1 million in one out of every five verdicts. The largess of juries has led lawyers and court watchers to refer routinely to the Bronx as "plaintiff city." Author Tom Wolfe made this point wryly in his novel *Bonfire of the Vanities*: "In a civil case a Bronx jury is a vehicle for redistributing the wealth."[31]

The atypical political ideology of the Bronx jury extends to criminal cases as well, prompting the following headline in a *New York Times* article: "Bronx Juries: A Defense Dream, a Prosecution Nightmare."[32] The infamous Larry Davis, purported to be a major drug dealer and multiple murderer, was acquitted *twice*—this after a period of time during which he was the most wanted fugitive in New York City. Nor was this an isolated case of leniency; the acquittal rate in the Bronx is 42 percent, in comparison with 29 percent in the rest of New York City and 25 percent in suburban Westchester County, just to the north. The Bronx is *not* "middle-America," and Bronx juries, which continue to give every benefit of the doubt to defendants, reflect the liberal political culture from which they are drawn.

One must always be cautious in making too much out of findings from one or two settings, as other factors, such as different case loads or weaker prosecutions, may have been responsible for the atypical verdict patterns in Middlesex County and the Bronx. But a number of broader studies of intrastate variations in jury verdicts reveal that the political atmosphere of communities *does* affect the way jurors approach cases. Although the political pendulum may have swung to the right throughout the nation, the particular balance between liberal and conservative sentiment varies from place to place. Such nuances of difference wend their way onto the jury.

Florida is a case in point. Like all southern states, it is relatively conservative; but it is far from homogeneous. On the basis of voting patterns, one study divided the seventy-seven counties in the state into three categories: very conservative, conservative, and moderate. Juries in the 38 very conservative counties convicted 68 percent of defendants; those in the 33 moderate counties convicted 63 percent; and those in the 6 moderate counties convicted only 56 percent.[33] These differences in jury behavior are rather sharp and unlikely to be the result of chance.

An analysis of California jury behavior in the late 1980s also attests to the impact of the political climate. Anyone remotely familiar with that state's politics would have little trouble characterizing the prevailing ideology of three adjacent counties—Los Angeles, Orange County, and San Diego. Los Angeles is moderate; San Diego is conservative; Orange County is ultra-conservative. Jury behavior matches this exactly: the jury conviction rates for Los Angeles, San Diego, and Orange counties for the three years between 1986 and 1988 are 75, 83, and 90 percent, respectively.[34] A coincidence? Unlikely; rather, juries to some degree are cast in the same manner as the body politic.

Another correlation between political atmosphere and jury behavior relates to the distinction between central cities and less urban locales. Large cities are almost always more liberal; New York City is more liberal than "upstate"; Chicago is more liberal than "downstate." And data from three states— California, Florida, and New York—show that by and large the conviction rate in big cities is *lower* than that in less populated areas.[35] Jurors in big cities, despite having to live with harrowing crime problems, are less partial to the prosecution than jurors in safer areas that are more politically conservative.

This presents a predicament for defendants in highly publicized cases who are subjected to adverse publicity in large cities. Jurors living in or around the site of the crime may be eager to avenge crimes that infuriated them. However, a change of venue may well get the case transferred to a remote place where there is lower public anger about the specific crime but more negative feelings toward defendants in general. The accused may be going from the frying pan into the fire.

The dominant theme everywhere is to crack down on criminals, so we are dealing with gradations and shadings when we contrast popular attitudes. Similarly, differences in jury behavior between left-leaning, middle-of-the-road, and right-leaning political cultures are not of seismic proportions. But there are differences, and a defendant facing charges in a deeply conservative environment has a much tougher battle than a defendant tried in a community that is more liberal. Jury politics is in part local politics—the application of common sentiments about crime and criminals to the case at hand.

Juries and Police

If there is any one proposition about jury behavior that is nearly incontrovertible, it is this: juries side with the police. This is the other side of the "jury toughness" coin. Police are widely perceived as the central force protecting lawful citizens from criminals, the good guys who risk life and limb going after the bad guys who imperil the community. Consequently, most jurors are willing to bend over backward to protect police officers accused of misconduct. Stories ordinarily considered far-fetched are believed when related by police; strange defenses are accepted; compelling evidence against police is scrutinized with a fine-tooth comb; and reasonable doubt is stretched to the limit. When it comes to police, jury leniency abounds.

A classic case emerged from the Democratic National Convention held in Chicago in 1968, where massive protests against the Vietnam War took place. Police responded with such fury and violence that a subsequent report commissioned by the government characterized the affair as a "police riot."[36] Among those victimized by the swinging clubs of the police were fifty newspeople covering the story, including *Chicago Daily News* reporter John Linstead, who required several stitches in his skull. The federal government prosecuted several officers for violating Linstead's civil rights, and at the trial it was shown that the only thing Linstead had done was to yell "Cut that out, you motherfucker!" in an attempt to intervene on behalf of some civilians being beaten up by police. Testimony of nine eyewitnesses and a film of the incident analyzed frame by frame all pointed to one verdict—guilty.

But that is not how things turned out: the officers were all acquitted. The jury apparently broadened its focus to consider whether or not police should be supported when they and the community confront disruption. The defense attorney shrewdly plied the law-and-order theme, arguing in his summation: "We have a thin, blue line between anarchy and law and order. Please do not, by returning a verdict of anything but innocent, make that thin blue line dissolve."[37] The jury accommodated, its conservative ideology absolving police in the face of very damning evidence.

The same pro-police bias often occurs when police are victims; God help the defendant accused of killing a cop—because juries won't. Conservatives consider slaying or assaulting a police officer an even worse offense than attacking a citizen, because it is perceived as attacking the upholders of law and order. A major survey of citizens' rating of crime seriousness placed killing a police officer at the very top of the list, as compared to other types of murder such as impulsively killing a spouse (which comes in 19th) or killing someone after a barroom argument (which ranks 36th).[38] To kill a police officer is to incur the community's wrath.

The tendency of jurors to take the police's side, whether police are victims or defendants, is often compounded by jurors' racial biases (to be discussed in detail in the next chapter). Many incidents that involve the police entail officers who are white and citizens who are black, so juries that are predominantly or exclusively white may "tilt" toward police because they tilt against blacks. The pro-police and anti-black biases become "double whammies" against the prosecution of allegedly malfeasant police. After the jury ruled in favor of Wrightsville, Georgia, sheriff's police accused of threatening, beating, and shooting at forty-eight blacks in a series of incidents, one juror said: "It wasn't only a matter of racial prejudice. It was also a matter of empathy for law enforcement officers and particularly on behalf of men who had served in the military, feeling that the sheriff was justified."[39]

Although jurors are usually sympathetic to police, there are circumstances when the pro-police posture diminishes. First, juries seem somewhat less receptive to the police's point of view when defendants have "clean hands." People who get into encounters with police typically have done

130

something wrong, and the issue is whether police have overreacted. But there are also cases such as that of Anthony Byrd, who was severely brutalized by police whose help he sought after having been robbed on a New York subway train. A jury found Byrd absolutely blameless in the entire incident and awarded him $2.7 million.[40] The implication is that police who go after criminals to subdue them are given more than the benefit of the doubt by juries, but juries balk at underwriting police heavy-handedness against completely innocent individuals.

A second situation in which juries may turn against police is when police officers themselves provide the damaging evidence against their colleagues. This rarely happens, because there is an unwritten norm among police called the "buddy code" that discourages police from informing on each other. When the code is broken and police testify about the wrongdoing of other officers, the jury's reflexive acceptance of police justifications for the use of force is suspended. This is what happened in Milwaukee when a police officer came forward twenty years after Daniel Bell was killed by police during a traffic incident to relate how his partner had planted a knife on the dead man's body to justify a claim of self-defense. Not only was the officer's partner convicted of reckless homicide and perjury, but a federal jury awarded $1.79 million to the family of the deceased in a civil rights suit.[41]

Another qualification of the jury's partiality toward police are cases of police acting sheerly out of self-interest rather than in pursuit of professional responsibilities. Police in uniform who abuse their authority as a means of dealing with private conflicts to which they are parties lose some of the respect they are normally given. Off-duty police accused of committing crimes seem to be treated by juries like anyone else.

Finally, let us not lose sight of the fact brought out earlier that all communities are not the same, nor are the juries that come from them. Those enclaves of liberalism that produce greater-than-average positive feelings toward defendants also feature some animosity toward police. This reversal of the normally pro-police bias of jurors was keenly noted by a Bronx prosecutor who must cope with it: "It's bizarre. Everything here is truly stood on its head. The jurors are overwhelmingly suspicious of cops. If you have a case involving cops [as the main prosecution witnesses], you are almost certain to lose."[42]

131

Conclusion

The day after Ronald Reagan was shot in Washington, D.C., when it was still not certain whether he would recover, a *New York Daily News* reporter was covering the courthouse beat. Earl Caldwell sensed something in the air as he walked around—a feeling that seated jurors and jurors-to-be were deeply affected by the previous day's events. Caldwell wandered into a murder trial, one that never made the papers, and sagely sized up what was going on:

On the streets yesterday, it was the way it always is now after an attempt has been made on the life of an important public figure. People were saying they were fed up, that it was time that something be done. But all of it was just words. . . .

In the courtroom, though, it was different. The jurors make decisions. They have the power to act, and yesterday the talk in the courthouse was that it was the worst possible time for a case involving killing and a gun to be put in the hands of the jury.[43]

Caldwell was speaking of the political climate. What we have shown in this chapter is that the same balance between liberalism and conservatism that often determines which politicians are elected also affects the way jurors view cases. The political ethos of the community wends its way into the jury room—making jurors more or less eager to convict.

The pro-defendant leniency of old has given way to toughness. Experience with crime, fear of crime, and anger about crime have engendered conservative responses. The net result has been a nationwide trend toward more convictions at the hands of juries. But not all jurors and juries are the same; the degree of toughness in some measure depends on the political climate of the environment from which juries are drawn. This applies also to juries' attitudes toward police: the counterpart to jury hostility toward defendants is support for police, but in areas where police are in disrepute, they cannot count on verdicts in their favor.

Notes

1. Walter Miller, "Ideology and Criminal Justice Policy: Some Current Issues," *Journal of Criminal Law and Criminology* 64 (June 1973): 141–162.
2. *In re Winship*, 397 U.S. 358 (1970).
3. Norbert Kerr, Robert Atkin, Garold Stasser, David Meek, Robert Holt, and James Davis, "Guilt Beyond a Reasonable Doubt: Effect of Concept Definition and Assigned Decision Rule on the Judgments of Mock Jurors," *Journal of Personality and Social Psychology*, 34 (1976): 282–293.
4. California Penal Code § 1096 [cited in Fred Inbau, *et al.*, *Cases and Comments on Criminal Procedure*, 2nd ed. (Mineola, N.Y.: The Foundation Press, 1980), p. 1413.]. The Massachusetts case is *Commonwealth* v. *Massachusetts*, 59 Mass. 295 (1850).
5. *People* v. *Malmenato*, 14 Ill. 2d 52, 150 N.E. 2d. 806 (1986).
6. Robert Bray and Audrey Noble, "Authoritarianism and Decisions of Mock Juries: Evidence of Jury Bias and Group Polarization," *Journal of Personality and Social Psychology*, 36 (1978): 1424–1430.
7. Stuart Nagel, "Bringing the Value of Jurors in Line with the Law," *Judicature* 63 (1979): 189–193.
8. Rita Simon and Linda Mahan, "Quantifying Burdens of Proof," *Law and Society Review* 5 (February 1971): 319–330.
9. Paula DiPerna, *Juries on Trial: Faces of American Justice* (New York: Dembner Books, 1984), p. 223.
10. Edmond Constantini and Joel King, "The Partial Juror: Correlates and Causes of Prejudgment," *Law and Society Review*, 15 (1980–81): 36.
11. Martin Kaplan and Lynn Miller "Reducing the Effects of Juror Bias," *Journal of Personality and Social Psychology*, 36 (1978): 1443.

12. William Blackstone, *Commentaries*, vol. 4 (London, England: Oxford, 1769), p. 342.
13. *Duncan v. Louisiana*, 391 U.S. 145 (1968).
14. Roscoe Pound and Felix Frankfurter (eds.), *Criminal Justice in Cleveland* (Cleveland: The Cleveland Foundation, 1922), p. 340.
15. *Ibid.*
16. Harry Kalven and Hans Zeisel, *The American Jury* (Chicago: University of Chicago Press, 1966), pp. 55–59.
17. *Ibid.*, p. 60.
18. James Levine, "Jury Toughness: The Impact of Conservatism on Criminal Court Verdicts," *Crime and Delinquency* 29 (January 1983): 71–87.
19. Kalven and Zeisel, *The American Jury*, p. 495.
20. Robert Roper and Victor Flango, "Trial before Judges and Juries," *The Justice System Journal*, 8 (Summer 1983): 186–198.
21. Data were obtained from National Institute of Justice, *Sourcebook of Criminal Justice Statistics 1988* (Washington, D.C.: National Institute of Justice, 1988).
22. Data was obtained from the 1985 through 1989 volumes of Judicial Council of California, *Annual Report*, Table A-26.
23. Martha Myers, "Judges, Juries, and the Decision to Convict," *Journal of Criminal Justice* 9 (1981): 289–303.
24. James Wilson, *Thinking about Crime*, rev. ed. (New York: Basic Books, 1983), pp. 13–25.
25. Stuart Scheingold, *The Politics of Law and Order: Street Crime and Public Policy* (New York: Longman, 1984), p. 78.
26. Harold Stanley and Richard Niemi, *Vital Statistics on American Politics*, 2nd. ed. (Washington, D.C.: CQ Press, 1990), p. 148.
27. *Ibid.*, p. 31.
28. Levine, "Jury Toughness":83; National Institute of Justice, *Sourcebook of Criminal Justice Statistics 1989* (Washington, D.C.: U.S. Government Printing Office): 160–161.
29. *Ibid.*, p. 159.
30. Sam Roberts, "On Bronx Juries, Minority Groups Find Their Peers," *The New York Times* (April 19, 1988), p. B1; John Kifner, "Bronx Juries: A Defense Dream, a Prosecutor's Nightmare," *The New York Times* (December 5, 1988), p. B1.
31. Tom Wolfe, *Bonfire of the Vanities* (New York: Farrar, Strauss, 1987), p. 392.
32. Kifner, "Bronx Juries," p. B1.
33. James Levine, "The Influence of Political Ideology on Jury Decision-Making," unpublished manuscript, Brooklyn College, 1982.
34. The analysis done for this book was based on data taken from the 1987, 1988, and 1989 volumes of Judicial Council of California, *Annual Report*, Table A-26.
35. James Levine, "Using Jury Verdict Forecasts in Criminal Defense Strategy," *Judicature* 66 (May 1983): 460–461; Levine, "Jury Toughness": 81.
36. Daniel Walker, *Rights in Conflict: The Violent Confrontation of Demonstrators and Police in the Parks and Streets of Chicago During the Week of the Democratic National Convention of 1968* (New York: New American Library, 1968).
37. "Verdict in Chicago," *Newsweek* (June 23, 1969): 92.
38. Peter Rossi, Emily Waite, Christine Base, and Richard Berk, "The Seriousness of Crimes: Normative Structure and Individual Differences," *American Sociological Review*, 39 (April 1974): 228–229.
39. Quoted in DiPerna, *Juries on Trial*, p. 170.
40. Patricia Hurtado, "Man Wins TA Lawsuit," *New York Newsday* (January 1, 1989), p. 3.
41. "Million Awarded for Killing in '58," *The New York Times* (December 18, 1981), p. A24.
42. Kifner, "Bronx Juries," p. B4.
43. Earl Caldwell, "In Our Courtrooms, .22 Aims Bulletins at Minds of Jurors," *New York Daily News* (April 1, 1981), p. 6. Reprinted by permission.

133

8

·······

Juror

Biases

"**J**urymen seldom convict a person they like or acquit one they don't," said the preeminent trial lawyer Clarence Darrow over half a century ago.[1] His words were echoed at a recent trial lawyers' convention. "Get each juror to think that 'there's a reasonable doubt' because he's a nice guy and I like him," advised one lawyer. "Juries vote based on their impressions, their feelings, their biases, and their prejudices, not the facts of the case," stated another.[2]

Judges, too, have theorized that biases influence verdicts. Judge Jerome Frank, whose ideas on fact-skepticism were discussed in Chapter 1, talked about prejudice as the "thirteenth juror." In his view, two witnesses whose testimony is never recorded are everpresent in the courtroom: "Mr. Prejudice" and "Miss Sympathy."[3] The routine admonitions by judges that jurors must disregard personal prejudice are dismissed as ritualistic incantations that often reach deaf ears. According to Judge Frank, deep-seated likes and dislikes cannot be so easily expunged.

The words of lawyers and judges have been echoed by jurors themselves. A New York City juror explained why his jury acquitted reputed mobster William (Billy the Butcher) Masselli: "We liked him."[4] A British professor who served as a juror reported that one of the other members of the jury steadfastly declined to believe a witness because he did not like the look of his face.[5]

But how valid are the opinions of a few lawyers, a judge, and a couple of jurors?

How much in fact do preconceived opinions about people, based on who they are rather than on what they did, affect the rendering of verdicts? Answers to these questions are the topic of this chapter.

The Nature of Jury Bias

By what process may biases of jurors influence verdicts? The most direct way is blatant discrimination: jurors act out their dislikes of certain kinds of people by construing the evidence in a way that works against the people they dislike. In its more extreme form, the hostility is so intense that the jurors disregard the evidence altogether; the verdict for all practical purposes comes *before* the trial.

There is another side to bias, a more subtle way in which one's preexisting attitudes about people may affect the judgment process. It is stereotyping—the use of unreliable generalizations about all members of a group that fail to account for individual differences within the group. Voluminous research has demonstrated that such exaggerated and distorted images of the characteristics of particular groups are pervasive in the United States.[6]

Everyone engages in stereotyping at one time or another for the simple reason that it is often necessary to make snap decisions about people when a more careful judgment is not feasible. In deciding whom to sit next to on a bus late at night or whom to ask for directions when we are in a strange neighborhood, we size people up according to visible cues—their race, age, appearance, and so forth. In our minds we have pictures of safe and unsafe people, stereotypes based on prior experience or what we have been taught, and we rely on them as shortcuts in making judgments. It is possible for jurors, also confronted with insufficient facts, to do the same thing in deciding verdicts.

This practice can have pernicious consequences. First, stereotypes can be all wrong; it is *not* true that most Irishmen are drunks; it is *not* true that most Jews are chiselers; it is *not* true that most blacks are thugs. Second, even when there is a grain of truth to stereotypes, they are always probability judgments and therefore may be erroneous when applied to a specific case. Just because most elderly women are honest does not mean that the one on trial is; the fact that many young males drive recklessly (as reflected in their higher insurance rates) does not by itself mean that the one accused of manslaughter was driving wildly.

Stereotyping, to a greater or lesser extent, pervades the criminal justice system. In fact, a special phrase was coined to describe the image that police carry in their minds about who is likely to be dangerous; the person to watch out for is called the "symbolic assailant."[7] Police must act quickly, sometimes in a split second, when they decide which cars to pull over, whether to draw their guns, and how tough to be in making an arrest. They make shorthand judgments based on people's personal characteristics, such as race, age, and gender, or some combination thereof. Often they are right but sometimes they are wrong—with potentially tragic consequences.

To what extent do jurors engage in stereotyping? It is possible that jurors, who are deciding things in a much calmer and less threatening environment than the police, are in a better position to study the facts free of preconceptions. But perhaps not; it may be that because jurors lack professional training and role constraints, they engage in more stereotyping. Indeed, a recent jury simulation that varied the defendants' race and the type of crime committed showed a tendency for mock jurors to engage in race-stereotypic thinking.[8] One thing is clear: like everyone else, *to some degree* they make categorical judgments about people based on lifelong experiences.

What are the consequences of stereotyping? Experimental research has shown that reliance on generalizations about types of people retards the reception of new information. One laboratory study showed that "the activation of a social stereotype elicits a selective evidence-processing strategy on the part of decision-makers."[9] In other words, greater attention is paid to external evidence consistent with the stereotype than to evidence that is inconsistent with the preconception; the latter tends to be neglected.

To what extent discrimination and stereotyping enter the juror's thinking is unclear. Jurors have a very special assignment, which they are told repeatedly must be accomplished in as objective and rational a manner as possible. Yet it is hard to cast aside biases entrenched over a lifetime, especially if issues raised by the case at hand trigger deep feelings about the defendant or victim.

In the rest of this chapter, we will be looking at some forms of bias that at times seem to affect jury decision making. The purpose is not to prove that racial or ethnic or religious or any other kind of hostility caused particular verdicts but to alert readers to the potential for such prejudiced outcomes. Bias is one element in jury politics, nothing more and nothing less.

Racism

It takes little knowledge of American history to realize how deeply bias against blacks is embedded in American culture. From the days of slavery to the days of Jim Crow to the violent resistance to civil rights in the 1960s, blacks have been subjected to unequal treatment. Segregation and discrimination have haunted blacks in many facets of life—in housing, in employment, in education, and in sports. It would be quite surprising if the jury was devoid of such racism.

An early case in which a conviction almost certainly was based on race was the Scottsboro case. In 1932, seven poor, young, black men (who became known as the "Scottsboro boys") were accused of raping two white girls on a freight train in Alabama. Twice they were quickly convicted by juries, and twice the convictions were overturned by the United States Supreme Court

136

for procedural irregularities, including the denial of counsel and the exclusion of blacks from the grand jury. One of the "boys," George Norris, was tried a third time; a jury again convicted him in short order and he served fifteen years in prison. Forty years later, he was pardoned by Governor George Wallace on the advice of the state parole board, which concluded that Norris was innocent from the outset.

In the half-century since the Scottsboro cases, race relations have improved. But racial prejudice still sometimes seems to sit as a "thirteenth juror." Some blacks are still convicted on the basis of dubious evidence, and defendants who have victimized blacks often get absolved despite persuasive evidence presented by the prosecution.

The jury trial of Lenell Geter is a case in point. The crime: the gunpoint robbery of a Kentucky Fried Chicken restaurant located in Balch Springs, Texas, netting $615. The time of the robbery: August 21, 1983 at 3:20 P.M. The defendant: a black engineer with no criminal record, making $30,000 a year. The site of the trial: Greenville, Texas (which some years ago had a road sign announcing it as "The Blackest Land—the Whitest People.") The race of the jurors: all white. The jury's verdict: guilty. The sentence (also imposed by the jury): life imprisonment.

The police had zeroed in on Geter after a Greenville woman notified them that a black man was hanging around a nearby park; she said he looked like a man wanted for another restaurant robbery. Although Geter was cleared of that robbery, police started following him and began circulating his picture to see if he was linked to other crimes. Five employees of the Kentucky Fried Chicken store picked Geter out of a photo lineup and eventually identified him as the robber. Not one iota of physical evidence was produced by the prosecution—no gun, no money, no clothing, no fingerprints.

At this point, you are probably wondering if Geter had an alibi; what better defense could there be but to show that he was somewhere else when the crime was committed? Geter was fortunate in this regard; not one, not two, but *nine* co-workers at the E-systems military and electronics research center said Geter was at work the day of the crime. Geter's supervisor testified that there was no way he could have completed all of the tasks he did that day and still make the 50-mile trip to the site of the crime. Another employee said that she had talked to Geter at about 3:00 P.M. about taking part in a Bible study group and a softball game, a conversation alleged to have taken place just twenty minutes before the robbery. All of these employees vouching for Geter's presence at the firm were white, so no one could accuse them of simply sticking up for someone of their own race. An apparently foolproof alibi—all to no avail.

What was going on in the jurors' minds? Geter was the perfect defendant—a mild-mannered, deeply religious, well-educated professional accused of a crime that made no sense from the standpoint of someone in his economic position. He had a perfect alibi; as one co-worker put it: "Unless old Captain Kirk [of the space program *Star Trek*] dematerialized him and beamed him over there [to the site of the crime], he couldn't have made it back by then. He was here at work. There's no question in my mind—none at all."[10] The prosecution's case was weak: eyewitness identifications based on fleeting glimpses of the criminal, no physical evidence whatsoever, no credible motive. Was this "guilt beyond a reasonable doubt"? Was this a man deserving of life imprisonment? What happened?

Perhaps the jury trusted the eyewitnesses' identifications and doubted the testimony of Geter's coemployees. Perhaps the jury had so much faith in the police that they could not imagine them going after the wrong man. Perhaps the jurors were simply convinced by the evidence before them. Dallas County prosecutors believed that; one of them said: "To say this is a conviction based on race is as far out in left field as you can get."[11]

But racial bias as an explanation of the verdict cannot be dismissed so quickly. The jurors no doubt genuinely believed in Geter's guilt, but what drove them to that conclusion? After the trial, one of Geter's supervisors at work had an explanation: "We're not bleeding hearts, we're conservative engineers who want criminals punished. . . . But there's not a shred of evidence that they're [Geter and his codefendant] guilty of the crime. If they were white, they wouldn't be in the situation."[12]

Who was right? The aftermath of the conviction helped resolve the debate. Another man arrested for a series of holdups in the Dallas area was linked to the Kentucky Fried Chicken robbery for which Geter had been convicted. That man was found with a blue athletic bag and long-barreled revolver that matched the bag and gun Geter allegedly used. After four of the five witnesses who had originally identified Geter picked the new suspect out of a lineup, Geter's conviction and life prison sentence were overturned at the request of the Dallas County District attorney's office. So Geter served 477 days in prison for a crime he did not commit, because an all-white jury accepted the prosecution's flawed case against a black man with impeccable credentials.

Race is not always held against blacks. Some juries are free of prejudice; some manage to set prejudice aside; and some are actually preferential toward blacks. Just as the Scottsboro and Geter cases were selected to reveal bias against blacks, racially unbiased decisions rendered by all-white or nearly all-white juries can be cited as well.

One such case was the civil rights suit brought against the Ku Klux Klan by Beulah Donald. Her nineteen-year-old son Michael had been randomly snatched off the streets of Mobile in 1981 by a group of whites angry about an integrated jury's failure to convict a black for killing a white police officer. Mr. Donald was put in a car, severely beaten with a tree limb, and hung from a tree to die; his throat was also slashed. Beulah Donald eventually sued the United Klans of America, the group responsible for the brutal murder of her son. In 1987, an all-white jury from this Deep South city ruled in favor of the plaintiff and awarded her $7 million in damages, bankrupting the Klan and forcing them to sell their national headquarters. Read Mrs. Donald's poignant words: "When the trial was over, the jurors came down and told me . . . that they felt for me. . . . I was just surprised that a white jury could do this."[13]

Case studies prove neither the presence of racism nor its absence. They tell us nothing about the true dimensions of racially biased jury decision making. Each case has its unique aspects that may have accounted for the outcome, and those cases that receive media or scholarly attention may not have much in common with routine cases involving blacks that go unscrutinized. However, systematic empirical research has also uncovered the existence of racial politics on the jury.

Capital punishment statistics are one body of data showing the influence of race on juries. In the South between 1945 and 1965, blacks convicted of killing whites received a disproportionately high number of death sentences,[14] although in recent years being a black defendant does not in and of itself seem to put one at greater risk of getting the death sentence.[15] But race still counts; since the resumption of the death penalty in 1977 after a ten year moratorium, it has been shown that it is the race of the *victim* that has impinged on the capital punishment decisions of juries.[16]

Thus, an examination of 2,000 murder cases adjudicated in Georgia showed that even after taking nonracial variables such as crime severity into account, defendants charged with killing white victims were 4.3 times more likely to receive a death sentence than those charged with killing blacks.[17] These data were brought to the Supreme Court's attention in a case challenging the application of the death penalty on the ground it was discriminatory. The Court, acknowledging in *McCleskey* v. *Kemp* that there is "some risk of racial prejudice influencing a jury's decision in a criminal case," refused to upset the death penalty in the case at hand because there was no specific showing that the jury took race into account.[18]

The four dissenting justices took umbrage, claiming that life-or-death decisions made by the jury should be unconstitutional if there is a statistical likelihood that race was a major consideration. Here are their stark words about racial politics on the jury:

> At some point in this case Warren McCleskey doubtless asked his lawyer whether a jury was likely to sentence him to die. A candid reply to this question would have been disturbing. First counsel would have to tell McCleskey that few details of the crime or of McCleskey's past criminal conduct were more important than the fact that his victim was white. . . . [T]he assessment would not be complete without the information that cases involving black defendants and white victims [as in *McCleskey* v. *Kemp*] are more likely to result in a death sentence than cases featuring any other racial combination of defendant and victim. The story could be told in a variety of ways, but McCleskey could not fail to grasp its essential narrative line: there was a significant chance that race would play a prominent role in determining if he lived or died.

Another kind of research that demonstrates racial bias is studies of civil court judgments. One very careful investigation of 9,000 jury trials in Cook

County (Chicago) over a twenty-year period revealed that blacks fare worse, both as plaintiffs and as defendants. Blacks won fewer cases than whites when they were suing; they received smaller awards than whites when they did win; and they lost more cases when they were being sued. A sophisticated multivariate analysis led to the conclusion that even after the nature of injuries and the distribution of case types were taken into account, jury verdicts are less favorable for black litigants.[19]

Mock jury research confirms these findings of racial bias on the jury. Marilyn Ford reviewed the literature on mock juries in the mid-1980s and concluded that racial biases were more persuasively demonstrated than biases related to any other characteristic of the defendant.[20] In a lengthy 1985 *Michigan Law Review* article entitled "Black Innocence and the White Jury" that comprehensively surveyed mock jury studies using race as a variable, Sheri Johnson retrieved nine recent experiments showing that the race of the defendant significantly affected determinations of guilt and three studies linking the victim's race to verdicts. She concluded that there is a widespread tendency among white jurors to convict black defendants in circumstances under which whites would have been acquitted.[21]

Race has been shown to be less prevalent as an influence in other areas of judicial decision making, such as sentencing, than previously assumed.[22] However, the jury more closely mirrors the society than prosecutors and judges do, so we may expect the jury to be more apt to reflect prevalent prejudices. Data limitations preclude rock-solid findings on the part played by racial bias in jury verdicts, but surely sentiments about race hover around the courtroom whenever blacks are plaintiffs, victims, or defendants.

Ethnic Bigotry

Another kind of bias that has historically characterized American society is racism's twin—ethnic bigotry. Ethnicity, one's national origin and heritage, has been the basis for much intolerance since the country's earliest days. Many people's vocabulary unfortunately includes derogatory words like wop, polack, spic, chink, and kike; they are all common enough to be in the dictionary. Even in the absence of such epithets, ethnic bigotry is a fact of life.

As with the racial factor, we can only speculate on the impact of ethnic biases on juries. There are almost no mock jury studies that have looked at ethnicity, but there are a number of cases in which its importance loomed large.

The early twentieth-century case of Leo Frank involves anti-Semitism. Frank was a Jewish businessman accused of beating and strangling thirteen-year-old Mary Phagan, who was an employee of Frank's pencil factory. Her body was found in the basement; her purse and the $1.20 in wages she had received earlier in the day were missing. Soon thereafter the janitor accused Frank of the killing, saying that he and Frank carried the body from the second floor to the basement. The case against Frank was weak: there was no motive; the only one testifying against Frank was the janitor, whose story about what happened had changed several times before the trial; Frank's background gave no hint of criminal behavior. But during the trial, crowds milling outside the courthouse chanted "Kill the Jew," a local newspaper referred to Frank as a "Jew Sodomite," and the all-white, all-Christian jury convicted Frank almost in an instant. The postscript to the story is even worse: Frank's death sentence was commuted to life imprisonment by the governor, an action that propelled a heavily armed mob to abduct Frank from prison and lynch him from an oak tree. Later events attested to Frank's innocence: in 1982, an eighty-two-year-old man came forward to state that as a fourteen-year-old office boy, he saw the janitor carrying the dead body all by himself; the State of Georgia subsequently pardoned Frank post-humously. Historians and journalists who have investigated this infamous case are nearly unanimous: the jury convicted Frank primarily because he was a Jew.[23]

The conviction of Nicola Sacco and Bartolomeo Vanzetti was said by many to have stemmed from anti-Italian bias. The two, left-wing political radicals who had emigrated to the United States from Italy, were tried for the murder–robbery of a factory paymaster and his guard that took place in April 1920. Evidence against them was thin, yet the jury found them guilty and they were executed. The weight of historical opinion is that the two defendants suffered from a wave of prejudice against those of southern and eastern European ancestry that reached a peak shortly after World War I.[24]

A more recent case is the 1987 trial of Ronald Ebens. He was accused of beating Chinese-American Vincent Chin to death outside a Detroit bar after an argument during which Ebens blamed Asians for the decline of the American automobile industry. Ebens pleaded guilty in state court to manslaughter, for which he received a sentence of probation and a $3,700 fine, whereupon the federal government prosecuted him for depriving Chin of his civil rights. During the latter trial, there was considerable testimony about the ethnic conflict entailed in the dispute; a dancer at the bar heard someone yell at Chin, "Because of you motherfuckers, we're out of work."[25] But the jury, which had no Asian members, acquitted Ebens. We can only guess the reason, but there was widespread sentiment in the local press that the jury was to some degree reflecting anti-Japanese sentiment in the Detroit area, which somehow got generalized into a prejudice against all Asians.

A caveat: the juries in the previous three cases may well have been focus-ing on the evidence. Although the verdicts worked against ethnic minorities, as usual there was *some* factual basis for the verdicts. But one might ask, Would the outcomes have been different had Frank *not* been a Jew, had Sacco and Venzetti *not* been Italians, had Chin *not* been Chinese? We'll never know, but it is very doubtful that the jurors were oblivious to the matter of ethni-city. It plays some part in jury decision making.

Religious Intolerance

Persecution of religious outgroups is a theme running through American history. In colonial days, Puritans, Quakers, and Anglicans all, at times, persecuted those who practiced a different religion from themselves. Such prejudices continued into the twentieth century, when Roman Catholics were subject to much hostility. Religious intolerance has lessened dramatically over the years, but even today unorthodox religions elicit considerable public contempt.

This intolerance is sometimes shared by juries. Take, for example, the federal income tax fraud trial of Reverend Sun Myung Moon, leader of the Unification Church. His evangelical religion, which for a time was quite successful in attracting young people who became devout adherents, was so vilified that followers were given the derisive nickname "Moonies." There is little wonder that Moon asked for a nonjury trial, out of fear that his religious views and leadership rather than his tax returns would be at issue. The request was denied, a jury considered the case, and in 1982 Moon was convicted.

Did the jury fail to heed the judge's warning that they act without religious prejudice, or was their action simply an evaluation of the complex financial data presented to them? It is worth pondering whether the same fate would have befallen the Reverend Billy Graham or the late Cardinal Cooke had these popular leaders in the religious mainstream done exactly what Moon did in regard to taxes and been subjected to trial by jury. Lacking any systematic data on the effect of religious bias on jurors, we can only surmise, but it does seem that members of minority religions that are in public disrepute have one strike against them when appearing before juries.

Sexism

The persistence of male chauvanism, the idea that males are and should be the dominant sex, does not need documentation. And because jurors share many of the attitudes held by the public from which they are drawn, it is not surprising that the gender of the victim/or the defendant can influence the way jurors construe the evidence. In the courtroom, sexism has manifested itself mainly in the form of juror disdain or indifference toward certain female victims rather than toughness against female defendants.

Recall the findings on jury nullification from chapter 6. For years male-dominated juries indifferent to women's rights were reluctant to convict men accused of rape unless the victim and the defendant were complete strangers or unless there was a physical assault in addition to the sexual attack. Women who were involved with men, sexually or otherwise, were in effect deprived of the protection of rape laws if they were attacked by someone they had agreed to be with.

The attitude that imprudent women are at the mercy of men is not a thing of the distant past. Consider the 1983 case of five men tried for the gang rape of a woman they met in a Holbrook, Massachusetts, bar. A sixth man who had been given immunity from prosecution testified that the woman, whom he described as a "happy drunk," was taken from the bar in her car to a secluded place where she was stripped, repeatedly raped by the group while pleading not to be touched, and then doused with beer. Defendants claimed that the woman submitted voluntarily, but none of them took the witness stand to testify in their own defense. How plausible is it that a woman would agree to participate willingly in this kind of activity with almost total strangers—even if she was somewhat intoxicated? It may seem very unlikely, but the jury of five men and seven women acquitted the defendants of all charges except one—damaging the woman's car![26] It is hard to explain this verdict except through the inference that the jurors were negatively inclined toward a woman perceived as flirtatious or promiscuous.

Such negative attitudes toward women have diminished considerably in recent years, and convictions in rape cases have increased. Indeed, in another Massachusetts case only one year after the Holbrook rape acquittal, a group of men were found guilty of raping a woman with whom they were drinking at Big Dan's bar. They were accused of dragging her from the bar where she was having a drink with another woman, hoisting her onto a pool table, and raping her consecutively to the cheers of bar patrons. The defense was that the woman agreed to take part in the group sex. The evidence against the Big Dan's defendants was a little stronger than in the Holbrook case because of some incriminating testimony from bystanders, and the men were convicted of aggravated rape. But despite the implausibility of the defendants' story that the woman consented to group sex on a barroom pool table in full view of a crowd of men, some experts on jury behavior who studied the case doubt that the men would have been convicted had there not been observers to corroborate the victim's version of events.[27]

The continued social acceptance of myths about rape continues to plague rape prosecutions tried before juries, particularly the erroneous notion that promiscuous women and prostitutes by nature are willing victims. An interview study with 331 jurors in Indianapolis, Indiana, revealed that the sexually active life-styles of women claiming to have been raped were held against them and augured to the benefit of defendants whom they had accused of rape.[28] As recently as 1989, several members of a Florida jury that acquitted a man of repeatedly raping a woman he abducted at knifepoint said after the trial that they reached that verdict because the woman's lace miniskirt worn without underwear was provocative.[29] Sexism is still a factor in rape cases.

There are, on the other hand, ways in which a woman's gender may help her. The stereotype of women as the "fair" sex at times has caused jurors to disbelieve that a woman could commit ghastly crimes. Some readers may remember the old nursery rhyme "Sugar and spice and everything nice, that's

143

what little girls are made of; frogs and snails and puppy dogs' tails, that's what little boys are made of." Even Judge Frank succumbed to this myth in referring to "*Mister* Prejudice" and "*Miss* Sympathy"; negative bias is associated with men and positive bias with women. This age-old idea that women are inherently nicer than men is still around and can benefit women on trial. But although this characterization of women may help them win cases in the short run by prompting jurors to believe in their innocence, in the long run it perpetuates the demeaning conception of women as weak and timid.

The feminist movement has clearly had an impact on the country, and juries have partaken in the growing recognition of the bad treatment from men that many women have had to endure. Not only are rape convictions up, but women are winning civil suits challenging discrimination based on gender. It seems unlikely that Kansas City television news anchorwoman Christine Craft, who was demoted because she was not pretty enough, would have won her 1983 suit against the station, let alone receive half a million dollars from the jury, in an earlier era when women were rarely even hired to be television journalists. However, despite its decline, sexism continues to play a role in jury decision making.

Class Biases

144

Cynics say money talks—in the courtroom as everywhere else. But the empirical findings on the impact of defendants' economic class on jurors are mixed. Although a study of one hundred Pennsylvania criminal court verdicts showed that the likelihood of conviction was directly related to the amount of status discrepancy between jurors and defendants, the experimental research has produced inconclusive findings.[30] All we can safely say at this point is that the process of adjudication before juries gives affluent litigants certain advantages.

One reason the more affluent may do better before juries is that they have more resources to bolster their defenses. Not only can they hire more competent lawyers, but they can afford to pay for services such as research and investigation which lawyers must engage in to defend their clients more adequately. Chapter 4 showed that money can help those on trial make a better case for themselves, and the stronger exculpatory evidence that such research produces in itself can sway the jury toward acquittal.

But wealth can assist a person in more subtle ways. First, people often stereotype wealthy persons as honorable and poor people as more prone to crime. Jurors looking at a well-attired defendant from an affluent background may surmise that *that* is not the kind of person who would steal, let alone kill. That is the reason that lawyers have defendants with low incomes dress in suits and ties when they testify; they are hoping to counter the bad image that lack of means sometimes conveys. Jurors "sizing up" a poor person may think about what "those" kind of people so often do—lie, cheat, fight, drink, and steal. That is a false generalization, but one that is sometimes hard to dispel—perhaps accounting for verdict patterns such as those discovered in an Indianapolis study showing jurors more likely to convict in sexual assault cases with weak evidence when defendants are unemployed.[31]

Another source of class bias is the relationship between socioeconomic status and style of speech. Research has shown that people of poor backgrounds who appear in court speak more timidly and less confidently than those with greater affluence, who come across more forcefully.[32] Language and speaking handicaps of the poor can undermine their credibility, just as the greater articulateness of those from middle and upper-class backgrounds can make them seem more believable.

Homophobia

Homophobia, the fear of and antagonism toward homosexuals, is widespread. As is true of racial and ethnic minorities, colloquial vocabulary has many opprobrious words for homosexuals—faggot, queer, homo, and so forth. Bias against gays manifests itself in many places, and the legal system is no exception.

In *Bowers* v. *Hartwick*, the Supreme Court ruled that there is no constitutional right of adults to engage in voluntary homosexuality; the Court upheld a Georgia law making the practice of homosexuality a crime punishable by several years' imprisonment under the state's sodomy statutes.[33] In so doing, the Court stressed that such deviant sexual practices have been deemed immoral throughout American history. Chief Justice Warren Burger went even further in his concurring opinion: "Condemnation of [homosexuality] is firmly rooted in Judeo-Christian moral and ethical standards. . . . To hold that the act of homosexual sodomy is somehow protected as a fundamental right would be to cast aside millennia of moral teaching."[34]

If the United States Supreme Court takes such a dim view of homosexuality, it would be naive to expect jurors to do otherwise. Individuals on trial for crimes against gays have sometimes been acquitted or found guilty of less serious charges in circumstances that seemed to warrant convictions on major charges. The classic example is the trial of Dan White, who admitted to walking into San Francisco's City Hall on November 27, 1978, and fatally shooting Mayor George Moscone and Supervisor Harvey Milk at point blank range. White, a Supervisor himself until he resigned on November 10, 1978, had won election on a conservative, anti-homosexuality platform (in a city with a large gay population). The mayor appointed homosexual leader Harvey Milk to replace White, an event that infuriated White and triggered his deadly foray into City Hall. Said White in his confession: "I saw the city as going kind of downhill."[35]

Charging White with murder, the prosecutor called the slayings "cold-blooded, premeditated executions." But the defense countered with a most unusual claim—that White's steady diet of candy bars, cokes, and cupcakes had created a sugar imbalance that made him emotionally unstable. This peculiar argument, disparaged by critics as the "twinkie defense," prevailed; the jury acquitted White of murder and instead found him guilty of manslaughter. Said the jury's foreman: "The killing was done out of a passion . . . given the stress he was under."[36] But many asked, How many people who carefully stalked into the top hall of government, shot two top officials to death, and then blamed it on too much junk food would have been given such leniency by a jury? The cynical explanation was that the jury was simultaneously disdainful of homosexuals and biased in favor of White, a Vietnam War paratrooper, ex-police officer, and former firefighter. Mayor Moscone's successor, Diane Feinstein, took this point of view, saying, "This is a very hard verdict to swallow."[37] The gay community reacted more angrily, going on a rampage the night of the verdict that resulted in injuries to 119 people and $1 million in damage to city buildings and police cars (many of which were torched).

A decade later on the opposite coast, another verdict seemed to stem in part from negative feelings about homosexuals. New York City art dealer Andrew Crispo went on trial for kidnaping and torturing a college English teacher. The two met when the teacher, answering a pay phone near a bar frequented by homosexuals, agreed to have sex with Crispo. They had a morning sexual encounter at Crispo's apartment, during which the teacher let Crispo beat him with a belt. What followed that evening led to the criminal charges: a six-hour sadomasochistic encounter at Crispo's art gallery entailing handcuffing, beatings, and whippings, which Crispo claimed were consensual acts. His victim said he consented to some "rough sex" but not to torture.

The jury acquitted Crispo. One juror later said that the English teacher had willingly entered a "master–slave" relationship, so anything that happened thereafter was of his own doing.[38] The embittered teacher accused both the judge and the jury of devaluing the lives of homosexuals: "In our society it is acceptable to brutalize and even murder gay men."[39]

It is possible that the jurors in the White and Crispo cases were bias-free; we cannot read their minds. And even if homophobia did have an impact on them, because there is no systematic data on juror reactions to homosexuals we cannot know if these two cases are anomalies. But homosexuality remains a sensitive issue and a source of heated political conflict, so intolerance of gays may well wend its way into the jury room.

The Defendant's Reputation

In the Soviet Union in the days of firm Communist rule, criminal trials introduced not only evidence of the defendant's alleged crime but background information of all kinds to determine what kind of a person he or she was.

Judgments were made about people's character, not just the deeds they allegedly committed. The quest was to find out whether the person was basically good or bad, and this assessment became the basis for determining culpability.[40]

In the American system, one's good name is supposed to be irrelevant to decisions about guilt or innocence except insofar as it impinges on the credibility of the defense. However, juries do engage in character assessment and will take a defendant's reputation into account if that comes to light.

One of the most damaging pieces of information for the defense is the criminal record of the person on trial. This is generally inadmissible, but if defendants take the witness stand, then prior convictions can be used to undermine the veracity of their professed innocence. Judges admonish jurors not to assume automatically that prior wrongdoing is indicative of present guilt, but it is hard to put aside the commonsense assumption that there is continuity in people's behavior. Bad reputations can adversely affect defendants, and mock jury research has indeed found that convictions are more likely when the defendant's record becomes known.[41]

The other side of the coin is the favorable effect of a good reputation. The high standing in the community of some public figures, such as successful politicians and sports heroes, can endear them to jurors. The classic example of this is the 1980 case of Bert Lance, a figure high in President Jimmy Carter's administration.

It is widely thought that the key to Lance's acquittal on bank fraud charges arising from his pre–White House days was his stature in the State of Georgia, where he was tried. The defense emphasized the man's many virtues, a not difficult job in light of Lance's statewide reputation as a family man with deep religious values, a decent banker quick to help out the poor, and a valiant defender of southern graces. People from all walks of life waxed eloquent about him at the trial, from President Carter's aging mother Lillian to Martin Luther King, Sr.

Was it the evidence concerning complex financial transactions that spared "Ol' Bert" (as he was affectionately referred to in Georgia)? Jurors who spoke out after the verdict said that they could not find any criminal intent, but that could be a rationalization on the jurors' part. A halo effect resulting from past exemplary activities may help people on trial, just as the blemish of previous criminal activities can hurt them.

Conclusion

After discussing the role of rational choice in judicial decision making in his classic book *The Nature of the Judicial Process*, Supreme Court Justice Benjamin Cardozo said this about judges: "Deep below consciousness are other forces, the likes and dislikes, the predilections and the prejudices, the complex of instincts and emotions and habits and convictions, which make the man, whether he be litigant or judge."[42] What is true of judges would appear to be true of jurors: they have biases of all kinds. They are not tabulae rasae, "blank slates" whose minds are waiting to be filled with details from trials.

What remains unclear is the extent to which biases affect judgments. Notorious cases abound in which pretrial sentiments about entire groups of people almost certainly influenced verdicts, some of which have been discussed in this chapter. But we do not yet know the true dimensions of bias in routine adjudication before juries. Racism, sexism, and other prejudices affect politics in many arenas, but assessing how much they seep into the political life of jurors must await further research. This much is clear: they are part of the conglomeration of personal sentiment, along with the jurors' reactions to the evidence, that jurors take with them into the jury room. What happens next—the transformation of individual perspectives into a collective judgment—is the topic of the next chapter.

Notes

1. Quoted in E. Sutherland and Donald Cressey, *Principles of Criminology,* 7th ed. (Philadelphia: Lippincott, 1966), p. 442.
2. Both lawyers were quoted in Stuart Taylor, "Trial Lawyers Trade Tips and Practice Presence," *The New York Times* (July 28, 1981), p. B20.
3. Jerome Frank, *Courts on Trial: Myth and Reality in American Justice* (New York: Atheneum, 1963), p. 122.
4. Alex Michelini and Bob Kappstatter, "Light at the End of Tunnel," *New York Daily News* (May 26, 1987), p. 3.
5. E. Devons, "Serving as a Juryman in Britain," *Modern Law Review,* 28 (September 1965): 561.
6. For a summary of research on stereotyping and additional citations, see Richard Schaefer, *Racial and Ethnic Groups,* 4th ed. (Glenview, Ill.: Scott Foresman/Little Brown, 1990), pp. 63–66.
7. Jerome Skolnick, *Justice Without Trial: Law Enforcement in Democratic Society,* 2nd. ed. (New York: Wiley, 1975), pp. 45–48.
8. Randall Gordon, "Attributions for Blue-Collar and White-Collar Crime: The Effects of Subject and Defendant Race on Simulated Juror Decisions," *Journal of Applied Social Psychology,* 20 (July 1990): 971–983.
9. Galen Bodenhausen, "Stereotypic Biases in Social Decision Making and Memory: Testing Process Models in Stereotype Use," *Journal of Personality and Social Psychology,* 55 (1988): 734.
10. Peter Applebome, "Facts Perplexing in Texas Robbery," *The New York Times* (December 19, 1983), p. 17.
11. *Ibid.*
12. Peter Applebome, "Racial Issues Raised in Robbery Case," *The New York Times* (May 31, 1983), p. A14.
13. Quoted in Jesse Kornbluth, "The Woman Who Beat the Klan," *The New York Times Magazine* (November 1, 1987), p. 39.
14. Marvin Wolfgang and Marc Riedel, "Race, Judicial Discretion, and the Death Penalty, *Annals of the American Academy of Political and Social Sciences,* 407 (May 1973): 119–133.
15. David Neubauer, *America's Courts and the Criminal Justice System,* 3rd. ed. (Pacific Grove, Calif.: Brooks/Cole, 1988), p. 371.
16. William Bowers and Glenn Pierce, "Arbitrariness and Discrimination under Post-*Furman* Capital Statutes, *Crime and Delinquency,* 26 (1980): 563–635.
17. David Baldus, Charles Pulaski, and George Woodworth, "Comparative Review of Death Sentences: An Empirical Study of the Georgia Experience," *Journal of Criminal Law and Criminology,* 74 (1983): 661.
18. *McCleskey* v. *Kemp,* 481 U.S. 279 (1987).

19. Audrey Chin and Mark Peterson, *Deep Pockets, Empty Pockets: Who Wins in Cook County Jury Trials* (Santa Monica, Calif.: Rand Institute for Civil Justice, 1985), p. 58.

20. Marilyn Chandler Ford, "The Role of Extralegal Factors in Jury Verdicts," *The Justice System Journal,* 11 (Spring 1986): 25.

21. Sheri Lynn Johnson, "Black Innocence and the White Jury," *Michigan Law Review,* 83 (June 1985): 1626-1636.

22. John Hagan, "Extra-Legal Attributes and Criminal Sentencing: An Assessment of a Sociological Viewpoint," *Law and Society Review,* 8 (Spring 1974): 357-383; James Gibson, "Race as a Determinant of Criminal Sentences: A Methodological Critique and a Case Study," *Law and Society Review,* 12 (1978): 455-478; Gary Kleck, "Racial Discrimination in Criminal Sentencing: A Critical Evaluation of the Evidence with Additional Data on the Death Penalty," *American Sociological Review,* 46 (1981): 783; William Wilbanks, *The Myth of a Racist Criminal Justice System* (Pacific Grove, Calif.: Brooks/Cole, 1987).

23. Leonard Dinnerstein, *The Leo Frank Case* (New York: Columbia University Press, 1968).

24. Richard Hofstadter, William Miller, and Daniel Aaron, *The United States: History of a Republic* (Englewood Cliffs, N.J.: Prentice-Hall, 1957), p. 633.

25. Quoted in Saul Kassin and Lawrence Wrightsman, *The American Jury on Trial: Psychological Perspectives* (New York: Hemisphere, 1988), p. 29.

26. "Jury Acquits Five on Rape Charges," *The New York Times* (June 18, 1983), p. 7.

27. Valerie Hans and Neil Vidmar, *Judging the Jury* (New York: Plenum, 1986), p. 217.

28. Gary Lafree, Barbara Reskin, and Christy Visher, "Jurors' Responses to Victims' Behavior and Legal Issues in Sexual Assault Trials," *Social Problems,* 32 (April 1985): 389-407.

29. "Nature of Clothing Isn't Evidence in Rape Case, Florida Law Says," *The New York Times* (June 3, 1990), p. 30. After the verdict, the Florida legislature passed a law precluding introduction into evidence of the nature of a rape victim's clothing.

30. Freda Adler, "Socioeconomic Factors Influencing Jury Verdicts," *New York University Review of Law and Social Change,* 3 (Winter 1973): 1-10; Eric Hoffman, "Social Class Correlates of Perceived Offender Typicality," *Psychological Report,* 49 (1981): 347-350; Robert Bray, Cindy Struckman-Johnson, Marshall Osborne, James McFarlane, and Joanne Scott, "The Effects of Defendant Status on the Decisions of Student and Community Juries," *Social Psychology,* 41 (1978): 256-260; James Gleason and Victor Harris, "Race, Socio-Economic Status, and Perceived Similarity as Determinants of Judgments by Simulated Jurors," *Social Behavior and Personality,* 3 (1975):175-180; James Gleason and Victor Harris, "Group Discussion and Defendant's Socioeconomic Status as Determinants of Judgments by Simulated Jurors," *Journal of Applied Social Psychology,* 6 (1976):186-191; Robert Gordon and Paul Jacobs, Forensic Psychology: Perception of Guilt and Income," *Perceptual and Motor Skills,* 28 (1969):143-146.

31. Barbara Reskin and Christine Visher, "The Impacts of Evidence and Extralegal Factors in Jurors' Decisions," *Law and Society Review,* 20 (1986): 435.

32. J. Conley, W. O'Barr, and A. Lind, "The Power of Language: Presentation Style in the Courtroom," *Duke Law Journal* (1978): 1375-1399.

33. *Bowers v. Hartwick,* 478 U.S. 186 (1986).

34. 478 U.S. 186, 196-197 (1986).

35. Robert Lindsey, "Disputed Parole Kindles Anger in San Francisco," *The New York Times* (January 5, 1984), p. A18.

36. Melinda Beck and Michael Reese, "The Night of Gay Rage," *Newsweek* (June 4, 1979): 31.

37. *Ibid.*

38. Patrick Clark and Don Gentile, "Jury Clears Crispo . . . ," *New York Daily News* (October 17, 1988), p. 3.

39. "Crispo Cleared of Kidnaping and Sex-Torture," *The New York Times* (October 17, 1988), p. 3.

40. Harold Berman, *Justice in the USSR: An Interpretation of Soviet Law,* revised ed. (New York: Vintage, 1963), pp. 302-308.

41. Valerie Hans and A. N. Doob, "Section 12 of the Canada Evidence Act and the Deliberations of Simulated Juries," *Criminal Law Quarterly,* 18 (1976): 235-253.

42. Benjamin Cardozo, *The Nature of the Judicial Process* (New Haven: Yale University Press, 1957), p. 167.

149

9

· · · · · · ·

Jury Room

Politics

For hours, days, and sometimes months, jurors play a passive role in the trial process. Then comes the fateful moment, after the judge gives them the final instructions, when the jurors are led off to the sanctity of the jury room. Now it is their turn to be in charge.

What happens next? The first order of business is selection of the foreperson, an unnecessary step in states where he or she is chosen by lot or in states where the first juror selected is automatically designated foreperson. Then comes a bit of fumbling around, as jurors grope for a procedure to follow for the deliberations. Someone usually suggests a straw poll, which is taken unless there is substantial dissent. Through secret balloting, a show of hands, or a verbal go-around, the breakdown of jurors' inclinations is revealed.

What does the initial survey usually show about the "lay of the land" in the jury room? According to Kalven and Zeisel's definitive interview study of Chicago and Brooklyn jurors, the jury is initially split 69 percent of the time.[1] Because most jurisdictions still require unanimity to reach a verdict in criminal cases, hopes of a quick and easy decision are dashed and the jury's work begins.

Jurors then embark on the complex task of trying to influence one another in order to arrive at a verdict and avoid a mistrial. This is quite an endeavor, as jurors emerge from the trial with decidedly different perceptions of reality and often bring to bear varying political sentiments. With so much at stake and such discord afoot, the situation would seem to be hopeless. But it isn't.

In about two-thirds of all juries, at least one person's original stance changes, and there is often substantial shifting of positions. Juries are enormously successful in finding a way out of their disagreements; hung juries are rare, occurring in only about 5 percent of all cases.[2] But it doesn't come easily; jurors engage in a host of complex interactions to resolve their conflicts: they argue, they coax, they pressure, they maneuver, they dominate, and at times they engage in bargaining. Communications, group dynamics, leadership, and politics—all are in the steaming cauldron of jury deliberations.

Persuasion

Jurors are obsessed with the facts of the trial and the law governing their cases. Eavesdrop on virtually any jury deliberations, and you will hear relentless discussion of the details of the evidence and the meaning of legal concepts. The struggle to reach a verdict is a serious business, and jurors take it seriously. Jokes about jurors flipping a coin so they can get home in time for dinner are totally off base; the California jury considering a libel suit against *Penthouse Magazine* deliberated three weeks in 1982 before returning a verdict for the defendant—after a trial that lasted five months!

Discussions are focused on legally relevant ideas and information. Jurors use all their reasoning and debating skills to try to convince others of their point of view. They bring in personal observations and experiences bearing on the case at hand to bolster their opinions (such as "I've been in fights, and I know how you throw a punch when you're trying to really hurt someone"; or "Alleys in this city are much too dark to get a good look at someone"). Frequently jurors will return to the courtroom to get a reading of parts of the transcript or to seek clarification from the judge on points of law. Normally, they try to change each other's minds by patiently considering minute details and repeatedly going over the logic of their arguments. Using words and ideas to influence others works: there are sometimes moments during which a juror genuinely "sees the light" and is converted to the opposite point of view.

Consider the case of the New York City jury ready to convict Allen Lewis for pushing talented flutist Renee Katz in front of a subway train, causing the seventeen-year-old girl to lose her finger and her budding musical career. One of the jurors who believed Lewis to be innocent made a point about the defendant's handwriting that turned the tide. The juror convinced his co-jurors that the full, rounded letters of the defendant's signature on his time sheet at work could not conceivably have been written by a nervous man who just moments earlier had severely injured and almost killed another person. One of the converts who changed his mind on the basis of this presentation was a philosophy professor, who later spoke in awe of his "remarkable, intelligent" co-juror.[3] This was a hideous crime that caused feelings to run high, but the voice of reason prevailed in the jury room. Whether or not Lewis was really innocent will never be known, but sound thinking and careful discussion led the jury to reverse its initial inclinations and acquit the defendant.

This is not to suggest that juries are passionless. The exact opposite is the case; the jury room is often charged with emotion. People lose their tempers, become sarcastic, get into shouting matches, and once in a while break into tears. During the jury deliberations in the mass murder trial of Juan Corona, one juror put down on paper the intensity of what he was going through. Said this juror, a war veteran: "I need some aspirins. God, I hate aspirins and yet here I am chewing them by the handful. I never got this strung-out in combat."[4]

This presents a bit of a paradox. On the one hand, jurors focus on the minutiae of their cases and engage in considerable thoughtfulness. On the other hand, below the surface are intense emotions that propel the discussion. Sometimes these emotions come out in the open, as during one Pennsylvania case dealing with Vietnam War protesters in which the deliberations were characterized by one juror as "blurred, quarreling, timeless periods of irrational arguments."[5] The Oliver North jury got so bogged down in conflict that it held a prayer meeting to get the group back on course.[6] But such open emotionalism is rare, and the deep feelings of the jurors are usually sublimated—emerging in the jury room as a relatively calm, respectful exchange of opinions.

So what can we conclude about the nature of the give-and-take in the jury room? It is in part an intellectual discovery process in which jurors use reason to correct their co-jurors' errors in reconstructing factual reality and interpreting the law. It is in part a debating society in which sounder arguments prevail over weaker arguments. It is in part a sober quest for truth drawing on the thoughtfulness and rich experiences of the jurors. It is in part the triumph of reason over emotion.

But it is more. Just as there is much more to the individual juror's decision process than an objective contemplation of the evidence, so too the joint decision process is driven by some complex group dynamics generally unknown to the jurors themselves. Jurors will almost always tell us that they switched their views and their votes simply because they came to realize that the others were right, and on one level this is precisely what happens. However, as we shall now see, there are deeper social and political reasons that account for the transformation from division to consensus. Jurors are often in the grip of ineluctable forces that impel them toward verdicts.

Number of guilty votes on first ballot	0	1–5	6	7–11	12	TABLE 9-1
Final verdict						First ballot
Not guilty (33% of all cases)	100%	91%	50%	5%	—	and final verdict in 225 Brooklyn
Hung (5%)	—	7	—	9	—	and Chicago
Guilty (62%)	—	2	50	86	100	criminal trials
Total	100%	100%	100%	100%	100%	
Number of cases	26	41	10	105	43	

Source: Adapted from *The American Jury,* by H. Kalven and H. Zeisel, p. 488. Copyright © 1966 by Little, Brown & Co., Inc. Reprinted by permission.

Peer Pressure

In the popular movie *Twelve Angry Men,* Henry Fonda plays a juror who, as the lone holdout for acquittal of a defendant, is able to convert all other eleven jurors to his point of view. It is a satisfying ending, but not only because audiences love to see the underdog win. It is also satisfying because many of the jurors who first opted for conviction were so clearly acting in response to internal values and prejudices, whereas Fonda's character (whose liberalism was not so apparent) came across as the voice of reason. The success of one juror's painstaking dissection of the evidence and clever argumentative techniques in sowing doubts in his co-jurors' minds is a glowing example of juror persuasiveness.

153

This all makes for a moving Hollywood drama, but what goes on in real life is just the opposite: people who hold the minority opinion, especially when very few in number, usually cave in. Minorities of one almost never succeed in converting everyone else. The best the lone dissenter can usually do is hang the jury—which itself is a relatively infrequent occurrence. Table 9-1, showing the relationship between the first ballot breakdowns and the final verdicts in the deliberations of 225 Brooklyn and Chicago juries, reveals that in nine out of ten cases the initial majority prevailed. The authors of this study were so taken by the profundity of their finding that they put it in italics: *"With very few exceptions the first ballot decides the outcome."*[7]

Recent experimental research using mock juries confirms the findings of the Brooklyn and Chicago study. Tanford and Penrod showed a videotape of a trial entailing three offenses to groups of six-person juries. Initial and final vote distributions were recorded, showing the effects of majority persuasion. The initial verdict preference of the majority was reversed only 6 percent of the time on the first charge and only 4 percent of the time on the other charges.[8] The side that has the votes at the outset will almost always have the verdict at the end.

Why? Social psychology provides a powerful answer: the strong pressures on minorities to conform to the majority viewpoint. It is very uncomfortable to feel that one is the "odd person out"—a dissident who is out of line with everyone else. People do not like to feel deviant or obstreperous, making things difficult for others in a group. Fitting in is a more comfortable experience.

The classic experiments of psychologist Solomon Asch illustrate this point. Asch gathered subjects in a room and asked them to make judgments about the length of lines drawn on cards. Everyone in the room was shown two cards, one of which had one line, labeled X, and the other of which had three lines of different lengths, labeled A, B, and C. Line X was *clearly* closest in length to Line C. All the participants were asked to make a determination about which of the lines on the card with three lines was closest in length to Line X.

All the line raters except the subject were confederates of Asch. The confederates had all been told to lie, so, when asked, each gave an incorrect answer—that Line A or Line B was closest to Line X. What was of interest in the experiment was what the nonconfederate subject would do after all the others had given the wrong answer. Remarkably, one-third of the subjects emulated the wrong answer, saying that Line X was closest in length to Line A or B. This occurred despite the fact that the subjects were deceiving their own eyes—the differences were clear-cut variations in physical reality as the lines were obviously of different lengths. Unlike the trial situation, which is replete with ambiguity, this was a simple perceptual task; yet many of the duped subjects chose to go along with the group judgment rather than rely on their own senses.[9] The urge to conform overpowered their good judgment.

Extrapolating these findings to the jury room, it is easy to imagine how uncomfortable it is to be a dissenter. As other jurors make sensible points, the dissenter's resistance may appear stupid or obnoxious. The dissenter may consider him- or herself to be an ordinary person in the mainstream of life, an average citizen, and may question: "What's wrong with me? What have I missed? Why am I being such a trouble-maker?" Given a quite plausible contrary view, it seems reasonable to give in.

There is in fact considerable evidence that jurors who find themselves in a small minority are timorous about advocating their position and prone to capitulate to the pressure of the majority. Jury deliberations from this standpoint are a wearing-down process, based on the relative power of the two opposing factions rather than on a free exchange among many autonomous individuals. Much of the time deliberations are a more-or-less time-consuming process of pressuring the minority into submission.

The first juror to join the majority camp makes it that much easier for other dissenters. In fact, there is experimental evidence that the "bellwether juror" who makes the initial switch legitimates the idea of capitulation so that the others with similar views almost always follow suit.[10] The open-mindedness of one juror is emulated by others, who no longer feel weak-kneed about abandoning their original position. Conformity becomes acceptable.

Most jurors reconcile themselves to having collapsed by praising the wisdom of their colleagues' arguments and accepting their own fallibility. According to one juror who wrote a book about the murder trial in which he participated, the final juror holding out for conviction yielded after a "sustained barrage" of abuse and hostility was directed at him. However, rather than criticize his pressuring co-jurors, the switcher had kind words: "I've come to respect all of you too much. I can't do this to you and I won't continue any longer. I change my vote."[11]

Respect is sometimes a two-way street, with the dominant group helping the holdout to relent by acknowledging the right to dissent and the legitimacy of alternative viewpoints. This "stroking" process can ease the way to capitulation by enabling the dissenter to maintain self-esteem at the same time he or she is crumbling. This was the tactic of what had become an eleven-person majority for conviction in the Juan Corona mass murder case. Rather than steamroll the remaining resister into compliance with them, the jury took a day off from voting after six full days of deliberation and told her to go with her convictions. On the eighth day she switched, remarking: "I think I've changed my mind. Yesterday you gave me a day's rest and I relaxed and I saw things differently. . . . Basically, I now think you people are right and I do think Corona guilty."[12]

But jurors are not always so gentle, and a number of capitulating jurors have described the agony of standing in the way of a verdict. Said one holdout who finally agreed to convict in a lovers' triangle case: "They wore me down. . . . I could never go through that again. They would have to shoot me first."[13] He yielded, despite continuing to harbor doubts about the defendant's guilt.

Thus, social and psychological pressure usually suffices to bring dissenters into line. Much of the soul-searching and argumentation that takes place in the jury room masks the almost irresistible powers of the majority to get its way. But as we shall now see, this generalization is too broad: minorities within the jury are not so powerless as they have been made to seem.

The Power of Holdouts

Referring back to Table 9-1, data show that when the jury is evenly split at the outset, half the verdicts are guilty and half are not guilty; the conformity principle does not come into play until some switching has taken place. Second, some minority contingents prevail; minorities of four or five once in a while do carry the day. This, in fact, is what happened in the Corona case: the first vote was 7-to-5 for acquittal; the final vote was unanimous for conviction.

Another phenomenon is revealed by the table: in 16 cases out of 225 the jury hangs. Holdouts can be quite obstinate, especially if they have intense political convictions underlying their opinions. From one standpoint they may be seen as independent thinkers; from another they are pigheaded fanatics. However they are labeled, they have the power to deadlock the jury and create a mistrial.

Thus, the federal government's espionage case against former FBI agent Richard Miller, who was accused of passing bureau secrets to the Soviet Union, ended in a hung jury. Despite *fourteen days* of deliberation after a three month trial held in Los Angeles in 1985, one juror adamantly refused to give in. A Tennessee jury reached a similar impasse during the deliberations over charges that two men hung a seventy-three-year-old man from an apple tree when he surprised them during a burglary. Said the district attorney: "I have never seen a jury more personally distraught that they couldn't convince a lone holdout."[14]

The strong-willed juror is the exception to the rule; it takes steel nerves and implacable resolve to hold firm in the face of unmitigated pressure. But it takes less fortitude to stick to your guns if you have an ally. Asch's experiments showed that the presence of only a single person giving the correct answer to the line-matching test was sufficient to get a substantial number of subjects to rely on their own senses rather than go with the crowd. And mock jury studies have shown that two dissidents are far more likely to resist group intimidation than one. So although intransigent holdouts are uncommon and hung juries are infrequent, jurors who are resolute can and do on occasion thwart the majority.

Bargaining

The dominant group in the jury room usually comes out on top, but it does not necessarily get everything it wants. The unanimity that juries so regularly achieve eclipses the fact that a certain give-and-take among different factions on the jury may have taken place. In virtually every walk of life, the settling of differences is often achieved by bargaining, and jurors act accordingly. In a classic work on American politics, political scientist Robert Dahl noted that American government is characterized by endless bargaining,[15] and a more recent treatise on the making of public policy noted that "no one institution is immune" from the imperative of bargaining.[16] Jurors fit right into these pronouncements: they bring their politics into the jury room, and they often use politics as a way of getting out of the jury room.[17]

Decision alternatives presented to juries provide ample opportunities for bargaining. Juries often have multiple options in criminal cases rather than the simple twofold dichotomy of guilty or not guilty. They may be presented with multiple charges, ranging in degree of seriousness; they may be considering a number of separate counts of the same crime; and they may be dealing with multiple defendants. The 1980 trial of Northern California Hells Angels, for example, entailed forty-four counts against eighteen defendants; the number of verdict possibilities was astronomical.

What this means is that jury verdicts can run the gamut from extreme harshness to extreme leniency. The jury can convict everyone of everything; they can acquit across the board; or they can do some convicting and some acquitting. There are even more gradations possible in civil cases, where jurors finding liability can assess damages anywhere from ten cents to ten billion dollars. Rather than there being one side within the jury that simply vanquishes the opposition, there is often the possibility of a mutual accommodation whereby both sides agree on middle ground.

Bargaining, an always appealing decision option when two adversaries are at loggerheads, is a particularly logical course of action for divided juries. The premise of this entire book is that value differences are often the underpinning of juror conflicts, and bargaining is a nice way of resolving such political discord—for all but extremists. Whereas juries can go around in circles endlessly quibbling and quarreling about the "real facts," they may well be able to settle things satisfactorily by concentrating on outcomes that provide something for everybody. The brokered verdict, which neither totally condemns nor totally absolves, can resolve the dispute among embattled jurors.

Bargaining among jurors is not just a theoretical contingency; it actually happens. Experimental evidence has shown that many mock jurors who prior to deliberations favor very tough or very lenient verdicts wind up accepting an intermediate position;[18] real jurors act similarly. Indeed, in a dissenting opinion in the *Apodoca* case, which sustained the use of nonunanimous juries in state courts, Justice Douglas took judicial notice of this phenomenon as a rationale for insisting on unanimity. Said Douglas: "Moreover, even where an initial majority wins the dissent over to its side, the ultimate result in unanimous jury States may nonetheless reflect the reservations of uncertain jurors. I *refer to many compromise verdicts on lesser-included offenses and lesser sentences."*[19] The correctness of this sage observation is borne out by any number of cases, as the following sections illustrates.

157

Compromise

Compromise is the type of bargain that takes the form: "You want A; I want C; let's settle on B." It entails splitting the difference, choosing an intermediate position between two extremes. It is commonplace in everyday life, from price negotiations in the marketplace to parents and children compromising over the child's bedtime to Congressional taxing and spending decisions. It also occurs in the jury room.

The monetary outcomes of civil law cases make juror compromising especially attractive; middle ground can be determined arithmetically. Juries divided over the proper damage award to be given to the plaintiff can simply average the individual amounts arrived at separately by each juror. Interviews with jurors in thirty-eight federal civil trials held in Philadelphia revealed that the jury engaged in averaging 40 percent of the time when they were embroiled in disagreements about how much to grant the plaintiff.[20]

Although judgments about liability are supposed to be distinct from the determination of damages, it is not unknown for jurors who would prefer to rule for the defendant to accept a judgment in favor of the plaintiff if the damage award is kept low. This apparently is what happened when the jury deliberated in the successful suit against the Liggett tobacco company for having caused cancer reported in Chapter 5. The four pro-defendant jurors ruled for the plaintiff on the condition that the eight pro-plaintiff jurors would agree to reduce the damage award from $5 million to $400,000.[21] Psychologist Edith Greene, who studied the civil jury's decision-making process in detail, concluded that "juror discussions about damages can be complex and motivated by subtle attempts at persuasion and compromise."[22]

In criminal cases, the most straightforward type of jury compromise occurs when jurors agree to convict on light or moderate charges rather than either convict on the toughest charges or acquit altogether. The infamous case of Joel Steinberg, who was convicted of manslaughter in the death of his adopted six-year-old daughter, is illustrative. Steinberg, a disbarred lawyer and routine cocaine user, was accused not only of striking a severe blow to the back of the girl's head but of failing to get help for twelve hours while she was still alive. Complicating the trial was the situation of Hedda Nussbaum, Steinberg's live-in lover, who allegedly had been viciously brutalized by Steinberg for years. She, too, waited to call medical authorities until it was too late. At first Hedda was also charged with murder, but later the charges were dropped and she became a government witness against Steinberg.

From the beginning of deliberations, the jury was deeply divided.[23] The facts were even more clouded than usual, and the allocation of moral responsibility between the two principals was a source of dispute. The jury initially split evenly into three factions: those who thought Steinberg guilty of murder (the "hard-liners"), those who favored first-degree manslaughter (the "middle-of-the-roaders"), and those who opted for second-degree manslaughter because they thought Hedda had struck the fatal blow (the "softies"). This was not a minor squabble; in the jury foreman's words, "We were almost hopelessly divided."[24] After eight days of high-tension drama and tedious recounting of testimony, the jury arrived at a verdict. They opted for first-degree manslaughter, the in-between outcome.

Although at one point the pro-murder contingent reached ten, that was the high-water mark. The hard-liners eventually realized that they would never get all twelve jurors to agree on a murder conviction. They then wilfully deviated from the judge's instructions that they first dispense with the murder charge before going to the lesser ones, and they concentrated their efforts on getting the "softies" to accept the first-degree manslaughter charge—no mean feat considering that some continued to feel that Nussbaum might have been the more culpable. Having accomplished that, the hard-liners themselves relented on the murder charge, even though in their hearts they believed it was warranted. The alternative was a hung jury, and it was thought preferable to establish some culpability and assure punishment rather than give Steinberg another opportunity to get exonerated.

Experts on the law decried the final result as a legal fiasco. A murder conviction was deemed tenable because a showing of "depraved indifference causing death" sustains the charge, and Steinberg's refusal to get aid for his dying daughter was a manifestation of such indifference. A second-degree manslaughter conviction was viable because the key element of that crime is recklessness that causes death, which could be inferred from the facts presented at the trial. But first-degree manslaughter required a showing of specific intent to do serious physical injury, which had not been demonstrated, and at one point in the pretrial proceedings the district attorney almost dropped that charge as unprovable. The jury convicted Steinberg of the one crime that he was arguably not guilty of committing!

The legally incongruous result prompted one law professor to say; "I think he got away with murder"; a lawyer specializing in cases of violence against women called it a "rogue verdict."[25] But although the outcome may have been wanting legally, it was unassailable politically; it was a compromise between two extremes. If one group believes in a level of culpability that warrants severe punishment and the other thinks relatively light punishment is in order, it makes sense to choose the position midway between the two extremes. As one of the jurors put it, "We didn't make everyone happy. There were people at either end of the spectrum who had to give."[26] In politics, including jury room politics, half a loaf is often better than none.

The Supreme Court has rejected appeals based on the logical shortcomings of verdicts.[27] In granting the jury the discretion to reach verdicts that do not make much sense legally, the Court's unanimous decision explicitly accepted the legitimacy of compromise as part of the normal deliberations process. Just as plea bargains fashioned by legally adept prosecutors and defense attorneys sometimes bear little connection to the facts, the negotiated verdicts reached by jurors are at times out of sync with reality.

Compromise may leave all sides somewhat displeased, and jurors at the extreme positions will sometimes grumble later that they were disheartened by the outcome. Exactly such regrets were expressed by one of the jurors in the Joel Steinberg case, who had agreed to the compromise verdict of manslaughter. A year after the trial, in a nationally televised reunion of five of the jurors, this juror bemoaned the verdict and berated herself for not making greater efforts to persuade her co-jurors to bring in a murder conviction, which she firmly thought was deserved.[28] But the moderate position between stern retribution and soft-hearted exculpation may comport

159

with jurors' sense of justice, as examined in chapter 5. And it is justice that is often the driving force behind jurors' thinking.

Logrolling

Logrolling is a practice long familiar to lawmakers. The term originated 200 years ago to describe the practice of land-clearing settlers who put aside their differences to help each other out; they would literally roll each other's logs that were too heavy to be removed by one person. The term now refers to arrangements by which members of a legislative body agree to support each other's bills. It is a simple device for getting majority support: you vote for my bill and I'll vote for yours. It's the equivalent of the colloquial expression "You scratch my back and I'll scratch yours."

This is a plausible option for divided juries deliberating the fate of multiple defendants simultaneously. Pro-prosecution forces agree to acquit one or more of the less blameworthy defendants, and the pro-defense side goes along with convicting the central figures in the crime. Conviction of the worst offenders is traded for acquittal of those who appear less culpable.

Logrolling by juries is an even more discreet phenomenon than compromise; it can sometimes be inferred but it can never be proved. For example, three New Orleans policemen were convicted of violating the civil rights of a black man during a brutal police interrogation conducted as part of a hunt for the killer of a white police officer, but four other officers were acquitted for their behavior during the same incident. One of the defense attorneys, shocked about the inconsistency of the verdict, exclaimed, "I find it unbelievable that they can look at the same evidence and acquit some and convict others."[29] The verdict seems baffling unless we bring in a plausible political explanation: defendants were traded off so that neither the pro-police nor the pro–civil rights forces would come away empty-handed. Defendants are treated differently in order to secure a resolution that gives something to both sides in a split jury.

The Negotiation Process

How do jurors, who are supposed to abide by the law and the evidence, engage in a practice that seems so out of kilter with their sworn duty? How can they indulge in such political expediency and still live with their consciences? How can they barter over truth and justice?

On rare occasions, the compulsion to arrive at a verdict pushes juries that are wracked with dissension into straightforward negotiations to resolve the conflict. Jurors put their cards on the table: this is what I want and this is what I'm willing to give up to get it. Jury wrangling over facts shifts to jury skirmishing over verdicts in an attempt to make a deal.

One of the most vivid portrayals of such explicit bargaining at work within the jury was provided by one of the jurors in the infamous "Chicago Seven" trial. In that trial, the defendants were accused of the federal crime of crossing state lines to incite a riot during the Democratic Party's national convention in August 1968 and of having created a conspiracy to implement their plans. Over the course of five months, jurors heard extensive contradictory testimony about the nature of the confrontation between protesters and police—who started the violence, whether there was preplanning, if police overreacted, and whether defendants were merely exercising their right to demonstrate. The jury at the onset of deliberations divided into two camps— eight pro-police jurors, who wanted to convict all seven defendants of everything, and four pro-demonstrator jurors, who sided with the defendants. At the end, after five days of anguished deliberations, the jury found all seven innocent of conspiracy, acquitted two of the less strident figures of all charges, and convicted five defendants of the single charge of incitement. The jury both compromised and logrolled, creating a "package" verdict acceptable to all.

How was this result achieved? The inside story was provided by one of the jurors who was instrumental in forging the deal.[30] This woman, a "hard-liner," unabashedly decided that a mediated solution was the only way to end the protracted and seemingly irresolvable conflict in which the jury found itself. She went into the adversary's "camp" and got them to agree to the principle of convicting some and acquitting others; she then managed to persuade her own side to settle for less than their optimal expectations. She candidly asserted that the negotiated verdict was reached "although a majority of jurors still felt all the defendants guilty on both counts—and three jurors felt that all of them were innocent."[31] This was a straight-out, above-board political deal.

Such brazen verdict brokering is highly unusual. A more congenial strategy is tacit bargaining—the use of a subtle communications process to signal intentions and expectations about desired outcomes. Studies of negotiations have uncovered all kinds of indirect methods that people use to reconcile their conflicts, often without saying a word.[32] Jury room discussion provides ample information not only about jurors' verdict preferences but also about the intensity of those preferences—just how firmly committed each person is.

If individuals start to reconsider the meaning of a fragment of testimony or the truthfulness of a particular witness, they are implying a willingness to shift positions on the ultimate outcome, and they are inviting a reciprocal loosening of views by the opposition. The stuff of juror exchanges are matters of record—whether the defendant was spiteful, how well the defendant and the victim were acquainted, in what direction a gun was pointed, whether the eyewitness had good vision, and so forth. But when jurors on either side change their earlier view of the facts, the change communicates an attitude of flexibility about the ultimate verdict.

161

The very definition of tacit bargaining is that it remains unspoken, so providing examples is difficult. It seems fairly clear, however, that this is what transpired in the 1983 case against Barbara Austin for shooting a man who was her boss and her lover. The jury was deadlocked: nine jurors favored a murder conviction and three wanted to acquit on the basis of insanity. The judge was informed that the jurors were at an impasse early in the second day of deliberations, but the judge sent them back for more discussion. Soon thereafter, some jurors on both sides started toying with the notion that the defendant was in a state of extreme emotional disturbance when she pumped five bullets into the victim in his law office. Little by little, other jurors embraced this position, a rendition of reality that perfectly fit the requirements of a manslaughter conviction. Through indirection, middle ground was reached. As one of the jurors put it, "We were deadlocked. . . . I guess you could call the manslaughter verdict a compromise verdict."[33]

So jurors need not resort to overt vote trading, an indecorous practice that does not square with judges' orders that jurors stick to the evidence. Jury bargaining is normally a delicate process in which give and take are couched in the most circumspect language. In most cases, negotiations among jurors—an intuitively appealing way out of the morass of deep-seated conflict—is covert to the point of invisibility.

162

Leadership

Although each juror has one vote, not all jurors have equal influence. Studies have shown that rates of participation in the discussion vary enormously,[34] and it appears that some jurors are listened to more than others. Power is thus stratified within the jury; some lead and others follow. The exercise of leadership can be a force that guides jurors to the final verdict.

Leadership Roles

There are three main effects that jurors exercising leadership can produce. First is what may be referred to as the "bulldozer role"—intimidating the minority. Sometimes the leader is adept at getting dissenters to collapse, or at least getting them to give in earlier than they may otherwise do.

This is not usually done in a domineering manner. It is accomplished by a steady banter of comments and questions directed at those who are holding out. Words, logic, persistence, sometimes charm, and once in a while belittlement are the tools of the leader's trade. The payoff is that less self-assured jurors, with fewer resources to fall back on, give in.

A good example was the case of Jean Harris, the wealthy prep-school headmistress accused of killing Dr. Herman Tarnower, renowned creator and popularizer of the "Scarsdale diet." Ms. Harris had been romantically involved with Tarnower for fourteen years and was grief-stricken when Tarnower became involved with another woman. She claimed at the trial that she had gone to Tarnower's house to commit suicide and that he was accidently killed when they struggled over the gun she had brought.

The jury, faced as usual with much uncertainty about the night's bloody events, initially voted 8-to-4 for a murder conviction. According to the report of a juror who at first thought Ms. Harris innocent, two jurors in the majority immediately "took charge," and over the course of the next eight days, "they were super-clear and logical as they tried to probe us and lead us."[35] Their leadership worked; despite the fact that the jurors were given six verdict options by the judge, they convicted the defendant of the most serious charge—premeditated murder. The temptation to bargain was squelched by the handiwork of two take-charge jurors.

A second leadership role is to help forge compromises. Ivor Kraft, a lawyer and professor of social work, has described how he and two other moderate jurors convinced a number of other jurors to abandon their extreme positions and move toward the middle:

> Repeatedly and slyly we reminded the doves [wanting leniency] of the bestial nature of the crime we were assessing. Repeatedly and cunningly, we reminded the hawks [wanting toughness] that the evidence concerning the exact motive and intent of [the accused] was uncertain or ambiguous. Against our patience and determination, they were as children. We milked our advantage of being in the middle position, the healing position.[36]

Once in a great while those who exercise leadership can totally reverse the inclinations of the majority. This is what Henry Fonda's character did in the movie *Twelve Angry Men,* and although the chances of converting eleven others as he did are minute, assertive jurors with leadership skills can convert a large contingent of jurors. The occasional times when minorities on the jury win out is often owing to the role played by particularly forceful jurors.

One such individual was Andrew Choa, a bank vice-president who served as a juror in the influence-peddling trial of John Mitchell and Maurice Stans, two cabinet members in the Nixon administration. After a ten-week trial replete with evidence about complex financial and governmental matters, the jury's initial vote was 8-to-4 for conviction. Choa, described by his bank colleagues as "to the right of Ivan the Terrible,"[37] was able almost single-handedly to convert the majority and win an acquittal for two conservative politicians whom he admired. Choa steadfastedly delved into the complex details about the comings and goings of people operating in the Washington, D.C., labyrinth of power—convincing everyone that what Stans and Mitchell had done was a standard practice of high government officials. Years later Choa denied playing a special role, saying that everyone on the jury made a contribution.[38] But it certainly appeared as if a particularly effective leader had wielded exceptional influence over his co-jurors.

The Making of a Jury Leader

Who becomes a leader? Sometimes it is the jury foreperson, who has the advantage of being able to have some control over the agenda and influence the order of speaking. Being in charge also enables one to speak at will without having to fight for recognition. People defer to legitimate authorities of all kinds, including those at the helm in the jury room.

Other jurors may also exert influence. The power structure within the jury sometimes mirrors the stratification within society, so those with higher status, whether they are foreperson or not, often play more central roles in the jury room. Over the years, men and those more affluent and better educated have spoken more than women and those less affluent and with less education.[39] The resources of jury leadership are self-esteem, verbal ability, and deference from others; and because these resources are unequally possessed in American society, it is not surprising that there is an uneven distribution of power within the jury. There have been some notable exceptions, but in general the more powerful you are in the country at large, the greater your capacity for leadership on the jury.

Judges' Influence on Jury Deliberations

164

In old England, judges had enormous control over jury deliberations. Not only was physical coercion used to get the jurors to reach a verdict, it was also used to get them to issue the *right* verdict. The classic case illustrating this practice was the trial dealing with unlawful assembly charges brought in 1670 against William Penn and William Mead, whose Quaker religious practices had gotten them in trouble with the Crown. After much time had elapsed and the jury had failed to convict the two, the court official said to the jury: "Gentlemen, you shall not be dismissed till we have a verdict that the court will accept; and you shall be locked up, without meat, drink, fire, and tobacco; you shall not think thus to abuse the court; we will have a verdict, by the help of God, or you shall starve for it."[40] The jurors never did relent, the not-guilty verdict was finally accepted, and one juror named Bushell eventually won a court case that abolished the right of the court to use force to get a sought-after verdict. The famous decision, known simply as *Bushell's Case*, established a firm precedent: neither British nor American judges can threaten or use physical punishment to bring jurors into line.

However, that does not mean judges have no power over what goes on in the jury room; far from it. It is judges who determine how long jurors must remain in deliberations when they are engulfed in conflict. Jurors will commonly report back to the judge that they cannot achieve unanimity, and just as commonly, judges will send them back to the jury room to do more work. The longer the judge keeps the jury going and rejects its pleas that further discussion would be futile, the more likely it becomes that the jury will come up with a verdict and avoid a mistrial.

There are dramatic instances of jurors snarled in dead-end discussions who ultimately arrive at unanimous verdicts because the judge would not let them quit. The trial of several lesser figures on riot charges in the Howard Beach, New York, racial attack case had just such an electrifying ending. After protracted deliberations the jury twice reported that they were deadlocked 11-to-1 for conviction; but the judge sent them back. Ultimately, the holdout capitulated.

Even jurors who are dead set on their views may reconsider if the judge keeps them working long enough. Imagine yourself as a juror who has just sat through a 3½-year trial involving 182 witnesses, 6,000 exhibits, and 100,000 pages of transcripts. Your jury deliberates for two weeks, gets nowhere, and throws up its hands as hung—only to be sent back to the jury room. Resuming deliberations, you enter a third, fourth, fifth, sixth, seventh, and finally an eighth week of deliberations. At some point you would probably say, "Enough! *Any* verdict is better than this."

This is *not* just a hypothetical example; it is precisely what happened in Belleview, Illinois, in 1987.[41] A judge kept the jury deliberating for two months before it finally decided for the plaintiffs suing the Monsanto Company for having spilled the toxic chemical dioxin in their Missouri community. One of the jurors, who had originally opposed awarding the plaintiffs $16 million in punitive damages, after the trial confessed to reporters: "In a way, I'm sorry I changed my mind. But . . . I was really tired. I just wanted peace of mind. . . . I agreed because I wanted to get out of there."[42] The case would have been ended, and the suit probably would have been dropped or settled out of court—but for the judge's determination to get a verdict.

It is not just the total duration of jury deliberations that can have a decisive impact on the outcome; it is the specific time intervals in which the jurors are required to do it. The Monsanto jurors faced a long ordeal, but perhaps what an Indiana jury had to endure in dealing with criminal charges against the Ford Motor Company was even more debilitating.[43] After an eight-week trial in which the prosecution tried to prove Ford guilty of reckless homicide for producing their Pinto automobile with deadly defects, the jurors deliberated for three days.

The final day was the most agonizing. At 5:45 P.M., the jury asked to be dismissed for the day; the judge said no. At 11:45 P.M. they said further deliberations would be fruitless; the judge sent them back. At 3:00 A.M., after deliberating more than halfway through the night, they returned a not guilty verdict. After twenty-five votes, the final holdout gave in. Keeping a jury deliberating into the wee hours of the night to the point of exhaustion has more than a touch of the bizarre to it, but it is just an extreme example of the power judges have to wrench a verdict out of juries otherwise destined to hang.

In criminal cases, it is the circumstance of sequestration during deliberations that can be especially upsetting. In addition to the disorientation of being completely cut off from one's normal life, there is the commonly felt claustrophobia of the jury room; jurors in lengthy deliberations report feeling

165

the walls closing in on them. For smokers, nicotine deprivation can be another problem. Combine these unsettling physical effects with the social pressures previously discussed and even the most conscientious juror may crave cloture. One of the jurors in the Hinckley case (cited in Chapter 5), after several days of deliberation, said: "I changed because of the pressure. I had the shakes all day. I had to get out of there."[44] Judges who keep jurors going in such a tense atmosphere are in a sense exerting pressure on dissenters to give in to the majority.

Allen Charges

In addition to prolonging deliberations, judges have another mechanism for intervening in the jury decision-making process. If jurors return to the courtroom with the news that they are stymied by irreconcilable differences, the judge can give them an *"Allen* charge," so named after the nineteenth-century Supreme Court decision of *Allen* v. *United States*[45] that upheld its use. In jurisdictions that permit *Allen* charges judges can lecture jurors who refuse to join the majority about the importance of reaching a verdict and their obligation to listen carefully to each other's views. Also known as the "dynamite" or "shotgun" charge because of its potential for breaking up a jury logjam, this special instruction can prod juries that would otherwise have been unable to reach verdicts into convictions, compromises, or acquittals. Its potency has been substantiated by a recent mock-jury study that found that jurors given *Allen* charges changed their votes more often and reported heightened coercive pressure from the majority than did a control group who were not given such instructions.[46]

A federal judge in Tennessee made use of an *Allen* charge to cope with a jury stalemated in the case against Ray Blanton, the former governor of Tennessee, who was charged with extortion stemming from the sale of liquor store licenses. The jury, mired in disagreement after about forty hours of deliberation, was reminded of the great expense of the seven-week trial and was cautioned that a retrial would bring out nothing new. The judge further urged jurors who were in the minority to consider the views of the majority and to agree with them if their consciences permitted. The jury unanimously convicted Blanton a few hours later, revealing how effectively judges can jolt deadlocked jurors.

Conclusion

Jurors who are initially divided in the jury room do just what they are supposed to do as they grope for verdicts; they talk, question, parry, conjecture, and debate. But it is often group dynamics, the unwitting part of deliberations, that brings jurors together. Jurors are remarkably successful at achieving unanimity (when necessary) because they get caught up in the same collective choice processes that enable small groups of all kinds to forge consensus out of conflict.

Political divisions, as well as differing perspectives about the evidence, often put jurors at loggerheads, and it is political processes that frequently extricate the jurors from their disputes. Politics is a cause of juror conflict, and politics sometimes resolves it. And when verdicts are obtained, they in turn become part of the larger political landscape. As we will see in Chapter 10, the consequences of jury decisions go well beyond the courtrooms in which they are announced.

Notes

1. Harry Kalven and Hans Zeisel, *The American Jury* (Boston: Little Brown, 1966), p. 488.
2. *Ibid.*, pp. 56–57.
3. Jill Smolowe, "Jurors Who Freed Subway Suspect Say His Handwriting Swayed Them," *The New York Times* (January 27, 1980), p. A20.
4. Quoted in Victor Villasenor, *Jury: The People vs. Juan Corona* (Boston: Little Brown, 1977), p. 164.
5. Paul Cowan, "The Long Ordeal of 12 Anguished Jurors," *The Village Voice* (February 8, 1973), p. 9.
6. David Rosenbaum, "Prayer Was the Turning Point, a Juror Says," *The New York Times* (May 5, 1989, p. A19.
7. Kalven and Zeisel, *The American Jury*, p. 488.
8. Sarah Tanford and Steven Penrod, "Jury Deliberations: Discussion Content and Influence Processes in Jury Decision Making," *Journal of Applied Social Psychology*, 16 (1986): 322–347.
9. For a succinct summary of Asch's work, see Roger Brown, *Social Psychology* (New York: Free Press, 1965), pp. 670–673.
10. Reid Hastie, Steven Penrod, and Nancy Pennington, *Inside the Jury* (Cambridge, Mass.: Harvard University Press, 1983), pp. 72–73.
11. Melvyn Zerman, *Call the Final Witness: The People vs. Darrell R. Mather as Seen by the 11th Juror* (New York: Harper & Row, 1977), p. 138.
12. Villasenor, *Jury: The People vs. Juan Corona*, p. 213.
13. Peter McLaughlin and Tony Burton, "Jury Thinks It Over, Doubts Buddy's Guilt," *New York Daily News* (May 15, 1980), p. 5.
14. "Jurors Are Deadlocked in Tennessee Killing," *The New York Times* (December 8, 1985), p. A22.
15. Robert Dahl, *A Preface to Democratic Theory* (Chicago: University of Chicago Press, 1963), p. 150.
16. Garry Brewer and Peter de Leon, *The Foundations of Policy Analysis* (Pacific Grove, Calif.: Brooks/Cole, 1983), p. 213.
17. Some of the material in this section on bargaining first appeared in James Levine, "Jury Room Politics," *Trial Lawyers Quarterly*, 16 (1984): 21–33.
18. Hastie, Penrod, and Pennington, *Inside the Jury*, p. 60.
19. *Apodoca v. Oregon* 406 U.S. 404 (1972); italics added.
20. John Guinther, *The Jury in America* (New York: Facts on File, 1987), p. 97.
21. Steven Brill, *Trial by Jury* (New York: American Lawyer Books/Touchstone, 1989), p. 414.
22. Edith Greene, "On Juries and Damage Awards: The Process of Decisionmaking," *Law and Contemporary Problems*, 52 (Autumn 1989): 241.
23. What happened in the Steinberg jury room was pieced together from the accounts of several jurors reported in Ronald Sullivan, "Steinberg Is Guilty of First-Degree Manslaughter," *The New York Times* (January 31, 1989), p. A1; Robert McFadden, "The Force of the Fatal Blows Persuaded Jurors of 'Intent'," *The New York Times* (January 31, 1989), p. A1; Scott Ladd, "Jury Finds Joel Is Guilty: 1st-Degree Manslaughter," *New York Newsday* (February 1,

167

1989), p. 3; Scott Ladd, "Steinberg's Jurors Recount Verdict That Almost Wasn't," *New York Newsday* (February 1, 1989), p. 5.

24. McFadden, "The Force of the Fatal Blows," p. A1.
25. Kevin McCoy, "A 'Rogue' Verdict?" *New York Daily News* (January 31, 1989), p. 22.
26. McFadden, "The Force of the Fatal Blows," p. A1.
27. *United States* v. *Powell*, 469 U.S. 57 (1984).
28. Interview with Connie Chung on CBS television, "Face to Face with Connie Chung," May 7, 1990.
29. Wendall Rawls, Jr., "Black Tells Texas Federal Jury of New Orleans Police Beating," *The New York Times* (March 11, 1983), p. A14.
30. Kay Richards, "Rereading of Indictment Leads to Compromise Plan for 'Chicago 7' Jurors," *The Oregonian* (February 28, 1970), p. 3.
31. Kay Richards, "Juror for Chicago 7 Convinced Panel Reached Proper Verdict," *The Oregonian* (March 1, 1970), p. 1.
32. Thomas Schelling, *The Strategy of Conflict* (Cambridge, Mass.: Harvard University Press, 1970), pp. 53–80; Charles Lindblom, *The Policy-Making Process*, 2nd ed. (Englewood Cliffs, N.J.: Prentice-Hall, 1980), 54–55.
33. Frank Faso and Don Singleton, "Guilty in Lawyer's Death," *New York Daily News* (January 23, 1983), p. 3.
34. See, for example, Fred Strodtbeck, Rita James, and C. Hawkins, "Social Status in Jury Deliberations," *American Sociological Review*, 22 (1957): 713–718. Also see Michael Saks, *Jury Verdicts: The Role of Group Size and Social Decision Rule* (Lexington, Mass.: Heath, 1977).
35. Lisa Zumar, "Written and Spoken Word: A Big Difference," from "A Juror's Diary," *New York Daily News* (February 28, 1981), p. 5.
36. Ivor Kraft, "Happy New Year–You're a Juror," *Crime and Delinquency*, 28 (October 1982): 594–595.
37. Hans Zeisel and Shari Diamond, "The Jury Selection in the Mitchell-Stans Conspiracy Trial," *American Bar Foundation Research Journal*, (1976): 151–174.
38. Paula DiPerna, *Juries on Trial: Faces of American Justice* (New York: Dembner Books, 1984), p. 89.
39. Fred Strodtbeck and Richard Lipinski, "Becoming First among Equals: Moral Considerations in Jury Foreman Selection," *Journal of Personality and Social Psychology*, 49 (1985): 927–936; F. Strodtbeck, R. James, and C. Hawkins, "Social Status in Jury Deliberations," *American Sociological Review*, 22 (1957): 713–718; F. Strodtbeck and R. Mann, "Sex Role Differentiation in Jury Deliberations," *Sociometry*, 19 (1956): 3–11.
40. Quoted in Hans and Vidmar, *Judging the Jury*, p. 22.
41. "Monsanto Liable in '79 Dioxin Spill," *The New York Times* (October 23, 1987), p. A12.
42. "Dioxin Case Juror Acted to Go Home," *The New York Times* (October 25, 1987), p. 26.
43. Reginald Stuart, "Pinto Trial Snarled as Judge Voices Concern Over Publicity," *The New York Times* (March 13, 1980), p. A18; Reginald Stuart, "Ford Auto Company Cleared in 3 Deaths," *The New York Times* (March 14, 1980), p. A1.
44. "2 Jurors Assert That Pressure Forced Them to Alter Votes," *The New York Times* (June 23, 1982), p. B6.
45. *Allen* v. *United States*, 164 U.S. 492 (1896).
46. Saul Kassin, Vicki Smith, and William Tulloch, "The Dynamite Charge: Effects on the Perceptions and Deliberation Behavior of Mock Jurors," *Law and Human Behavior*, 14 (1990): 537–550.

CHAPTER 9

The city of Miami exploded on the evening of May 17, 1980. The underlying causes of the riot in the black community of Liberty City, which killed fourteen, injured hundreds, and resulted in $100 million in property damage, are many and complex: terrible living conditions in the ghetto, unfair treatment of blacks by city authorities, inadequate political representation, and resentment against Cuban immigrants who were faring better. The immediate cause of the deadly riot was simpler: jury verdicts.

Figure 10-1 shows the boarded-up storefront of a market burned out during the riot. Two names are scrawled on it, JONES and McDUFFIE. JONES refers to Johnny Jones, the black superintendent of the county school system and the highest black official in the state of Florida. A month earlier, in the face of rather skimpy evidence, Jones was convicted of corruption for trying to use school funds to get himself $9,000 worth of luxury plumbing. McDUFFIE refers to Arthur McDuffie, a black insurance executive beaten to death by white Miami police officers after a traffic incident. The afternoon of the Liberty City riot, an all-white jury had acquitted the police officers in the McDuffie case of all criminal charges in the face of compelling evidence against them, including the testimony of the chief medical officer of Dade County, who said the head injuries to McDuffie were the worst he had seen in 3,600 autopsies.

In one sense, these two jury verdicts were only two unrelated decisions about

10
· · · · · · ·
The Impact
of Jury
Verdicts

FIGURE 10-1

The impact

of jury

verdicts

on Miami's

Black

Community

Source: D. Gorton/NYT Pictures

170

whether guilt had been proved beyond a reasonable doubt, but they represented much more to the black community: they stood for long-standing, festering, intolerable racial injustice. McDuffie's sister, in a voice choked with emotion, said what virtually all blacks were feeling: "We despise the verdict. We hate it and it hurts us to our hearts. I feel like my people are nobody."[1] The verdicts triggered violence because they symbolized the continuation of the racial inequality that still existed 115 years after the end of the civil war, 26 years after *Brown* v. *Board of Education*,[2] and 17 years after Dr. Martin Luther King's "I Have a Dream" speech. To the black community in Miami the verdicts were political statements that reaffirmed the historical tradition of white supremacy.

In this chapter we will see that jury verdicts often have ramifications that go far beyond their impact on the parties in the case. Just as the United States Supreme Court's decisions "trickle down" to the society at large, jury verdicts have consequences that in a sense "trickle up and out " to the legal system, the political system, and the lives of ordinary people. And as the fury in Miami so tragically demonstrated, verdicts can bring about thunderbolts as well as raindrops. Juries have power.

Verdicts as Legal Benchmarks

Although juries decide relatively few civil or criminal cases, what they do in the few cases that do come before them serves as a benchmark for the resolution of cases without juries. Lawyers look to jury verdicts for guidance, using them to gauge how cases at hand would likely turn out if they went to trial. These verdicts, in the words of Professor Marc Galanter, cast a shadow on the daily workings of the legal system; how a case is resolved at the pretrial stage is to a considerable extent governed by expectations about what would happen to the case if it went to the jury.[3] Verdicts are markers and signals telling litigants, lawyers, and judges what certain kinds of cases are "worth" in the jury's view. They communicate the real politik of the jury room—the law as modified by the jurors' political perspectives. In appraising how a case should be handled and whether it should be dropped, negotiated, or fought, it is not enough to get a good reading of the law and to make a careful estimate of the evidence; how the jury will react must be taken into account.

Effects of Verdicts on Civil Settlements

A routine part of the negotiation process entailed in the settling of lawsuits is an assessment of the way juries have been handling certain kinds of cases. Not only is much information about jury verdicts passed by word of mouth among lawyers, but there are special publications that report who wins, who loses, and the nature of damage awards. Just as major-league baseball players who are in conflict with club owners over salaries will often reach settlements based on the relatively few cases that actually are decided in arbitration, plaintiffs and defendants in the civil courts are guided by the small but influential set of cases resolved by jurors. Sometimes the "bottom line" in negotiations are discussions among lawyers entailing predictions about probable jury behavior, based on what juries dealing with similar cases have already done.

It is the *actual behavior* of juries that counts, apart from what the law says or what moral precepts might dictate. If jurors are using large damage awards against doctors in medical malpractice cases to express their anger at the medical profession, it is *that* fact of life that will affect settlements— not the formal rules of negligence. If corporate defendants are faring worse than individuals because of "deep pocket" thinking on the part of jurors, that becomes a reality in negotiations—despite the fact that jurors are not *supposed* to take the resources of defendants into account in rendering judgments. If, because of sympathy based on age, juries side with the elderly when they are sued, plaintiffs simply will have to settle for less. All the political elements that juries bring to bear in reaching verdicts become sources of leverage in the bargaining process, whether they are legitimate or not. The law and the facts may be the starting points of negotiations, but what the plaintiff legally deserves (if anything) is adjusted on the basis of perspectives jurors are likely to take.

This is not mere conjecture. A classic study of automobile injury settlements found that "the basis . . . of settlements in serious cases seems on

171

both sides to be an estimate of the likely recovery of the claimant before a jury. . . . Both sides come to this estimate by comparing a given case *in its many dimensions* against other, similar, cases that have gone to trial."[4] The key phrase is "in its many dimensions"; anything that enters the consciousness of jurors affects what plaintiffs will be willing to accept and what defendants are forced to pay. The point is that the decisions of past juries enter into present-day bargaining among the parties: all of the jurors' predilections become part of the jockeying among litigants and their attorneys.

Libel cases are a good example of this phenomenon. In settling two lawsuits brought against CBS television by public officials in Philadelphia and Chicago, CBS agreed to pay hundreds of thousands of dollars, acknowledging that they had been influenced by well-publicized suits against the media in which juries awarded the plaintiffs millions of dollars.[5] The successful suits of Carol Burnett against *The National Enquirer,* of a former Miss Wyoming against *Penthouse Magazine,* and of the president of Mobil Oil against the *Washington Post* cast a shadow over libel litigation by showing that juries were quite upset about the way the press was delving into people's personal lives and invading their privacy. Even though a landmark Supreme Court decision had ruled that public figures could win libel suits only if they showed malice on the part of the organization that printed erroneous material, jurors took a somewhat different path and gave the individuals additional protection. It was *that* reality, jurors' sympathizing with celebrities whose reputations were damaged, that mattered—not just the technicalities of libel law.

172

Thus, judges are correct in telling disappointed civil court jurors whose cases are settled during the trial or deliberations that the jurors' presence played an important role in the outcome. Even the jurors who show up for jury duty but who never get to serve play a role; they are the people with whom lawyers must reckon in gauging whether to settle and, if so, for how much. One irritated panelist who had waited in the large juror hall without being called was assuaged by a jury clerk in a slightly offensive but realistic manner: "Relax, you don't think you are being used, but you are—just by breathing. You wouldn't believe how many cases have been settled this morning without coming to trial. When these lawyers see all you hot bodies out here, they decide to give in."[6]

Such assurances by court personnel do not placate everyone. When an anti-trust trial that had run twenty-one months was settled between Fotomat franchises and a giant film processing concern, one juror deprived of the chance to render a verdict took umbrage: "I feel that the jury was essentially used as a bargaining chip."[7] Disappointing as such abrupt terminations of trials are for those who have patiently sat through them, the role of "bargaining chip" is of the utmost importance. The settlement in the Fotomat case was surely induced and influenced by predictions about how a real jury was responding to the accumulating evidence. Whether the jury is actually seated and is hearing the evidence, or whether there is only a remote possibility that a jury will be called, projections of prior jury behavior govern the resolution of cases settled out of court.

Jury Forecasting and Prosecutorial Discretion

Most criminal cases are resolved before the trial, either by unilateral dismissals by prosecutors or by plea bargaining by defendants. These pretrial decisions are made on the basis of many factors: the strength of the evidence, the seriousness of the charges, the victim's willingness to testify, and the priorities of the prosecutor's office. But in the background of all these assessments is a critical issue: how would the case "sell" to a jury? Whether charges are pressed and, if they are, what kind of deal is struck, often depends on perceptions about whether the case can be won. Prosecutors and defense attorneys look at the small number of jury trials that take place to ascertain how juries typically respond to various charges and defenses, to different kinds of defendants and victims, and to the adequacy of the evidence. The predicted outcomes of hypothetical jury trials are often the rock-bottom reality of plea bargaining; they establish the risks prosecutors and defendants take in placing a case in the uncertain hands of a jury.

Thus, all the propensities of jurors discussed in previous chapters are implicit ingredients in the pretrial give-and-take. The "going rate" that prosecutors and defense attorneys attach to various charges, what both sides are willing to accept as punishment or the basis for punishment, depends in large measure on the inclinations of juries that adjudicated similar cases. Jury politics in the past affects plea bargaining in the present.

The phenomenon of jury nullification (analyzed in Chapter 6) sometimes has the effect of curtailing or even halting prosecution of certain offenses. For many years, the jury's reluctance to convict defendants tried for drunk driving dissuaded prosecutors from pressing charges except in the most egregious cases. Similarly, Quebec authorities reportedly stopped prosecuting doctors for performing abortions after three successive juries between 1973 and 1976 refused to convict a physician who had performed illegal abortions.[8]

Juries send messages, and one message to prosecutors is this: don't waste your time; you'll get nowhere with us. Prosecutors are conviction-oriented, so rather than see themselves suffer a string of defeats, they sometimes have cases dismissed—despite the fact that the law has clearly been broken. Jury verdicts are a significant source of input in the exercise of prosecutorial discretion.

Verdicts as Guidelines for Punishment

In Chapter 8, it was shown that judges can influence juries. The reverse is also true: juries' behavior can provide cues to judges about what the socially acceptable outcome of a case would be. Juries by their very nature reflect the political attitudes of the community, and their vantage point sometimes instructs judges about how they ought to use their discretion.

Now that "just deserts" has become a prevailing philosophy in sentencing, judges more than ever seek guidance in assessing the moral repugnance of crimes as well as the grounds for mitigation. Interpretation of jury verdicts is one means judges may use to gauge what the community thinks should be done to those who are convicted. The proclivity of juries to treat defendants accused of mercy killings somewhat leniently (discussed in Chapter 5) may thus be one factor prompting judges to mete out less severe punishments than they do for other murderers.

Jury Verdicts and Deterrence

The effects of jury verdicts extend beyond the legal system. Tough decisions by juries can act as intimidating forces keeping people who would violate the law in line. On the other hand, jury leniency may be a signal to those contemplating breaking the law that their wrongdoing will go unpunished. Thus, juries play a role, albeit a modest one, in the deterrent capabilities of the law.

Deterrence is a major goal of the legal system. The idea of deterrence is that the punishment of some criminals and civil law violators serves as an example to others. By coming down hard on a few people, the legal system scares large numbers of potential violators into compliance with the law.

Deterrence is a good theory, but it is hard to put into practice. For sanctions to have an impact, a number of things must happen: (1) there must be a sufficiently high probability of getting punished so that breaking the law represents a substantial risk; (2) punishment must be severe enough that it outweighs whatever benefit accrues from the wrongdoing; (3) punishments that are meted out must be communicated to the audience of potential lawbreakers; and (4) those on the verge of breaking the law must be acting rationally at the time.[9] Deterrence often fails when these conditions are not met.

Juries have relatively little capacity to enhance the law's deterrent effectiveness. They normally play a minor role in determining the certainty or severity of punishment, so what they do is of little consequence to the crime-prone population. However, jury convictions that are widely publicized can contribute to deterrence by intimidating those on the brink of committing crimes.

The drunk driving cases are apropos. The recent trend toward more convictions may well be telling those accustomed to driving while intoxicated that their endangerment of the community will no longer be tolerated. Because juries are no longer overlooking this type of offense, fear of tough treatment if caught may cause some people to refrain from driving while drunk.

Acquittals can also deter. The spate of verdicts acquitting battered women who strike back at the men who have abused them may well give some men pause before they continue their attacks on women. If jurors let women "off the hook" for taking matters into their own hands, even to the extent of killing their abusers, some men may begin to fear retaliation. This was the clear hope of a jury in 1987 who acquitted Stella Valenza of attempting to kill her husband, a man who in addition to routinely beating his wife, forced her to have oral and anal sex at gunpoint. One of the female jurors said in

174

an impassioned statement that the verdict came with a message: "Let men beware."[10]

Civil court verdicts also may send messages. For years it was commonly thought that the various open-housing laws on the books were not being enforced, and real estate brokers in many cities continued to engage in a host of racially discriminatory practices, including steering black apartment seekers away from exclusively white buildings and neighborhoods. But a series of verdicts awarding damages to aggrieved blacks who sued such brokers began to make it clear that the racial prejudices that sometimes affect jurors' verdicts were no longer operative in this field of law. One housing expert has concluded that there has been a "very, very substantial decrease" in housing discrimination due to the stiff penalties imposed by juries.[11]

Deterrence is complicated business. No single institution is single-handedly capable of deterring everyone bent on breaking the law. But juries do have some impact on the legal system's ability to instill fear in the hearts of those considering breaking the law. Anthropologist E. Adamson Hoebbel once said that laws are rules that have teeth that bite;[12] juries can help sharpen the teeth.

Political Reverberations of Jury Verdicts

What juries do can have political repercussions. Jury verdicts can cause politicians to make changes, and they can cause changes in politicians. Juries end their service at the conclusion of their cases, but their verdicts may act as catalysts in the political process.

The effects of the many corruption cases heard by juries in the 1980s are a good example. In Chicago and in New York, juries returned many convictions against high officials, including some against judges. These verdicts were major blows to the party machines based on the exchange of money for power that had dominated those cities for decades.

At times, the fortunes of particular politicians may be affected by verdicts. In the Watergate scandal, the jury convictions of top officials in the Nixon administration, including the attorney general and the chief of staff, signaled to the nation that the government's lies and abuses of power were being taken quite seriously. In the aftermath, the Republican Party paid dearly, losing many congressional seats they had held for years and losing the presidency itself in 1976 to Democrat Jimmy Carter, whose campaign condemned the Republicans for allowing Watergate to happen.

Political movements seeking power are also sometimes affected by what juries do. The "sanctuary movement," which attempts to help victims of right-wing Central American governments who seek refuge in the United States, was given a tremendous boost when one of their members was acquitted of transporting illegal aliens by a jury in Corpus Christi, Texas. Said one of the group's members at a symposium in Arizona: "Emotionally and psychologically it has a tremendous impact on the movement [and] on the public."[13]

Verdicts that penalize political movements can have the exact opposite consequences. The 1990 decision of an Oregon jury to assess $12 million against the White Aryan Resistance (W.A.R.), a white supremacist group linked to the anti-black and anti-Semitic "skinheads," had the effect of destroying the group. According to lawyers for the plaintiffs, the family of an Ethiopian man bludgeoned to death by the W.A.R., the verdict sent a "signal" to the "organized hate business" that they could no longer function.[14]

Jury decisions regarding politicians and political activists are not always life-or-death verdicts, but they can affect a movement's future viability. The jury may think it is just deciding evidentiary matters, and sometimes that is the case; but others may render a more far-reaching interpretation of the jury's actions. The jury, at times, is a key player in local and national politics.

Economic Consequences of Jury Verdicts

The economic system can also get jolted by jury verdicts. Large damage awards in civil cases can have enormous impact on the beneficiaries of such largess as well as on those forced to pay. And just as the power structures that run governments can be affected by verdicts, so too can major institutions in the business world.

176

Companies can be put on the brink of bankruptcy. The extraordinary $10.53 billion damage award against Texaco for interfering with Pennzoil's attempted purchase of Getty put Texaco in a situation in which it was fighting for survival. Many economic interests were at stake: the value of Texaco stock to shareholders, the jobs of Texaco's employees, amounts owed to Texaco's creditors, taxes due from Texaco, and the livelihood of people and businesses in communities where Texaco is a major presence. The jury's verdict threatened the survival of the nation's third-largest oil corporation.

Jury action rarely puts companies on the verge of extinction, but large damage awards can so unsettle businesses that they must alter some previously profitable practices. For example, Merrell Dow Pharmaceuticals halted production of its morning-sickness drug Bendectin seven days after a jury in 1983 awarded $750,000 to the family of a girl born with a deformed hand whose mother had taken the drug while pregnant. The company held to its position that the drug was "absolutely safe" but said that negative publicity engendered by the verdict, rising insurance premiums, and the potential of additional litigation made it economically unsound to continue producing the drug.

Sometimes the economic impacts of verdicts are indirect. When a police officer who was accidentally shot in a police operation won a $3.5 million damage suit against South Tucson, Arizona, the award bankrupted that small city. This in turn deprived creditors of money they were owed and forced property owners to accept higher taxes. A single damage award, correct as it may have been, turned the economic structure of the community upside down.

There is one other possible economic impact of jury verdicts that needs mentioning. Some people allege that large damage awards in negligence cases have forced insurance companies to raise their premiums and have even made certain enterprises uninsurable. Others claim that exorbitant product liability awards have adversely affected the vitality of a whole range of businesses. Out of such concerns has emerged a political coalition attempting to curb the power of juries by either putting maximum limits on the awards juries can make to plaintiffs or giving judges more control over the amounts awarded.[15] Critics of these proposals respond that the impact that the jury has on insurance rates and business profitability is small in comparison with other market factors.

Symbolic Impacts of Jury Verdicts

This chapter began with a description of the devastating Miami riot of 1980 that was precipitated by a pair of jury verdicts. The rage unleashed by these decisions was not a response to the verdicts' tangible effects. Arthur McDuffie was dead, and nothing could bring him back. A guilty verdict might have resulted in prison sentences for the offending police officers, but that would not have corrected the underlying inequities and grievances that plagued the black community. The jury's action had virtually no effect on living conditions in the ghetto.

It was the symbolism of the decisions that was so infuriating. As is so often the case in jury trials, there was a stark conflict of values: police power versus black dignity. The jury chose the former, and the community reacted violently. No matter what the underlying facts of trials, which are always in dispute, the society often sees the jury as taking sides. Those identifying with the winners take delight; those siding with the losers are embittered.

A decade after the McDuffie and Jones verdicts that wreaked so much havoc on Miami, another verdict that symbolized social inequality tore the city apart. In December 1990, it was Puerto Ricans who exploded in reaction to a federal jury verdict that failed to convict police officers of conspiracy in the beating death of Leonardo Mercado, a Puerto Rican drug dealer. Said one lifelong resident of Miami's small Puerto Rican community: "It's not just because of the Mercado trial. Cubans get everything; we get nothing."[16] Once again, the jury inadvertently fomented trouble by bringing to a head long-standing grievances about inegalitarian conditions in the community.

It is the populist nature of jury decision making that gives such poignancy to some of its verdicts. The jury is seen as expressing the will of the people, so when it speaks, it speaks with authority. When it provides support, its actions are keenly appreciated; when it offends, it offends badly; and when it stings, it really stings.

177

Conclusion

In 1977, Alabama's attorney general, who was personally prosecuting a fiercely racist man for a Birmingham church bombing fourteen years earlier that killed four young black girls, made the jury vividly aware of the ramifications of their verdict. "Let the world know," he said in his summation while holding up pictures of maimed bodies and shattered religious objects, "that this is not the way the people of Alabama felt then or feel now."[17] The jury's guilty verdict did not bring back the girls or reconstruct the church, but it symbolized a new respect for the rights of blacks in what had been a citadel of segregation.

The Birmingham verdict, like many verdicts, had an impact beyond the disposition of a court case. Juries are far more than cogs in the legal machine who resolve the relatively few cases that go to trial. They also affect the mundane, day-to-day resolutions of criminal and civil cases that never get to court. They sometimes catalyze significant changes in the political and economic system. And at times they carry messages of great symbolic significance that are taken very seriously by the communities that receive them.

De Tocqueville was again correct: "It would be a very narrow view to look upon the jury as a mere judicial institution: for however great its influence upon the decisions of the courts, it is still greater on the destinies of society at large."[18] It is very important to understand the jury politics analyzed in this book, because the consequences of jury verdicts gravely affect American life.

178

Notes

1. Quoted in John Crewdson, "10 Die in Miami Riot; Arson and Looting Persist for 2nd Day," *The New York Times* (May 19, 1980), p. 1.
2. *Brown* v. *Board of Education,* 347 U.S. 483 (1954).
3. Marc Galanter, "Jury Shadows: Reflections on the Civil Jury and the 'Litigation Explosion,' " in *The American Civil Jury* (Washington, D.C.: The Roscoe Pound-American Trial Lawyers Foundation, 1987), pp. 15–42.
4. H. Laurence Ross, *Settled Out of Court: The Social Process of Insurance Claims Adjustment* (Chicago: Aldine, 1970), pp. 114–115. Italics added for emphasis.
5. Jonathan Friendly, "CBS Agrees to Pay in Two Libel Suits," *The New York Times* (May 7, 1983), p. 9.
6. Quoted in Paul DiPerna, *Juries on Trial: Faces of American Justice* (New York: Dembner Books, 1984), p. 210.
7. Quoted in "For a Juror, Mixed Emotions: 2-Year Case Ends Out of Court," *The New York Times* (May 7, 1983), p. 9.
8. Lynn Mather, "Policymaking in State Trial Courts," in John Gates and Charles Johnson (eds.), *The American Courts: A Critical Assessment* (Washington, D.C.: CQ Press, 1991), p. 139.
9. For extended explanations of deterrence theory, see James Levine, Michael Musheno, and Dennis Palumbo, *Criminal Justice: A Public Policy Approach* (New York: Harcourt, Brace, Jovanovich, 1980), pp. 350–379; and Franklin Zimring and Gordon Hawkins, *Deterrence: The Legal Threat in Crime Control* (Chicago: University of Chicago Press, 1973).
10. Steward Ain and Joseph McNamara, "Tearful Stella Cleared," *New York Daily News* (December 5, 1987), p. 3.

11. Lee Daniels, "Housing Discrimination: Study of City Is Updated," *The New York Times* (March 19, 1982), p. B7.

12. E. Adamson Hoebbel, *The Law of Primitive Man: A Study of Comparative Legal Dynamics* (Cambridge, Mass.: Harvard University Press, 1954), p. 26.

13. Wayne King, "Texas Official's Acquittal Buoys Democrats," *The New York Times* (March 18, 1985), p. 24.

14. Robb London, "Sending a $12.5 Million Message to a Hate Group," *The New York Times* (October 26, 1990), p. B20; also see "White Supremacist Leaders Penalized for Inciting Death," *The New York Times* (October 23, 1990), p. B6.

15. Stephan Daniels, "The Question of Jury Competence and the Politics of Civil Justice Reform: Symbols, Rhetoric, and Agenda-Building," *Law and Contemporary Problems,* 52 (Autumn 1989): 269–310.

16. Steven Holmes, "Puerto Ricans' Alienation Is Cited in Miami Rampage," *The New York Times* (December 5, 1990), p. A24.

17. B. Drummond Ayres, "Case Goes to Jury in Birmingham in '63 Church Bombing Fatal to 4," *The New York Times* (November 18, 1977), p. A18.

18. Alexis de Tocqueville, *Democracy in America.* Translated by Henry Reeve, revised by Francis Bowen, edited by Phillips Bradley. (New York: Alfred A. Knopf, 1946), p. 282.

THE IMPACT OF JURY VERDICTS

11
. . . .
The Verdict
on Juries

The preceding ten chapters have presented considerable material about jurors and juries. We have discussed the jury's history; we have presented cases galore; we have introduced ample social science research about jury functioning. The evidence is in; the trial is over; it is time for the verdict. When all is said and done, how good are juries?

Alas, the answer may be somewhat disappointing. But having been time and again confronted with a major theme of this book—that trials *never* produce absolute truth or absolutely unimpeachable verdicts —we will not be surprised. The evidence on juries is conflicting, so any assessment of the jury must be made tentatively and with humility.

What have we discovered? Lawyers, and to a lesser extent judges, try to influence jurors with varying degrees of success. Jurors try hard to be objective, scrutinizing the evidence; but unavoidably they bring in their own values. They seek justice, but justice is a slippery concept that means different things to different people. Some laws in effect are nullified by jurors; most are accepted at face value. There are jurors who will convict almost anybody; there are jurors who will convict almost nobody; most fall somewhere in between. Some jurors fall prey to racial, ethnic, and other prejudices; others do not. In the end, the jury relies on its own devices, generally reaching a consensus through the interplay of persuasion, peer pressure, and old-fashioned politics.

Where does that leave us? To make a sound assessment, we need to apply some criteria about what we seek from juries to the evidence that we have assembled about how juries work. That is what we shall now do—pit our ideals against reality in order to reach a judgment. The verdict on juries that follows is a mixed one, neither totally positive nor totally negative. The jury does pretty well.

Assessing the Jury

Rationality

One of the most important expectations we have of jurors is that they use their minds to seek the truth. Separating the truly innocent from the truly guilty is a cardinal function of jury behavior. So a key question for us is, How good are juries at finding out the facts?

There is a recurring feeling in many circles that the jury is simply incapable of getting things straight, that the material presented in many cases is just beyond their comprehension. Jury critics are fond of reciting trial transcripts filled with complex technical evidence and asking how jurors can possibly untangle it. Thus, a *Wall Street Journal* article scathingly quotes testimony from the antitrust suit brought by MCI Communications Corporation against the American Telephone and Telegraph Company (AT&T):

> *Attorney:* Why were the revenues being placed in jeopardy?
>
> *Witness:* The major reason is, as I said, the breadth of services that we felt—well, for instance, 50% of the market, more than 50% of the market was being foreclosed in the refusal to FX and CCSA interconnect. There are additional parameters. There was the double connection at the double loops of the terminal to the customers' premises under certain circumstances."[1]

If the above excerpt from a trial sounds like gibberish, imagine how difficult it is for jurors to cope with such testimony day after day, week after week. Not all cases are of such complexity, but there is almost always a mass of detail and alien-sounding jargon with which to contend. Are jurors up to the task of fathoming it all, let alone coming up with the right verdict based on it?

That is a tough question. Certainly, jurors make mistakes—sometimes with grievous consequences, as when they convict the wrong person of serious crimes. Years ago, Judge Jerome Frank and Barbara Frank wrote a book aptly entitled *Not Guilty*, in which they discussed a number of cases in which jury verdicts were conclusively demonstrated to have been wrongful.[2] And Baldwin and McConville, in their study of British jury verdicts, reached the following grim conclusion: "On the evidence of our research, we concluded that jury trial was an unpredictable method of discriminating between the guilty and the innocent."[3]

There are any number of recent cases, such as the Lenell Geter case discussed in Chapter 8, in which jury errors have come to light. William Bernard

Jackson's conviction was even more horrendous: he served five years in a maximum security Ohio prison for committing two gruesome rapes that a look-alike was later found to have committed in a string of at least thirty-six rapes. Said Jackson upon his release: "They took away part of my life, part of my youth. I spent five years down there, and all they said was, 'We're sorry.' I didn't get no compensation for the time I did, no money, no job, nothing. And they can never make up those five years."[4] What would Jackson have to say about jury rationality?

But occasional miscarriages of justice do not make for sound generalizations. We rarely find out for certain that the jury has blundered; and even when we disagree with verdicts, there is almost always the possibility that *they* are right and *we* are wrong. The facts rarely speak for themselves, and juries normally have some sane reconstruction of the facts that justifies their verdict. The adversary system provides alternative viewpoints in every case, so there is normally a rational basis for the conclusions that juries reach.

One other point must be borne in mind in assessing juror rationality. Open-and-shut cases in which guilt or innocence seems obvious are usually settled by bargaining; it is the relatively close cases that go to the jury. To expect juries to get the facts right every time when their task is so often a difficult one would be to expect the impossible. It is unfair to use perfection as the standard against which to judge the jury.

The ultimate question is, Who could do any better? Judges are by no means Einsteins, and even if they were, it is human experience rather than sheer intelligence that is necessary to make sense out of the hodgepodge of evidence produced at the typical trial. Remembering what was said is no small part of competent fact finding, and the collective memory of twelve jurors (or even six) is likely to be better than that of one individual. Moreover, the pooling of opinions in a collaborative decision-making process provides a mechanism for testing out ideas, distinguishing sense from nonsense; jury deliberations are sounding boards. Jurors *are* attentive; they *are* conscientious; they *are* thoughtful. They err, but to err is human; there is no solid research showing that anyone else would be less fallible. Despite occasional lapses, the best evidence available suggests that the jury is a fairly competent fact-finding institution.[5]

Legality

Juries are dedicated to following the law. They make genuine attempts to figure out the meaning of legal concepts as best as the sometimes incomprehensible instructions given by judges permit. They get the gist of the law's standards, although legal complexities sometimes escape them. They follow the law because they believe in it; most of the criminal and civil law norms accord with their own political sentiments.

However, on occasion jurors do "bend" the law as explained in Chapter 6—making exceptions, qualifications, and amendments as they see fit. Self-defense is one of the best examples; jurors are more generous than penal codes and legal precedents in giving people the right to deal with attackers. In certain very limited circumstances, jurors convict so rarely that their actions are tantamount to nullification of the law. They will put their politics above the law when the law contravenes their most heartfelt convictions.

Although outright abandonment of the law or even rewriting of it is rare, juries do something that many others in the criminal justice system also do: they prioritize. They apply a double standard, indeed a triple or quadruple standard, concerning how much proof they want in order to convict. Nobody is outraged that police ignore littering, that prosecutors dismiss most loitering charges, and that judges throw out many petty drug possession cases. Triviality is reason enough for authorities to spare offenders the sanctions of the law, and jurors follow suit. The law is the law, but it sometimes gets winked at when it is directed at nonserious misconduct.

The occasional deviation from the law in which jurors engage is often a source of criticism; it should not be. If judges routinely rework the law (and there is not much doubt of it), why shouldn't jurors have the same opportunity to keep the law in touch with current political sentiments?

The law needs to respond to the society's changing needs, and jurors are in an excellent position to know what those needs are. If jurors adjusted the law every time a case was entrusted to them, the result would be anarchy. But this is far from what happens, and the relatively modest fine tuning of the law in which juries engage is no cause for dismay. Jury politics, with its democratic underpinnings, is as sound a guideline as any for bringing about the legal evolution without which the law would become moribund.

Justice

Juries are devoted to justice; it is their beacon. Early empirical research on juries in the 1950s discovered that juries are vitally concerned with handing down morally proper verdicts, and everything that has come to light since then confirms the validity of this finding. Jurors are attuned to the entire context of cases, the whole range of circumstances that determine levels of blameworthiness. They are very concerned with seeing to it that people get what they deserve.

Do juries accomplish what they strive to do? If we could devise some nice formula for applying the concept of justice to particular cases, we could answer the question. Unfortunately, justice means entirely different things to different people. The Bernhard Goetz case that opened this book was heard by jurors passionately devoted to justice, but was their acquittal of the famous subway shooter on all but a gun possession charge just? You might think so, and I might disagree; there is no objective way of determining who is right. What is just and what is unjust depend on one's political beliefs.

Jurors, in seeking justice, often try to strike a balance between competing values. They search for middle ground whenever there is reasonable justifica-

183

tion for it. Although at times their verdicts have all the markings of practical compromises between warring factions on the jury, from another standpoint such verdicts often comport nicely with a sense of justice. Many of those on trial are neither paragons of virtue nor evil incarnate, and the position that the jury takes between two extremes is therefore quite appropriate. Justice comes in many shades of gray.

The ultimate test of the jury as a dispenser of justice is a political one. Jury justice is as close as our legal system gets to popular justice, meting out rewards and punishments according to common conceptions of right and wrong. At times this produces results that some of us will find unsatisfactory, but the total product of all verdicts is probably as just a set of outcomes as is possible. In his first inaugural address, Abraham Lincoln made the point as well as anyone: "Why should there not be a patient confidence in the ultimate justice of the people? Is there any better or equal hope in the world?"[6]

Accountability

Lincoln's profound words bring us to the final criterion against which to judge the performance of juries—accountability. Do juries give ordinary people an opportunity to get their views incorporated into the day-to-day running of the legal system? Is the jury a democratic element in what is an institution dominated by professionals and politicians? Do jurors represent a populist influence on decisions otherwise largely made by elites? The answer to all of these questions is decidedly yes.

This book has made it abundantly clear that popular ideologies, individual prejudices, views on policy, and visions of justice permeate the jury decision-making process. To be sure, not *everyone's* views get equally represented. But there is no doubt about it: jury verdicts *do* reflect majoritarian political sentiment.

The accountability of juries to the public is a mixed blessing. On the one hand, giving juries a voice in the legal system is a means for popular will to counterbalance the prerogatives of officials who may be indifferent to or out of touch with the people; it is a potential check on despotism. On the other hand, majorities at times support some dubious if not outright awful values, such as racism and sexism. Because "the people" are behind a verdict does not make it right.

As I assess the jury, I feel this bind acutely. Many verdicts are appalling to me, such as the acquittal on all charges of several New York City transit police officers who fatally beat and kicked graffiti scrawler Michael Stewart after arresting him. Evidence against the police was so substantial that even the normally pro-police Mayor, Ed Koch, called for a further review of the officers' conduct. Ultimately the city settled the civil suit brought by Stewart's family, agreeing to pay them $1.5 million.

Disheartened as I was by the jury's action exonerating the officers, I found myself agreeing with the defense of the verdict put forth by the president of the transit police union. He argued, persuasively, that the jury's perspective represented the best opportunity to get a reasonable view of all the equities of the case. In a letter to the editor of *The New York Times* in response to an editorial that had questioned the verdict, he spoke a profound truth: "The jury system is the purest example of American democracy, and no one—not even the Mayor—is above it."[7]

That vindication of a controversial verdict is compelling. It stresses the populist nature of the jury's makeup and functioning. The theory set forth in chapter 1 that juries reflect dominant social values has been amply supported by the research presented in the rest of this book. Jury verdicts resonate with the tenor of the times.

The jury makes the legal system somewhat accountable to the public—for better and for worse. If one of the jury's virtues is its compatibility with popular will, then the jury must be defended even when it reaches decisions that some of us believe are wrong. Democratic politics do not always produce glorious policies, and the outcomes of jury politics also can have shortcomings. Yet jury verdicts are what they are—legal decisions tempered by the infusion of popular feelings. Juries clearly pass the accountability test.

Improving Jury Performance

The verdict is in: the jury is all right, but it is imperfect. It does a decent enough job of finding the facts and applying the law, but it sometimes gets confused. It brings to bear social values, but it is somewhat hamstrung in controlling the outcomes of cases. There are many strains of the society represented on juries, but the jury is by no means a cross section of the community. It is a good institution that could be better.

Now for the "sentence": the jury's place in our legal system warrants reaffirmation. At the same time, however, some changes in its functioning seem in order. What follows are some very tentative suggestions for reform.

There are three goals to be accomplished in tinkering with the rules under which juries operate. First, we need to enlighten the jurors—to give them additional information to help them make their decisions more rationally. Second, we need to give more power to the jury, whose role should be enhanced, not contracted. Third, we need to democratize the jury system, further expanding the participation of all segments of society and reducing the continuing biases in jury selection.

None of the proposals that follow is foolproof; each has its costs and its drawbacks. Professor Robert Lineberry's "TANSTAAFL" principle applies to jury reform as it does to any other area of policy making: "There ain't no such thing as a free lunch."[8] I tender these suggestions for change very gingerly, knowing full well that each has strengths and weaknesses. These proposals are a call for discussion and experimentation, in the hope that we can find ways of making a very beneficial institution of the legal system work even better.

Jury Enlightenment

A major function of jury decision making and a significant goal of virtually all jurors is getting the facts right. Jurors almost never want to see an innocent person convicted, and most of the time they prefer that those who did commit crimes be convicted. The trouble is that trial procedures often leave jurors in the dark, baffled as to what really happened. We need to figure out methods for opening jurors' eyes and enabling them to better use their brains.

Proposal 1: Let jurors take notes. Jurors should be allowed to take notes. This is permitted in some jurisdictions at the discretion of the judge, with apparently salutary effects. Although some worry that jurors might get so caught up in jotting things down that they would be distracted from what is currently being said, there is no reason to believe that this would be any more of a problem than in the classroom where note taking is routine. Jurors need to be able to store certain evidence that makes an impression on them in an easily retrievable manner and to have a way of reminding themselves of points that they think may be worthy of discussion during deliberations.

A modest experiment done by a judge in Du Page County, Illinois, produced positive results. He invited jurors in a couple of cases to take notes and found that twenty-one out of twenty-four accepted the invitation, winding up with an average of thirteen pages of notes. When the jurors were later polled about their reactions, they uniformly expressed satisfaction.[9]

A much more rigorous experiment done in Wisconsin produced mixed results. Juries hearing sixty-seven criminal and civil trials were randomly divided into two groups—those in which note taking would be permitted (the experimental group) and those in which note taking would remain prohibited (the control group). Results of post-trial questionnaires submitted to judges, lawyers, and jurors showed that the jurors' notes were remarkably accurate and the note-taking process was not distracting. However, it did not prove to be much of a memory aid regarding either the testimony or the judges' instructions. Despite the uncertain utility of the note-taking process, juries liked having the option at their disposal.[10]

Proposal 2: Let jurors question witnesses. One step beyond note taking is permitting jurors to ask questions of witnesses. One of the most frustrating things for jurors is to be sitting on the edge of their chairs waiting for an attorney to ask a critical question of a witness, only to have the matter skipped over entirely. Lawyers are human; they do not think of everything that may be relevant. Besides, lawyers' interest in winning rather than getting at the truth may sometimes dissuade them from getting into the very issues that would be most instructive for making a sound judgment about what happened. Giving jurors a more active role in the fact-finding process may avert some wrongful verdicts.

Involvement of jurors in the witness interrogation process has had a mixed reception in the courts. The Court of Appeals for the Fourth Circuit has condemned juror questioning as "fraught with peril."[11] This sentiment was echoed by two disapproving justices on the Eighth Circuit, who have claimed that the practice destroys juror open-mindedness, impairs the attainment of justice, and is "inherently prejudicial."[12]

But the Court of Appeals for the Fifth Circuit, in upholding juror questioning, gave a compelling justification for allowing jurors to have some input:

> There is nothing improper about the practice of allowing occasional questions from jurors to be asked of witnesses. If a juror is unclear as to a point in the proof, it makes good common sense to allow a question to be asked about it. If nothing else, the question should alert trial counsel that a particular factual issue may need more extensive development. Trials exist to develop truth. It may sometimes be that counsel are so familiar with a case that they fail to see problems that could naturally bother a juror who is presented with the facts for the first time.[13]

There has been some experimentation with allowing jurors to ask questions. When it has been tried, jurors normally submitted their questions to the judge, who, after first screening them for appropriateness, submitted them to the witnesses. A study of the use of such a practice in the second circuit of the federal judicial system showed that jurors availed themselves of this opportunity in two-thirds of the twenty-four trials in which it was allowed.[14]

Juror questioning of witnesses was also tested in Wisconsin's trial courts during the same experiment that tested note taking. Although jurors' questions were not shown to have uncovered important information that otherwise would not have come to light, jurors who were permitted to ask questions were much more satisfied with the thoroughness of the trial testimony than their counterparts who were not authorized to ask questions.[15] A replication of the Wisconsin experiment in which judges in thirty-five states allowed juror questioning has produced similar results: jurors think it helps them get at the truth.[16]

Proposal 3: Provide jurors with trial videotapes. Videotaping the trial to permit "instant replays" of confusing or forgotten testimony in the jury room would be quite enlightening to jurors. Under current practice, jurors can normally request a rereading of parts of the transcript, but this lacks the nuances of a witness's performance on the stand that can be captured on tape. Inflections and expressions can be very important in deciding who is lying and who is telling the truth, and these elements are missing when a court reporter intones the trial record in a monotone. Modern equipment now permits trials to be recorded rather inconspicuously, and in fact many jurisdictions currently permit live television coverage. Why not share the fruits of such endeavors with jurors?

Proposal 4: Use plain language in instructions. There is substantial evidence that jurors find instructions about the law given to them by judges very confusing. The terminology is often arcane, and the phraseology is frequently cumbersome. Moreover, judges are often loathe to elaborate on what they have said when jurors come to them for clarification during deliberations. Pity the poor jurors in a conspiracy case dealing with organized crime who, when they asked the judge to explain the word "nationwide" in the charge, got this response: "You're going to have to use your own common sense and knowledge."[17]

The net result is that even highly intelligent jurors get frustrated or mixed up when trying to decipher what they were told. A University of Texas professor who served as a juror bemoaned in an article about his experience that "the jurors in this case were intentionally kept ignorant of the law."[18] A number of studies have shown that the true meaning of the law is often misunderstood by the jury.[19] Reflecting on these studies, jury experts Saul Kassin and Lawrence Wrightsman rightly conclude that *the problem is not jury comprehension, but the comprehensibility of judges' instructions.*[20]

But there is hope! Additional research has shown that rewriting the legal instructions in "plain English" with the help of semanticists significantly improves the jurors' comprehension.[21] Complementing this approach are two methods being tested in the federal court system: furnishing jurors with written copies of charges for use in the jury room and providing them with tape recordings of the charges playable in the jury room. The jurors' politics may still on occasion impel them to deviate from the law in reaching a verdict, but they should at least be in a position to know what they are doing.

Jury Empowerment

Juries should have more power, not less. The jury passes muster as a fact-finding body; juries give due (although not unflinching) respect to the law; and juries' sense of justice is as good as anyone's. Politics enters juries' judgments, but this is all to the good; the jury is a perfectly legitimate conduit for the transmission of public sentiments into the administration of justice. Juries have a right to be heard.

The twentieth century has seen the curtailment of jury power. Constraints have been placed on it and prerogatives removed from it. The following proposals are suggested, again cautiously, to reverse this trend.

Proposal 5: Permit jury nullification. Chapter 6 explained that, in a number of ways, juror assessments of the law and its application come into play in jury decision making. However, with the exception of two states, jurors are no longer given the explicit right to ignore laws and to base their decisions on conscience. By and large, nullification comes in through the back door.

Giving juries permission to interpret the law as they see fit or to refuse to apply it when it would be unconscionable to do so would clearly add to the politicization of the jury's role. The jury's legislative role would become more explicit and more honorable. A leading scholar on the topic of nullification says that nullification will probably happen more often if juries are told that it is permissible to engage in it.[22] If this means that the democratic impulse to keep the law consistent with public sentiment gets fuller venting, what is wrong with that?

Police, prosecutors, and judges are ever engaged in the creative process of converting the law on the books to the law in action. Juries, under proper limits to avoid utter arbitrariness, should be afforded at least equal opportunities. Jury nullification was supported by almost all of the Founding Fathers, including politicians as diverse as Thomas Jefferson and Alexander Hamilton;[23] we ought to think about bringing it back.

Proposal 6: Let juries pass sentences. Jury sentencing, except in capital cases, is on the way out. Arguably, this is an unfortunate trend, further undercutting the jury's power. The current approach to sentencing is to base punishments on the concept of "just deserts"—giving people what they deserve. We have pointed out that juries' decisions about guilt in criminal cases and about liability in civil cases are often predicated on the jurors' concept of blameworthiness. Their gut level concern often is, who should pay and how much?

Juries, to preclude the possibility of disproportionate sentences, sometimes may acquit those who are in fact guilty (discussed in Chapter 5). If juries were at least able to recommend sentences, if not set them altogether, they may be more inclined to stick closer to the facts and use control over punishment as a way of working justice into the decision matrix. People who kill others in cold blood might be convicted as murderers instead of being found guilty of manslaughter if juries could consider mitigating circumstances in determining the length of imprisonment.

The conservative ethos of today may well prompt juries to be tough in most cases of violent crime, but so be it. We may not all agree with most sentences recommended by juries but meting out punishment is one of the most political acts imaginable; giving juries a voice in the process seems an appropriate way of allowing the public pulse to manifest itself.

Proposal 7: Eliminate judges' control over verdicts. Judges currently have the right to direct verdicts in favor of defendants if they feel that the prosecution has not provided sufficient evidence to justify a conviction. They also can upset guilty verdicts that are totally inconsistent with the evidence. Thus, judges are able to intervene in the resolution of cases that presumably were entrusted to juries.

189

This stripping of jurors' power supposedly is done in the interest of more rational decisions. But who is to say that the judge is right and the jury is wrong? In 1982, a judge in White Plains, New York, overturned a jury's verdict that Luis Marin was guilty of murder for setting a motel fire that killed twenty-six people. The judge based this decision on the grounds that the jury had engaged in twisted logic and had been unduly swayed by the brilliant summation of the prosecutor. This elicited a bitter response from the prosecutor: "To set aside this verdict, is to call them a bunch of speculators and brand them as fools."[24] He had a valid point: why are the good faith efforts of twelve people scouring the record over the course of six days of deliberation less reasonable than one man's opinion, judge or not?

One step beyond the elimination of directed verdicts and of judgments notwithstanding the verdict is the elimination of the jury waiver. Current practices in many states permit defendants to opt for a juryless trial, although some states require assent from the prosecutor as well. But it is not just the adversaries who have a stake in the outcome of trials; the community also is affected, especially in criminal cases. It is arguable that juries as emissaries from the community should never be deprived of control over verdicts, bearing in mind that political considerations so often creep into the decisions. Perhaps trials and juries should be inextricably linked.

Jury Democratization

190

We have come a long way from the terribly skewed juries of the key man system of jury selection. Jury panels have been tremendously broadened, and many other sources of bias such as the old "housewives exclusion" have been eliminated. The jury now is much more representative of the entire society. But we can do better.

Proposal 8: Further eliminate jury exclusions. Although the categories of people entitled to automatic exclusion from jury service have been shortened, some important groups are still barred. Repealing the current rules that prohibit those convicted of felonies from serving on juries would significantly increase black representation because a disproportionate share of convicts are black. Permitting resident aliens to serve would help redress the tremendous underrepresentation of Hispanics, many of whom are not citizens. The court system is dominated by whites, yet in many parts of the country those charged with crimes who come before the courts are overwhelmingly black or Hispanic. Getting rid of the convict and alien exclusions would give these defendants a much greater opportunity to be heard by a jury with some of *their* peers on it.

Proposal 9: Increase juror pay. Jurors get puny wages. The prospect of getting ten or fifteen dollars a day, less than half the minimum wage, is quite a disincentive to many who are called for jury service.[25] The poor and lower middle class are the least able to give up most of their income for a minimum of one or two weeks, and many of them consequently disregard their subpoenas or manufacture gimmicks to get excused. People faced with being unable to make ends meet contribute to the "no show" problem, and because they are more likely to be of lower economic status, this contributes to class bias in the composition of juries.

There is another problem that arises from inadequate juror compensation. On occasion, jurors who suffer from economic travails due to jury service might subconsciously take their resentment out on defendants by coming down hard on them as a way of getting even. Jurors who are hard pressed economically might also be ill disposed to sit through lengthy deliberations out of concern for the money they are losing.

There are two ways to cope with these problems. First, juror pay could be raised substantially. Payments to jurors represent a tiny fraction of the total expenses of the legal system, so even doubling juror pay would still leave the jury as one of the system's worst funded institutions. Savings accrued from using modern techniques for making juror utilization more efficient and averting wasted hours spent sitting in the jury hall may go a long way toward coming up with the money to pay for the increased wages for jurors.

Another way of compensating jurors is to make employers continue to pay regular salaries to their employees who are on jury duty. Many employers do that now, and employees who benefit from these policies are much less reluctant to serve. This might be too big a burden for small businesses to afford, but it is certainly not unreasonable for large corporations who employ the bulk of Americans to subsidize jury functioning as a public service.

Proposal 10: Eliminate peremptory challenges. The ostensible purpose of peremptory challenges is to enable both sides in a trial to eliminate jurors who would seem to be biased, even if nothing said during the voir dire allows those jurors to be challenged for cause. What we saw in Chapter 3 is that in fact both sides use this device in an attempt to pack the jury with supporters. Although theoretically the peremptory challenge can no longer be used by prosecutors to exclude *all* blacks from a jury, many blacks still are removed, leaving juries disproportionately white. Moreover, other groups such as women can still be excluded en masse.

To rectify this problem, I suggest the elimination of peremptory challenges. To be sure, this will enable some bigots to get on juries who would otherwise be rejected. But the peremptory challenge is a two-edged sword: a hostile extremist to one side is a desirable partisan to the other. Why not just let all panelists serve unless their words during the voir dire show that they are so predisposed to a particular verdict that they are incapable of even considering the evidence?

This is not a harebrained idea. Justice Thurgood Marshall advocated it in his concurring opinion in *Batson* v. *Kentucky,* which struck down peremptory challenges based on race. Said Marshall:

> I join Justice Powell's eloquent opinion for the Court, which takes a historic step toward eliminating the shameful practice of racial discrimination in the selection of juries. I nonetheless write separately to express my own views. The decision today will not end the racial discrimination that peremptories inject into the jury-selection process. That goal can be accomplished only by eliminating peremptory challenges entirely.[26]

Eliminating peremptory challenges would bring the jury selection process in the United States more in line with the British system. In England, the voir dire is limited primarily to eliminating potential jurors who have some relationship to those involved in a case, and the peremptory challenge is rarely utilized.[27] The first twelve or so who are called from the panel serve. There has been no evidence that this method produces a greater number of erroneous verdicts, and it certainly tends to promote a more diverse set of jurors. In an institution as inherently political as the jury, further democratization of jury selection processes is in order.

Conclusion

Adjudication is a speculative, judgmental enterprise. It requires common sense, ethics, and political instincts. It defies computerization, it is only peripherally helped by a college education, and judges have no inherent special talent for it. It is a natural endeavor for ordinary people—which is exactly what jurors are.

The epigram at the beginning of this book is from Alexis de Tocqueville. His words bear repeating: "The jury is, above all, a political institution, and it must be regarded in this light in order to be duly appreciated."[28] The studies, cases, and analyses discussed in this book confirm the wisdom and the timelessness of his observation. Juries and politics are inseparable, for better and for worse.

It is mostly for better. Although there are doubters who rightfully draw our attention to the many instances of "jury-railroading" throughout American history,[29] the jury's misdeeds are democratic misdeeds. Just as allowing people to elect their leaders on occasion puts demagogues and charlatans in government, accepting as inevitable a certain number of verdicts that seem unthinkable may be necessary. De Tocqueville's words are again on target: "Thus the jury, which is the most energetic means of making the people rule, is also the most efficacious means of teaching it how to rule well."[30]

24. James Ferron, "Stouffer's Conviction Is Set Aside; Judge Finds Case Not Proved," *The New York Times* (April 15, 1982), p. A1.

25. British economic Roger Bowles has convincingly argued that those called for jury duty do an implicit cost–benefit analysis in deciding whether to serve willingly or to try to get excused. See Roger Bowles, "Juries, Incentives, and Self-Selection ," *British Journal of Criminology,* 20 (October 1980): 368–376.

26. *Batson* v. *Kentucky,* 476 U.S. 79, 102–103 (1986).

27. John Baldwin and Michael McConville, "Criminal Juries," in Norval Morris and Michael Tonry (eds.), *Crime and Justice: An Annual Review of Research,* II (Chicago: University of Chicago Press, 1986), p. 297.

28. Alexis de Tocqueville, *Democracy in America.* Translated by Henry Reeve, revised by Francis Bowers, edited by Phillips Bradley. (New York: Knopf, 1946), Vol. I, p. 282.

29. Theodore Becker, *Comparative Judicial Politics: The Political Functioning of Courts* (Chicago: Rand McNally, 1970), p. 325.

30. de Tocqueville, *Democracy in America,* p. 287.

194

Jurors get a rare opportunity—for some a once-in-a-lifetime opportunity —to participate in the governmental process. Jurors make critically important decisions, sometimes life and death decisions. They use their heads; they use their hearts; they use their souls. They become politicians in the best sense of that word: they make public decisions with the interests of the public in mind. They deserve our congratulations.

Notes

1. David Blum, "Jury System Is Found Guilty of Shortcomings in Some Complex Cases," *The Wall Street Journal* (June 9, 1980), p. 1. Reprinted by permission of *The Wall Street Journal*, © 1980 Dow Jones & Company, Inc. All Rights Reserved Worldwide.
2. Jerome Frank and Barbara Frank, *Not Guilty* (Garden City, N.Y.: Doubleday, 1957).
3. John Baldwin and Michael McConville, "Criminal Juries" in Norval Morris and Michael Toney (eds.), *Crime and Justice: An Annual Review of Research, II* (Chicago: University of Chicago Press, 1980), p. 291.
4. "Ohio Doctor Accused of 36 Rapes; Man Jailed for 2 of Them Is Freed," *The New York Times* (September 24, 1982), p. A16.
5. See Valerie Hans and Neil Vidmar, *Judging the Jury* (New York: Plenum, 1986), chap. 8, for a review of the literature on jury competence.
6. Abraham Lincoln, First Inaugural Address (March 4, 1861).
7. William McKechnie, "Let the Stewart Verdict Close the Case" [Letter to the Editor], *The New York Times* (December 6, 1985), p. A34. Reprinted by permission of the author.
8. Robert Lineberry, *Government in America*, 4th ed. (Glenview, Ill.: Scott Foresman, 1989), p. 22.
9. Victor Flango, "Would Jurors Do a Better Job If They Took Notes?" *Judicature*, 63 (April 1980): 437.
10. Larry Heuer and Steven Penrod, "Increasing Jurors' Participation in Trials: A Field Experiment with Jury Notetaking and Question Asking," *Law and Human Behavior*, 12 (1988): 245–251.
11. *DeBenedetto* v. *Rubber Co.*, 754 F.2d. 512, 517 (4th Cir., 1985).
12. *U.S.* v. *Alvin Johnson*, 892 F.2d. 707, 711 (8th Cir. 1989, concurring opinion of C. J. Lay joined by J. McMillan).
13. *United States* v. *Callahan*, 588 F.2d. 1078, 1086 (5th Cir.), cert. denied 444 U.S. 826 (1979).
14. Leonard Sand and Steven Reiss, "A Report on Seven Experiments Conducted by District Court Judges in the Second Circuit," *New York University Law Review*, 60 (June 1985): 423–497.
15. Heuer and Penrod, "Increasing Jurors' Participation in Trials": 252–253.
16. Larry Heuer and Steven Penrod, "Juror Notetaking and Question Asking: A Field Experiment," Paper presented to the Annual Meeting of the Law and Society Association, San Francisco, June 1990.
17. "Jury Is 'Confused' in Jersey Mob Case," *The New York Times* (June 18, 1980), p. B6.
18. Richard Schott, "Trial by Jury: Reflections of a Juror," *Trial Magazine* (May 1977): 59.
19. A. Elwork, B. D. Sales, and J. Alfini, *Making Jury Instructions Understandable* (Indianapolis: Bobbs-Merrill, 1982).
20. Saul Kassin and Lawrence Wrightsman, *The American Jury on Trial: Psychological Perspectives* (New York: Hemisphere, 1988), p. 149. The italics are in the original.
21. R. Charrow and V. Charrow, "Making Legal Language Understandable: A Psycholinguistic Study of Jury Instructions," *Columbia Law Review*, 79 (1979): 1306–1374.
22. Steven Barkan, "Jury Nullification in Political Trials," *Social Problems*, 31 (October 1983): 39.
23. For statements in favor of jury nullification by Hamilton and Jefferson, see Justice Gray's dissenting opinion in *Sparf and Hansen* v. *United States*, 156 U.S. 51 (1896).

1

Name Index

Subject Index

Jury nullification (*continued*)
    legislative role of juries and, 101–105
    local sentiments about laws and, 108–109
    uses of, 105–108
Jury panel, skewing of, 42–46
Jury pool, constitutional deficiency of, 41–42
Jury redefinition, 104
Jury room politics, 150–167
    bargaining and, 156–162
    judges' influence and, 164–166
    leadership and, 162–164
    peer pressure and, 153–155
    persuasion and, 151–152
    the power of holdouts and, 155–156
Jury selection, strategies in, 51–55. *See also* Jury selection processes
Jury Selection and Service Act (1968), 43
Jury selection processes, 38, 40–58
    haphazardness of the *voir dire*, 46–50
    right to a representative jury panel, 40–42
    "scientific" jury selection, 55–57
    selection strategies, 51–55
    skewing of the jury panel, 42–46
    use of peremptory challenges, 50–51
Jury size, 27–29
Jury tampering, 75–76
Jury toughness, trend toward, 123–127
Jury trials
    annual numbers of, 36
    avoidance of, 34–36
    waiver of, 27
Jury verdicts, 169–178
    deterrence and, 174–175
    economic consequences of, 176–177
    as legal benchmarks, 170–174
    political dimensions of, 8–9
    political reverberations of, 175–176
    symbolic impacts of, 177
Justice, 79–98
    aggravating circumstances and, 92–93
    in civil cases, 95–97
    death penalty and, 94–95
    Goetz case and, 3–4
    juries and, 183–184
    jurors intuitions about, 81–83

liberal versus conservative versions of, 120
    mitigating circumstances and, 83–92
    proportionality of punishment and, 93–94
Juvenile court delinquency proceedings, 26

Kent State killings, 16
Kerner Report, 113
"Key man" system, 43
Ku Klux Klan/American Nazi Party case, 12
Ku Klux Klan civil rights case, 138–139

Lance trial, 147
Language, jury instructions and, 188
Lateran Council, 23
Law of evidence, 25
Laws
    changing attitudes toward, 109–115
    local sentiments about, 108–109
    unpopular, 105–106
Lawyers, role in influencing juries, 63–66
Leadership, in jury deliberations, 162–164
Legal ambiguity, 13–14
Legal benchmarks, jury verdicts as, 170–174
Legality, jurors and, 182–183
Legal realism, 15
Lewis case, 151–152
Liability of defendant, 31–32
Libel cases, 172
Liberalism, 26
    versus conservatism, 119–121
Liberty City riots, 169–170
Liggett tobacco company case, 158
Little case, 61–63
Local political culture, 127–129
Lockhart v. *McCree*, 48, 59
Logrolling, in jury deliberations, 160
Los Angeles child molestation case, 12, 69

McCleskey v. *Kemp*, 139, 148
McDuffie case, 169–170, 177
McKeiver v. *Pennsylvania*, 26, 38
McMartin preschool case, 12, 69
Magna Carta, 23
Majority pressure, in jury deliberations, 153–155
Massachusetts v. *Anne Capute*, 84
Master wheel, 42–44

Media, role in influencing juries, 73–75
Mens rea, 82
Mercado trial, 177
Merrell Dow case, 176–177
Miller case, 156
Miller v. *California*, 13
Miss Wyoming/*Penthouse* case, 172
Mistrial, 31
Mitchell/Stans influence-peddling trial, 163
Mitigating circumstances, 83–92
Mobil Oil/*Washington Post* case, 172
Mock juries, 65, 70
    racism and, 140
    research on, 10
Money, role in influencing juries, 66
Monsanto Company trial, 165
Mothers Against Drunk Driving (MADD), 90

Negligence cases, 177
Negotiation, in jury deliberations, 160–162
Nonrepresentativeness issue, 41
Nonspecific bias, 47
Nonunanimous jury verdicts, 29
North case, 91–92, 152
Notetaking, by jurors, 186
Nullification. *See* Jury nullification
"Numbers test," 42

Obscenity laws, 13
One-day-one-trial system, 45
Opening statement, 30
Overcriminalization, 108, 120

Pacific Mutual Life Insurance Co. v. *Haslip*, 39
Palko v. *Connecticut*, 38
Pay for jurors, increasing, 190–191
Peer justice concept, 22
Peer pressure, in the jury room, 153–155
Pennzoil case, 81–82, 176
Penthouse libel case, 151
People v. *Malmenato*, 132
Peremptory challenges, 50–51
    eliminating, 191–192
Persuasion, in the jury room, 151–152
Plaintiff, 31
Plea bargaining, 34
Pleadings, 31
Poindexter case, 92
Police, juries and, 129–131
Policies, unpopular, 106

TO THE OWNER OF THIS BOOK:

We hope that you have found *Juries and Politics* by James P. Levine useful. So that this book can be improved in a future edition, would you take the time to complete this sheet and return it? Thank you.

Instructor's name: _____

Department: _____

School and address: _____

_____

1. The name of the course in which I used this book is: _____

_____

2. My general reaction to this book is: _____

_____

_____

3. What I like most about this book is: _____

_____

_____

4. What I like least about this book is: _____

_____

_____

5. Were all of the chapters of the book assigned for you to read?   YES   NO

If not, which ones weren't? _____

_____

6. Do you plan to keep this book after you finish the course?   YES   NO

Why or why not? _____

_____

7. On a separate sheet of paper, please write specific suggestions for improving this book and anything else you'd care to share about your experience in using the book.

OPTIONAL:

Your name: _____   Date: _____

May Brooks/Cole quote you, either in promotion for *Juries and Politics* or in future publishing ventures?   YES   NO

Sincerely,

James P. Levine